FIGHTING WORDS

RACE AND RESISTANCE ACROSS BORDERS IN THE LONG TWENTIETH CENTURY

Volume 1

Series Editors:
Tessa Roynon, University of Oxford (Executive Editor)
Elleke Boehmer, University of Oxford
Victoria Collis-Buthelezi, University of the Witwatersrand
Patricia Daley, University of Oxford
Aaron Kamugisha, University of the West Indies, Cave Hill
Minkah Makalani, University of Texas, Austin
Hélène Neveu Kringelbach, University College London
Stephen Tuck, University of Oxford

PETER LANG
Oxford • Bern • Berlin • Bruxelles • New York • Wien

FIGHTING WORDS

Fifteen Books that Shaped
the Postcolonial World

Edited by Dominic Davies,
Erica Lombard and Benjamin Mountford

PETER LANG
Oxford • Bern • Berlin • Bruxelles • New York • Wien

Bibliographic information published by Die Deutsche Nationalbibliothek.
Die Deutsche Nationalbibliothek lists this publication in the Deutsche National-
bibliografie; detailed bibliographic data is available on the Internet at
http://dnb.d-nb.de.

A catalogue record for this book is available from the British Library.

Library of Congress Cataloging-in-Publication data:

Names: Davies, Dominic, 1988- editor, author. | Lombard, Erica Louise, 1986- editor, author. | Mountford, Benjamin, 1980- editor, author.
Title: Fighting words : books that shaped the postcolonial world / Dominic Davies, Erica Lombard and Benjamin Mountford (eds).
Description: Second edition. | Oxford ; New York : Peter Lang, 2019. | Series: Race and resistance across borders in the long twentieth century ; 1 | Includes bibliographical references and index.
Identifiers: LCCN 2019018958 | ISBN 9781789974225 (alk. paper)
Subjects: LCSH: Books and reading--Political aspects--History--20th century. | Books and reading--Political aspects--History--19th century. | Books and reading--Social aspects--History--20th century. | Books and reading--Social aspects--History--19th century. | Postcolonialism--Historiography. | Imperialism--Historiography. | Books--History--20th century. | Books--History--19th century.
Classification: LCC Z1003 .F45 2019 | DDC 028/.90904--dc23 LC record available at https://lccn.loc.gov/2019018958

Cover image by Erica Lombard.
Cover design by Peter Lang Ltd.

ISSN 2297-2552
ISBN 978-1-78997-422-5 (print) • ISBN 978-1-78997-427-0 (ePDF)
ISBN 978-1-78997-428-7 (ePub) • ISBN 978-1-78997-429-4 (mobi)

This revised paperback edition was first published in 2019.

First published in 2017 by Peter Lang Ltd, International Academic Publishers,
52 St Giles, Oxford, OX1 3LU, United Kingdom
oxford@peterlang.com, www.peterlang.com

© Peter Lang AG 2019

Dominic Davies, Erica Lombard and Benjamin Mountford have asserted their right under the Copyright, Designs and Patents Act, 1988, to be identified as Editors of this Work.

All rights reserved.
All parts of this publication are protected by copyright.
Any utilisation outside the strict limits of the copyright law, without
the permission of the publisher, is forbidden and liable to prosecution.
This applies in particular to reproductions, translations, microfilming,
and storage and processing in electronic retrieval systems.

This publication has been peer reviewed.

Contents

TESSA ROYNON ET AL.

Introduction to *Race and Resistance Across Borders in the Long Twentieth Century*   ix

List of Figures   xiii

Acknowledgements   xv

Preface to the Second Edition   xix

DOMINIC DAVIES, ERICA LOMBARD AND
BENJAMIN MOUNTFORD

Introduction. Fighting Words: Books and the Making of the Postcolonial World   1

DOMINIC DAVIES

1   From Communism to Postcapitalism: Karl Marx and Friedrich Engels's *The Communist Manifesto* (1848)   27

IMAOBONG UMOREN

2   Anna Julia Cooper's *A Voice from the South* (1892): Black Feminism and Human Rights   43

CHRISTINA TWOMEY

3   Ambivalence, Admiration and Empire: Emily Hobhouse's *The Brunt of the War and Where it Fell* (1902)   57

REILAND RABAKA
4 W. E. B. Du Bois's *The Souls of Black Folk* (1903):
Of the Veil and the Color-Line, of Double-
Consciousness and Second-Sight 73

PRIYASHA MUKHOPADHYAY
5 *Wake Up, India: A Plea for Social Reform* (1913): Annie
Besant's Anticolonial Networks 89

JANET REMMINGTON
6 Sol Plaatje's *Native Life in South Africa* (1916):
The Politics of Belonging 103

ELLEKE BOEHMER
7 Making Freedom: Jawaharlal Nehru's *An Autobiography*
(1936) and *The Discovery of India* (1946) 121

ROUVEN KUNSTMANN
8 Joseph B. Danquah's *The Akan Doctrine of God* (1944):
Anticolonial Fragments? 135

JOHANNA RICHTER
9 The Resistant Forces of Myth: Miguel Ángel Asturias's *Men of Maize* (1949) 151

RUTH BUSH
10 The Hip-Hop Legacies of Cheikh Anta Diop's *Nations nègres et culture* (1954) 167

ASHA ROGERS
11 Culture in Transition: Rajat Neogy's *Transition* (1961–1968) and the Decolonization of African Literature 183

JOHN NARAYAN

12 Frantz Fanon's *The Wretched of the Earth* (1961): The
    Spectre of the Third World Project   201

BENJAMIN MOUNTFORD

13 'The Match is in the Spinifex': Frank Hardy's *The Unlucky
    Australians* (1968)   215

MICHAEL R. GRIFFITHS

14 Provenance, Identification and Confession in Sally
    Morgan's *My Place* (1987)   231

ERICA LOMBARD

15 Freedom Fighter/Postcolonial Saint: The Symbolic Legacy
    of Nelson Mandela's *Long Walk to Freedom* (1994)   247

ANTOINETTE BURTON AND ISABEL HOFMEYR

Afterword: Plotting a Postcolonial Course in Fifteen Chapters   263

Notes on Contributors   269

Index   275

TESSA ROYNON ET AL.

Introduction to *Race and Resistance Across Borders in the Long Twentieth Century*

When The Oxford Research Centre in the Humanities (TORCH) was launched in January 2013, one of its inaugural and flagship networks was 'Race and Resistance Across Borders in the Long Twentieth Century'. Conceived and convened by two of the current Peter Lang series editors (Elleke Boehmer and Stephen Tuck), the pioneering steering group included two of our current editorial advisory board members, Justine McConnell and Imaobong Umoren. Tessa Roynon was soon to join the growing group of postgraduate, early career and established scholars in the disciplines of History, English, Modern Languages, Classics, African Studies and Anthropology. From its inception, 'Race and Resistance Across Borders' has brought together researchers in the history, literature and culture of anti-racist, anti-colonial and transnational or internationalist movements in Africa, Asia, the Caribbean, Europe, Latin America and the United States.

The core aims of the initial interdisciplinary network remained constant even as we were established as a full research programme, still under the auspices of TORCH, at the end of 2014. It was in that same year that this book series of the same name came into being. Both the programme and the series focus on 'the history and culture of activists, artists and intellectuals who have worked within and against racially oppressive hierarchies in the first half of the twentieth century and beyond, and who have then sought to define and to achieve full equality once those formal hierarchies have been overturned', as our brief has it. Both the series and the programme further aim to explore 'the ways in which such individuals – writers, scholars, campaigners and organizers, ministers, and artists and performers of all kinds – have located their resistance within a global context and forged connections with each other across national, linguistic, regional and imperial borders'.

As our webpages document (www.torch.ox.ac.uk/race-and-resistance-across-borders-in-the-long-twentieth-century), our activities at TORCH amply fulfil these aims through a series of dynamic seminars, workshops, conferences, film screenings and book launches on both a large and modest scale. These have included (among many others) high-profile events on Malcolm X in Oxford, a reading by 2015 Man Booker Prize winner Marlon James, discussions on topics ranging from Israel/Palestine to Exhibit B, student-led workshops on the Black Lives Matter movement and the Rhodes Must Fall Oxford movement, and the hosting of the *Callaloo* Annual Conferences in 2014 and 2016. We are unified by our commitment to advancing diversity at Oxford in the curriculum, the student body and faculty at once. Our programme is now much valued for its role in generating fresh thought and resistant action.

Thanks to the initiative of Peter Lang's commissioning editor, Laurel Plapp, we have seized the opportunity to disseminate fresh and high-quality scholarship in lasting formats to an international readership. Given our theoretical emphasis on the transnational and intercultural nature of the anti-racist and resistance movements that are our subject, it was immediately self-evident that this series demanded editors located all over the globe in a diverse range of institutions and whose combined expertise constitutes multiple disciplines and perspectives. We were therefore delighted when Victoria Collis-Buthelezi (Witwatersrand), Aaron Kamugisha (University of the West Indies, Cave Hill), Minkah Makalani (University of Texas, Austin), Hélène Neveu Kringelbach (University College London) and Patricia Daley (Oxford) agreed to join as co-editors.

In the same spirit, we have been fortunate to form an editorial advisory board that constitutes a veritable powerhouse in the field: Funmi Adewole (DeMontfort University), Joan Anim-Addo (Goldsmiths, University of London), Celeste-Marie Bernier (University of Edinburgh), Alan Cobley (University of the West Indies, Cave Hill), Carolyn Cooper (University of the West Indies, Mona), Zaire Dinzey-Flores (Rutgers, State University of New Jersey), Tanisha Ford (University of Delaware), Maryemma Graham (University of Kansas), Christopher J. Lee (Lafayette College), Justine

Introduction to Race and Resistance Across Borders

McConnell (King's College London), Pap Ndiaye (Sciences Po), David Scott (Columbia University), Hortense Spillers (Vanderbilt University), Imaobong Umoren (University of Oxford/London School of Economics), and Harvey Young (Northwestern University).

It is with great pride that we see our book series, *Race and Resistance Across Borders in the Long Twentieth Century*, launch at Peter Lang. There could be no better inaugural volume than this one – *Fighting Words* – which has been so brilliantly edited by Dominic Davies, Erica Lombard and Benjamin Mountford. 'Can a book change the world?', they ask on their opening page. In launching this series, we testify to our own conviction that it can.

Elleke Boehmer, Victoria Collis-Buthelezi, Patricia Daley, Aaron Kamugisha, Minkah Makalani, Hélène Neveu Kringelbach, Tessa Roynon, Stephen Tuck
May 2017

Figures

Figure 1.1: A stamp of the Soviet Union, issued in 1948 to mark the hundredth anniversary of the first publication of *The Communist Manifesto* in 1848, and bearing the now iconic portraits of Marx and Engels. 29

Figure 2.1: Anna Julia Cooper. Courtesy of the Moorland-Spingarn Research Center, Manuscript Division Howard University, Washington, DC. 48

Figure 3.1: Emily Hobhouse in England: St Ives, Cornwall. Courtesy of the Free State Provincial Archives, VA1435. 59

Figure 4.1: The first page of W. E. B. Du Bois's handwritten draft of Chapter 13, 'Of the Coming of John'. Courtesy of the University of Massachusetts Amherst Libraries, with the permission of The Permissions Company, Inc., on behalf of the David Graham Du Bois Trust. 79

Figure 6.1: Sol Plaatje during his editorship of *Tsala ea Batho*, c.1913–1914. Courtesy of the Kimberley Africana Library. 107

Figure 7.1: The cover of the 1953 edition of *Jawaharlal Nehru: An Autobiography* by Jawaharlal Nehru, published by Bodley Head. Artwork © Random House. Reprinted by permission of The Random House Group Limited. 124

Figure 8.1: GYE NYAME ('Except God'), featured on the frontispiece of *The Akan Doctrine of God*. Courtesy of the Lutterworth Press. 142

Figure 11.1: The inaugural editorial by Rajat Neogy, *Transition*, Issue 1 (1961), 2. Reprinted with permission of Indiana University Press. 191

Figure 13.1:	Frank Hardy, with his tape recorder by his side, during a discussion about the Gurindji plan to move to Daguragu. With kind permission of Robin Jeffrey.	218
Figure 15.1:	Tributes to Mandela in a fishmonger in Woodstock, Cape Town, and on the side of the Cape Town Civic Centre building.	254

Acknowledgements

It is sometimes suggested that scholarly research can be a lonely pursuit. One might imagine book history to be an especially solitary and silent place – populated by historians and literary scholars, busily working away at their texts, alone between the covers. For us the experience of editing this particular book history could hardly have been more different. An interdisciplinary collection, bringing together scholars from a range of academic and geographical perspectives, *Fighting Words* is above all the product of a series of conversations and discussions about books and their influence between a group of writers who care deeply about books and their histories. As editors, we have cherished these conversations, and our understanding of books, book history and the postcolonial world have all been profoundly enriched by them.

In seeking these riches, however, we have accumulated many debts.

Above all, we extend our thanks to our contributors for their enthusiasm, dedication and hard work. Special mention must be reserved for Elleke Boehmer, Rouven Kunstmann, Priyasha Mukhopadhyay and Asha Rogers, who began this journey with us one sunny spring afternoon back in Oxford, and without whom we would never have reached our destination. We also acknowledge the support of our friend and colleague, the late Jan-Georg Deutsch, during the early stages of this project, and express our sadness that he is not with us to see it here at the end. Finally, we wish to thank Antoinette Burton and Isabel Hofmeyr, whose collection of essays inspired our own, and who have generously offered their responses to this volume in the Afterword.

Since 2014, Ertegun House, Oxford; the Oxford University Press John Fell Fund; the Oxford Global History Centre; the Sudbury Oxford Transnational History Foundation; the Oxford Faculty of English Language and Literature; the Oxford History Faculty; Corpus Christi College, Oxford; The Oxford Research Centre in the Humanities (TORCH) and, in particular, the Race and Resistance Network based there; and The

Faculty of Arts at the University of Melbourne (which supported the 2015 'Writers and Readers Conference') have all offered financial and other support for the conversations and discussions which have now come together as *Fighting Words*.

That coming-together has also relied heavily on the expertise of the editorial and production teams at Peter Lang, Oxford. In particular, Laurel Plapp and Tessa Roynon have lent us their guidance, support and patience throughout, reminding us at every step (as if book historians needed reminding) that behind every good book lies a good publisher. We also thank the series editors of *Race and Resistance Across Borders in the Long Twentieth Century* for their faith in the project.

Several archives and libraries have also graciously extended to us permission to include quotations and reproductions from their valuable collections; detailed acknowledgements are available in the relevant notes and bibliographies for each chapter. We offer particular thanks to the dedicated team at the National Army Museum for their assistance in accessing Lieutenant Brooke's diary.

To all these colleagues and supporters, whose involvement has profoundly improved the pages that follow we extend our heartfelt thanks. Responsibility for the failings that remain we reserve for ourselves.

Dominic Davies would like to thank the AHRC and British Academy, institutions that have both supported him as he devoted time to this collection. Special thanks go to the community at the Oxford Postcolonial Writing and Theory seminar and for the numerous academic and personal friendships it has fostered; to Jane and Simon, who have been pillars of generosity for almost thirty years; and to Emma, for her loyalty and companionship.

Erica Lombard is grateful to the University of Johannesburg for the Postdoctoral Research Fellowship during which the bulk of her work on this collection was completed; and to the Oxford Postcolonial Writing and Theory seminar community, which has been a valued source of ideas, friendship and solidarity. Special thanks to the Lombards and Culwicks, particularly to Rosemary Lombard for being an ever-generous sounding board, and to Arlyn.

Ben Mountford wishes to thank: the Hardy and Hardy-Rix families (especially Alan, Gailia, Shirley and Brian); Robert Bickers; Brenda Croft;

Acknowledgements

Ted Egan; John Goldschmidt; Luke Grimes; Peter Hudson; Bob Jeffrey; Keir Reeves; Penny Smith; Charlie Ward; the National Library of Australia; his colleagues at the Australian Catholic University and his former colleagues at La Trobe University and Federation University. As always, Ben owes the greatest of dues to the families Mountford, Courtney, Gibson and Wilson, and to Jennie, Darcy and Flora for always sharing their books with him.

Bendigo, Cape Town and Oxford
April 2017

Preface to the Second Edition

In the introduction to *Fighting Words*, which was penned in the final months of the tumultuous year 2016, we observed that the book was appearing at a time when the project of decolonization was gaining increased traction not only within academia, but also in popular social and political discourse more widely. The important work of Rhodes Must Fall (RMF), both in Cape Town and Oxford, along with movements such as Black Lives Matter, created seismic shifts that allowed for a renewed analysis of the lingering colonial legacies, discriminations and privileges still embedded in Britain's most enshrined institutions. Importantly, the resolve of such critiques has been strengthened rather than stifled by the recent resurgence of a vocal imperial nostalgia. In the two years since we wrote our original introduction to *Fighting Words*, the advances made by these and other movements both within and outside the academy have meant that calls to decolonize higher education, and society more widely, are also entering the mainstream. We hope that this paperback reissue of *Fighting Words*, and the story it tells of 'restless motion, anticolonial movement and ungovernability at all scales' – or 'postcolonial history from the bottom up', as Antoinette Burton and Isabel Hofmeyr write in their afterword to the book – may contribute something worthwhile to these evolving dialogues.

A few months after the 2017 publication of the first edition, we launched *Fighting Words* at a special seminar hosted by the 'Race and Resistance Across Borders in the Long Twentieth Century' research programme at The Oxford Research Centre in the Humanities (TORCH). The 'Race and Resistance' programme, originally conceived by Professors Elleke Boehmer and Stephen Tuck, was one of Oxford's first institutionally sanctioned spaces where historians, literary critics and cultural theorists could come together to discuss anti-racist, anticolonial and transnational or internationalist movements from across the Atlantic, the Global South and beyond. It is a space that has been and remains a home for many members of RMF and related groups; *Fighting Words* and the history of its fruition is deeply intertwined with the programme. When Peter Lang's Commissioning Editor, Laurel Plapp, approached the organizers of 'Race and Resistance' to propose a new book series of the same name, they seized the opportunity, bringing on board a team of series editors located in a diverse range of institutions all over the globe. *Fighting Words*, which explores how theories and movements of anti-imperial and anticolonial resistance across the planet have been shaped by books as they are read across the world, was the series' inaugural volume.

There was no better place, then, to launch *Fighting Words*, and comments and questions subjected the collection to the appreciative yet rigorous critical reception with which regular attendees of the 'Race and Resistance' seminar will be familiar. As some of these readers commented, the collection's subtitle assumes a postcolonial world, in the singular, but whose world is this? Is there only one world to be shaped? What histories does the assumption of a singular postcolonial world risk occluding? And relatedly, does the collection's emphasis on 'the book', even as it is embraced in a flexible and sometimes abstract form by our contributors, similarly invest weighty tomes with a certain imperialistic monumentalism? When monuments and their symbolism are rightly being contested, does a return to 'the book' as a contained material object risk reinforcing rather than undoing those forms and genres that were once such important tools of empire? If these are not entirely new questions, they are ever important ones, and we believe the essays collected here continue to answer them in different and productive ways.

Fighting Words originated as a response to the pressing debates of our moment, but it also demonstrates that these kinds of resistant conversations and confrontations have taken place across the long twentieth century and the globe, finding different expressions and emphases according to time and context. Erica Lombard's fierce cover design, which blends together the opening pages of the anticolonial texts discussed in this book, captures something of this enduring spirit of resistance. In this moment, we hope that the books addressed here – these fifteen points of entry into the ongoing project of decolonization – will increasingly find their way into and shape the syllabi and intellectual terrain of contemporary higher education.

Again, as in our first edition, we extend our sincerest thanks to all our contributors, colleagues, friends and families, as well as to our supportive colleagues at Peter Lang and TORCH, for coming with us on this next stage of the journey.

D. Davies, E. Lombard & B. Mountford
London, Cape Town & Melbourne
December 2018

DOMINIC DAVIES, ERICA LOMBARD AND
BENJAMIN MOUNTFORD

Introduction
Fighting Words: Books and the Making of the Postcolonial World

Can a book change the world? If books were integral to the creation of the imperial global order, what role have they played in resisting that order throughout the twentieth century? To what extent can anti-imperial and anticolonial resistance movements across the planet be traced back to, or be found to have their ideas rooted in, materially circulating texts? These questions undergird the fifteen chapters of which this collection is comprised, which together examine how the book as both a cultural form and material object has fuelled resistance to empire and shaped the contours of the postcolonial world in the long twentieth century.

The case studies presented illuminate the multiple ways in which books have facilitated the circulation of anti-imperial ideas, as they themselves have circulated as objects and commodities within regional, national and transnational networks. To track the diverse and multifaceted genealogies and afterlives of the fifteen resistant books discussed in this collection, *Fighting Words* brings together scholars from various disciplinary backgrounds, including history, literary criticism and cultural studies, and combines studies of overlooked resistant writing with re-evaluations of more canonized texts. The chapters cover a broad geographical terrain, spanning a number of colonial and anticolonial contexts, local and transnational networks of circulation, and historical and ongoing anti-imperial struggles.

Paper Empires: Books and Imperial History

In June 1900, Lieutenant George Cecil Brooke of the British Army was bound for Tianjin. An officer with the First Chinese Regiment, which had been raised at the British concession of Weihaiwei in 1898, Brooke and his men rushed to join the international force being assembled for northern China. To many observers, it seemed like a significant moment in the history of modern imperialism. At Tianjin and Beijing, Westerners, Japanese and Chinese Christians had been besieged by the anticolonial popular movement known as the 'Boxers' and by Qing army troops. Outraged at the threat to foreign diplomats and residents in China, an Eight Nation Alliance (comprising forces from the United States, Britain, Germany, Russia, France, Italy, Austro-Hungary and Japan) set out to liberate their legations and suppress the Boxers. In the weeks and months that followed, the Alliance occupied Tianjin and Beijing, exacting a brutal and disproportionate retribution for the damage done to foreign interests in China. As the Empress Dowager Cixi and her Court fled the Chinese capital it seemed as if the age of high imperialism, which had been defined by the scramble for Africa since the 1880s, might come to a head in the East – in a new scramble for China.

In his study of British imperialism in China, James Hevia has argued that British diplomatic and military agents tended to view imperialism and colonialism as violent pedagogical activities: 'teaching and learning by means of gun and pen'.[1] Throughout the period that Hobsbawm famously called the 'Age of Empire' (1875–1914) books played a central role in these processes – documenting and influencing the lives of both colonizers and colonized.[2] Likewise, a Briton travelling to China in the interwar period

---

1   James Hevia, *English Lessons: The Pedagogy of Imperialism in Nineteenth-Century China* (Durham, NC and London: Duke University Press, 2003), 4. See also James Hevia, 'Regulating the Facts of Asia: Military Reports and Handbooks', in *The Imperial Security State: British Colonial Knowledge and Empire-Building in Asia* (Cambridge: Cambridge University Press, 2012), 107–51.
2   Eric Hobsbawm, *The Age of Empire, 1875–1914* (London: Abacus, 2007).

Introduction 3

'might have been directed before he arrived by his superiors to read up on the country, or on the history of its foreign presence, or else might have read up out of curiosity, choosing a book from the ship's library for the long voyage East'.[3] Like many soldiers and marines, Lieutenant Brooke maintained a journal. In it he recorded his activities in the field and his observations, hopes and anxieties. Across the first two pages, he scrawled 'Notes from "Deeds That Won the Empire" by "Fitchett"' – a book that was becoming widely known to readers across the British imperial world – followed by a list of great military and naval triumphs, from the Spanish Armada to the Peninsula War.[4]

An Australian clergyman, educator and author, the Reverend William Henry Fitchett had been asked by a British naval commander in 1896 to write a series of commemorative reflections on significant moments in British imperial history. Published in the Melbourne *Argus*, pirated in India, reprinted in London, reissued as a shilling collection and finally released in London and New York as a single volume, Fitchett's *Deeds That Won the Empire* (1897) took on a life of its own. Tutors prescribed it for their students, a sixpenny version sold 100,000 copies and a Braille edition meant even the blind could marvel at the extent of British imperial endeavour. Beginning with epigraphs from Wordsworth and Kipling, Fitchett led his readers through a grand narrative of imperial warfare that culminated in the high drama of Waterloo, Cadiz and Trafalgar. It was a book, he promised, to gird the young for the future tests and travails of empire: 'There is a real danger that for the average youth the great names of [the] British story may become meaningless sounds, that his imagination will take no colour from the rich and deep tints of history. And what a

---

3   Robert Bickers, *Britain in China: Community, Culture and Colonialism, 1900–1949* (Manchester: Manchester University Press, 1999), 22.
4   Quotation courtesy of the National Army Museum. George Cecil Brooke, diary for 1900, George Cecil Brooke Papers, National Army Museum, 2004-09-244-1; A. A. S. Barnes, *On Active Service with the Chinese Regiment: A Record of the Operations of the First Chinese Regiment in North China from March to October 1900* (London: Grant Richards, 1902).

pallid, cold-blooded citizenship this must produce!'⁵ Certainly the British Admiralty saw the book's value, eventually equipping all the Royal Navy's warships' libraries with copies.⁶

Whether George Cecil Brooke came across Fitchett's book in a ship's library or elsewhere, that his 1900 journal begins with notes from *Deeds That Won the Empire* serves as just one small reminder of the importance of books, and of reading and writing more broadly, in framing experiences of empire. In his China journal, Brooke records sharing technical books with his comrades (on practical topics such as military engineering, field orders and military law), includes notes on warfare and military history and, on occasion, elevates his reflections on the day-to-day with poetry and inspiring quotations from sources as diverse as Tennyson and the Quran. As he made his way out East, Lieutenant Brooke, like many other players at the edge of empire, wove books and reading together with lived experience, scripting and enacting his own role in the great imperial drama unfolding in China.⁷

As this story suggests, books have played an important role in the expansion and justification of empire. However, they have also proved powerful tools for those seeking to critique and resist imperial rule, and to challenge the legacies of empire in a postcolonial world. It is this narrative of resistance that *Fighting Words* seeks to explore. Antoinette Burton and Isabel Hofmeyr argue that we might understand the book as 'a material form and a geopolitical influence' that has had a particular currency in the making and unmaking of empire.⁸ Put another way, books are tangible

---

5   W. H. Fitchett, *Deeds That Won the Empire: Historical Battle Scenes* (New York: Charles Scribner's Sons, 1898), v–vi.
6   A. G. Thomson Zainu'ddin, 'Fitchett, William Henry', *Australian Dictionary of Biography* <http://adb.anu.edu.au/biography/fitchett-william-henry-6179> accessed 30 October 2016.
7   On books, imperial drama and 'self-conscious actors' at the Boxer Uprising, see Robert Bickers, 'Introduction', in Robert Bickers and R. G. Tiedemann, eds, *The Boxers, China and the World* (Plymouth: Rowman & Littlefield, 2001), xv–xvii; Robert Bickers, 'Paul Cohen, the Boxers, and Alfred, Lord Tennyson', *The Chinese Historical Review* 14/2 (2007), 192–5.
8   Antoinette Burton and Isabel Hofmeyr, 'Introduction: The Spine of Empire? Books and the Making of an Imperial Commons', in Antoinette Burton and Isabel Hofmeyr,

Introduction 5

objects that both have particular properties and transmit ideas in specific ways; in each of these capacities they can effect various kinds of political, ideological and cultural change in the world. *Fighting Words* itself demonstrates the productive agency of books, for its own origins may be traced back to another book: Burton and Hofmeyr's edited collection, *Ten Books That Shaped the British Empire: Creating an Imperial Commons* (2014), each of whose ten chapters makes a case for a book that 'shaped the modern British Empire, both through the ideas they articulated and the material forms those ideas took'.[9] Encompassing a range of books – from Charlotte Brontë's *Jane Eyre* and Macaulay's *History of England* to M. K. Gandhi's *Hind Swaraj* and C. L. R. James's *The Black Jacobins* – the collection draws out the complex and diverse ways in which texts engaged with imperial power and shaped a range of imperial and anti-imperial conversations, creating what its editors call 'an imperial commons'.[10]

Ten Books was launched in Oxford in December 2014 at *The Global History of the Book: 1780 to the Present*, a conference that explored the global and local, transnational and inter-imperial, as well as textual and intertextual, dimensions of book history. In the process of curating the conference programme, the organizing committee (of which the editors of the present collection were a part) found the necessarily narrow scope of Burton and Hofmeyr's collection irresistibly provocative. We found ourselves asking what other texts might have been included in the collection, and which books we would nominate for their influence not only on the British Empire, but on the colonial and postcolonial world more broadly. These questions were addressed by two lively soapbox-style panels, in which speakers made pithy, passionate and polemic short pitches for the inclusion of these alternative books in the critical conversation. As each orator took their turn on the soapbox, the discussion became markedly noisier and disrupted. Speakers and members of the audience argued over the global and transnational resonance of books on the imperial hero (Steevens's *With*

---

eds, *Ten Books That Shaped the British Empire: Creating an Imperial Commons* (Durham, NC and London: Duke University Press, 2014), 2.
9   Burton and Hofmeyr, 'Introduction', 2–3.
10 Burton and Hofmeyr, 'Introduction', 3–4.

Kitchener to Khartoum); race and geopolitics (Dilke's *Greater Britain*); and magical realism (Rushdie's *Midnight's Children*); as well as works from the Western canon (Shakespeare's *The Tempest*). As these sessions progressed, however, the conversation increasingly centred on books that actively *resisted* empire in its various forms, such as Jawaharlal Nehru's *The Discovery of India*, Nelson Mandela's *Long Walk to Freedom* and Karl Marx and Friedrich Engels's *The Communist Manifesto*.[11] Although *Ten Books* devotes considerable attention to anti-imperial sentiments (particularly in chapters devoted to *The Black Jacobins*, *Hind Swaraj* and *A Century of Wrong*), the overall balance of the collection leans towards books that were 'carrier[s] of imperial opinion and authority'.[12] Taking inspiration from both its predecessor and these dynamic soapbox panels, *Fighting Words* sets out to explore more specifically the significance of books as anti-imperial instruments. If books constituted, in Burton and Hofmeyr's estimation, a 'Spine of Empire', the chapters that follow explore how they also broke the back of imperial culture in the long twentieth century.

The fifteen books discussed in this volume, we contend, have each in different ways played a significant role in highlighting and challenging the oppressive realities and damaging legacies of imperialism and colonialism during the long twentieth century.[13] The historical period covered by these books is a *long* twentieth century indeed, stretching in fact from the mid-nineteenth century to the present. Of course, the 'postcolonial world' referred to in this book's subtitle is in one sense a temporal concept, although the period it designates could be considered to have begun centuries ago,

---

11   The dynamic, participatory format proved a hit at the conference, and has since been replicated with similar results at related gatherings in Australia, South Africa and the US.
12   Burton and Hofmeyr, 'Introduction', 2.
13   Burton and Hofmeyr acknowledge that 'perhaps the best example of a book conscripted into an imperial role' was, of course, the King James Bible. See Burton and Hofmeyr, 'Introduction', 1. Similarly, we want to point out that the Bible, and surely also the complete works of Shakespeare, have had an unprecedented impact (indeed, one soapbox presentation at the *Global History* conference made the case for *The Tempest* as a postcolonial world-shaping text), but we follow Burton and Hofmeyr in putting these to one side in order to curate a specifically *postcolonial* reading list.

after the *onset* of colonialism and the beginnings of numerous anticolonial and other anti-imperial movements, rather than simply after Indian independence or decolonization in the 1950s and 1960s. In this regard, the word 'postcolonial' can be understood more helpfully as a condition rather than a strict temporal demarcator. It indicates a broad and notably global order forged in and shaped by a sustained period of intense imperial rivalry and mass subjugation frequently justified by racial discourses. That nationalism and the nation-state were the main political ideologies and dispensations to emerge from this imperial age is reflected in many of the books documented in this collection, from Annie Besant's *Wake Up, India* (1913) and Nehru's *Discovery of India* (1946) to Cheikh Anta Diop's *Nations nègres et culture* (1954). But many of them also broke out of the boundaries of their nationalist containers to be taken up in explicitly transnational ways, from the antinational East African vision of Rajat Neogy's *Transition* magazine (1961–8) to the global reach of *The Communist Manifesto* (1848).

Placing particular emphasis on the global, transnational and translocal resonances of specific books, the chapters that follow chart these texts' contributions to the creation of an *anti*-imperial commons, no less complex than its imperial counterpart. Included are contributions from eleven academics who participated in the original conference or related events, and four more whose chapters were commissioned to broaden the scope of discussion. Written for the general reader, the following case studies will have a particular resonance for those interested in postcolonial literature; imperial, transnational and global history; and of course, the global history of the book.

Going Viral: Global Histories of the Book

If this brief genealogy begins to account for our use of the term 'fighting words' as the title of this collection, its subtitle, which speaks of books that have shaped the postcolonial world, deserves further unpacking. What exactly do we mean by 'the book' in this discussion? And how might books have shaped the world, and the postcolonial world more specifically?

Before addressing these questions directly, it is necessary to stress that by focusing on books, we do not intend to diminish the importance of other cultural forms (such as music, oral traditions, performance, art and so on) in the making of history and culture, and, more specifically, in influencing anticolonial resistance in the twentieth century. A focus on any one of these media could fill multiple analogous volumes, which would in turn make welcome companions to this collection. Yet, the history of books and texts has long played an essential role in how we understand the past.[14] Repositories and transmitters of human knowledge (and often objects of great beauty and value), books and other texts have naturally been coveted by scholars, offering windows onto the societies that created them. From novels to political treatises, books crystallize the ideological tensions and power dynamics at play in a given geohistorical moment, whether that of their initial publication and circulation or of their succeeding reception and interpretation. In the twentieth century a growing number of academics began to conceive of their work as part of book history, *l'histoire du livre*, print culture or the sociology of texts. Differing slightly 'in shades of meaning and emphasis', as Rimi Chatterjee writes, 'all [these] forms of the discipline have running through them a concern with the materiality of the text: who makes it and how, who sells it, who uses it, and what happens to it after that'.[15]

Of particular interest to book historians are the connections that develop between those who produce and use books, together with the mediators who facilitate and influence those connections. Agents and antiquarians; publishers and patrons; retailers and reviewers; bibliographers and bootleggers; censors; editors; illustrators; teachers; distributors; librarians; and, of course, writers and readers – all are scrutinized under the book historian's

---

14   Leslie Howsam, 'The Study of Book History', in Leslie Howsam, ed., *The Cambridge Companion to the History of the Book* (Cambridge: Cambridge University Press, 2014), 1.
15   Rimi B. Chatterjee, *Empires of the Mind: A History of the Oxford University Press in India under the Raj* (New Delhi: Oxford University Press, 2006), 2. For a detailed survey of the evolution of book history through the twentieth century, see David Finkelstein and Alistair McCleery, *An Introduction to Book History* (New York: Routledge, 2005), 7–27.

gaze. Often these histories, which take place outside of the actual text of the book *per se*, inform the way in which their arguments and stories are communicated and consumed, and come to bear in important social and political ways on their contents. 'The life of books and their makers occupies', Chatterjee continues, 'a territory between the realm of ideas – where world-changing movements have their source – and the realm of commerce and material culture, which provides the impetus and the battleground for competing ideas'.[16] For example, *The Communist Manifesto* was published first in direct response to the social ills of Britain in the late 1840s, yet it was the subsequent boom in translations in the twentieth century that led it to inform anticolonial movements worldwide. The lives of the fifteen books considered in this study, and of the ensemble cast of makers and users that facilitated their production, distribution and reception, form an essential part of the chapters that follow.

Over the last few decades, scholars have been increasingly interested in the transnational and global dimensions of book history. Unsurprisingly, this preoccupation reflects the broader trend within the humanities and social sciences towards seeking a better understanding of the intensifying *global* forces shaping cultural production and reception. The rise of global history has shifted scholars' focus onto histories of political, economic and cultural interaction across regional and national political boundaries, necessitating new and more nuanced disciplinary and geographical categorizations. 'For the moment, at least', historian John Darwin notes, 'writing the history of nations and states seems much less important than tracing the origins of our world of movement, with its frenetic exchange of goods and ideas, its hybrid cultures and its fluid identities'.[17] Book historians have entered this discussion with enthusiasm, noting the centrality of their topic to the global transfer of ideas and cultural 'convergence' that have

---

16 Chatterjee, *Empires of the Mind*, 2.
17 John Darwin, *After Tamerlane: The Rise & Fall of Global Empires, 1400–2000* (London: Penguin, 2008), 12.

shaped the modern world.[18] They have revealed the transnational lives of producers and consumers of books and, indeed, of the physical book itself.

Like most book historians, contributors to this collection embrace a rather flexible, and sometimes abstract, definition of 'the book'. Although the majority of chapters featured here deal with printed texts bound in codex form, we do not consider the book to be a fixed concept limited (in the words of one cynic) to 'tree flakes encased in dead cow'.[19] Allowing for a more exploratory view of the book, interested historians have extended their analysis to encompass a range of textual forms, from record labels to clay tablets to eBooks. Like Sydney Shep, who speaks of 'the restless book', we seek to emphasize the multiplicity of forms involved in the material, political and literary histories of the books discussed in this volume.[20] Some originated as pamphlets or academic theses, handwritten manuscripts or speeches delivered orally. Another, *Transition*, never appeared as a case-bound book – though several seminal novels of decolonization began their lives in its pages. The inclusion of this East African literary magazine as one of our fifteen 'books' is intended to expand our understanding of the relationship between print and resistance in the decolonizing world, for its varied cultural and political impacts depended as much on its unbooklike ephemerality and versatility as on its status as a print object. The afterlives and legacies of the fifteen books included here are as wide-ranging as their diverse origins, and many have ramified into other cultural forms after their initial publication. Frank Hardy's *The Unlucky Australians* (1968), for example, helped to inspire a documentary film, a hit pop song and an illustrated children's book. Mandela's *Long Walk to Freedom* (1994), meanwhile, has been adapted as a children's book, a comic series, a film, and countless other mythologizing media narratives. As is particularly the case for Mandela's autobiography, global communication technologies in

---

18 See Chris Bayly, *The Birth of the Modern World* (Malden, MA: Blackwell, 2004), x–xx.
19 Quoted in Finkelstein and McCleery, *Book History*, 2.
20 Sydney Shep, 'Books in Global Perspectives', in Leslie Howsam, ed., *The Cambridge Companion to the History of the Book*, 55.

Introduction

the latter half of the twentieth century have progressively destabilized 'the book' as a rigid concept.

Yet, even when they remain within the realm of the printed and bound text, books and their meanings inevitably shift and evolve as they move through space and time, crossing linguistic, cultural and geographical boundaries. Hofmeyr observes that 'when books travel, they change shape', emphasizing how texts 'are excised, summarized, abridged, and bowdlerized by the new intellectual formations into which they migrate'.[21] Invoking the scientific method of the replication of experiments, James Secord has developed the term *literary replication* to describe how books and the ideas they express circulate in and permeate society by being 'replicated' in various forms, from reviews and extracts to adaptations and conversations.[22] As Shep notes, the term replication also carries genetic connotations (as in DNA replication), raising the further suggestion that books are comparable to organisms that adapt to their environments through the process of replication.[23] We would suggest that the metaphor of a virus is especially resonant here. Through replication and subsequent mutation, a virus may adapt so effectively to its host environment that its spread reaches epidemic proportions, crossing regional and national borders with ease (consider the global transmission of *The Communist Manifesto*, for example, or Mandela's *Long Walk to Freedom*). Alternatively, it may have a significant effect in a limited geographical region, such as J. B. Danquah's *The Akan Doctrine of God* (1944) in Ghana, or lie dormant until it finds conditions in a different context more conducive to its flourishing, like Anna Julia Cooper's *A Voice from the South* (1892).

21 Isabel Hofmeyr, *The Portable Bunyan: A Transnational History of* The Pilgrim's Progress (Princeton, NJ: Princeton University Press, 2004), 2–3.
22 James A. Secord, *Victorian Sensation: The Extraordinary Publication, Reception, and Secret Authorship of* Vestiges of the Natural History of Creation (Chicago and London: Chicago University Press, 2000).
23 Shep, 'Books in Global Perspectives', 65.

Building Resistance: Books and the Making of the Postcolonial World

In his seminal work on *Ecological Imperialism*, historian Alfred Crosby reads the relative success or failure of the export of European flora and fauna as an effective demarcator of the extent of European penetration in colonial societies, as well as the capacity of indigenous communities to resist imperial incursion.[24] For book historians interested in the colonial and postcolonial world, tracing the book's viral spread has proved similarly illuminating. Clearly, books played an important role in transmitting the cultural norms and ideas of the metropole to colonial peripheries, propagating the presumed intellectual and industrial pre-eminence of the imperial powers. Advances in printing technology and communications developed in Europe carried works by imperial writers around the globe with unprecedented speed and on an unprecedented scale. In so doing, they contributed to the instantiation of cultural, social and political inequalities that continue to shape the world today.

Working together in the annexe of Oxford's Ertegun House in 2014, buildings first constructed as offices for scholars working on the *Oxford Dictionary of National Biography*, participants in the *Global History of the Book* conference were highly conscious of the longstanding influence of iconic Western publications in shaping knowledge across vast intellectual spaces and, in turn, producing cultural conventions imbued with deeply unequal and materially consequential relations of power. This 'colonial knowledge', the anthropologist Nicholas Dirks has argued,

> both enabled colonial conquest and was produced by it [...]. Cultural forms in newly classified 'traditional' societies were reconstructed and transformed by and through colonial technologies of conquest and rule, which created new categories

---

24 Alfred W. Crosby, *Ecological Imperialism: The Biological Expansion of Europe, 900–1900* (Cambridge: Cambridge University Press, 1986).

and oppositions between colonizers and colonized, European and Asian, modern and traditional, West and East, even male and female.²⁵

As Finkelstein and McCleery have pointed out, 'grand projects' like *The Oxford English Dictionary* 'had tremendous social and cultural effects, acting as guardians of accuracy, setters of standards, summarizers of important intellectual material', often with negative ramifications for the world's colonized populations.²⁶ Commenting on the proliferation of textual production by imperial administrators, anthropologists, cartographers and fiction writers alike across the British Empire, Elleke Boehmer declares: 'To colonize something was to pile writing upon it'.²⁷

Yet, the reach and efficacy of this textual virus, as for European imperialism more generally, varied across the colonial world from region to region, and between different groups of colonizing and colonized peoples. In certain parts of the globe, such as Australia and New Zealand, the advance of European print culture (and with it European languages) came as part of the great 'white deluge', whose scale and intensity overwhelmed the capacity of Indigenous peoples to resist invasion.²⁸ In the years and decades that followed, the gradual emergence of an imperial press and communications system – accompanied by a colonial publishing culture centred on London – played a vital role in binding Australia and New Zealand (and to a lesser extent Britain's other white dominions) to the 'mother country'.²⁹ Elsewhere, the impact of European print culture was more ambiguous.³⁰ Harish Trivedi

---

25   Nicholas B. Dirks, ed., *Colonialism and Culture* (Ann Arbor: University of Michigan Press, 1992), 2–3.
26   Finkelstein and McCleery, *Book History*, 4.
27   Elleke Boehmer, *Colonial & Postcolonial Literature: Migrant Metaphors* (Oxford: Oxford University Press, 1995), 97.
28   Finkelstein and McCleery, *Book History*, 90–1; on the 'white deluge', Bayly, *Modern World*, xx.
29   Martin Lyons and John Arnold, eds, *A History of the Book in Australia, 1891–1945: A National Culture in a Colonised Market* (Brisbane: University of Queensland Press, 2001); Simon J. Potter, *News and the British World: The Emergence of an Imperial Press System* (Oxford: Oxford University Press, 2003).
30   On the linguistic history of empire, Nicholas Ostler, *Empires of the Word: A Language History of the World* (London: HarperCollins, 2005).

contests the conviction of Lucien Febvre and Henri-Jean Martin that the printed book is 'one of the most effective means of mastery over the whole world'.[31] In India, Trivedi demonstrates, the arrival of Western 'books' had curiously counterproductive consequences:

> When the British did finally begin to publish books in India in the 1770s, their first productions were [...] translations into English from Sanskrit of foundational works of Indian law, scripture and literature. These did not appear to promote or strengthen British rule in India in any obvious manner, but led on the contrary to an exciting discovery of the greatness of Indian culture and civilisation dating from a period when Britain had not had so much to show for itself.[32]

Moreover, as with English education in India, 'what began as a form of colonial imposition was soon turned around to be deployed as an effective instrument of resistance to colonial rule'.[33]

Boehmer emphasizes that colonial systems and technologies of rule paradoxically facilitated anticolonial and nationalist movements: a 'cross-nationalist circuitry was [...] made possible and shaped by worldwide colonial (what we would today term neocolonial) nexuses of communication and exchange'.[34] If the 'colonial facilitation of nationalist interconnection may seem an irony', Boehmer notes, it is nonetheless 'a subversive one'.[35] Boehmer builds here on Edward Said's pioneering work on the ways in which cultural and textual production were both complicit with and, crucially, subversive of imperial rule. In the preface to *Culture and Imperialism*, Said observes that 'though imperialism implacably advanced during the nineteenth and twentieth century, resistance to it also advanced'.[36] There was, Said argues, 'a kind of historical necessity by which colonial pressure

---

31 Quoted in Harish Trivedi, 'The "Book" in India', in Robert Fraser and Mary Hammond, eds, *Books Without Borders: Volume 2, Perspectives from South Asia* (Basingstoke: Palgrave MacMillan, 2008), 14.
32 Trivedi, 'The "Book" in India', 15.
33 Trivedi, 'The "Book" in India', 27–8.
34 Elleke Boehmer, *Empire, the National and the Postcolonial, 1890–1920: Resistance in Interaction* (Oxford: Oxford University Press, 1998), 12.
35 Boehmer, *Empire*, 13.
36 Edward Said, *Culture and Imperialism* (London: Chatto & Windus, 1993), xxvi.

created anticolonial resistance', the one being the underside of the other.³⁷ It is for this reason that the books studied in this volume necessarily had to position themselves as – and therefore often became – fighting words.

This observation clearly resonates with books such as Frantz Fanon's *The Wretched of the Earth* (1961) – written in direct response to the violent oppression of colonial rule, as John Narayan shows – and with Miguel Ángel Asturias's indigenous American mythological novel *Men of Maize* (1949), whose resistance to multiple phases of colonial occupation is explored by Johanna Richter. But it is an intimate relationship also built more subtly into other chapter studies included here: Sol Plaatje's *Native Life in South Africa* (1916), as Janet Remmington argues, was at once a damning critique of imperial Britain's neglect of its black subjects and an appeal to the same metropolitan centre for aid, which strategically utilized the Empire's print networks for its own ends.

Indeed, if, as Catherine Hall notes, colonialism was never 'a single unified phenomenon', the scholar's task is to 'investigate the threads of connection between' different colonial cultures.³⁸ Exploring the history of empire and decolonization through the history of the book requires a similarly flexible approach. In *Ten Books*, Burton and Hofmeyr conceive of books 'not just as mobile objects but as themselves dispersed events' in which imperial power could be found 'on offense or defense in the fits and starts of its multiple embodiments'.³⁹ 'What came up and off the printed page in the age of empire', they argue, 'illuminates [...] a variety of pathways between texts and power rather than a singular, evolutionary, quantifiable or predictable one'.⁴⁰ As the following chapters will show, in the age of decolonization, the relationship between books of resistance and the structures of power with which they engaged has been equally complex. Moreover, as they have mutated through processes of circulation, translation

---

37 Said, *Culture and Imperialism*, 44.
38 Catherine Hall, 'Introduction: Thinking the Postcolonial, Thinking the Empire', in Catherine Hall, ed., *Cultures of Empire: A Reader* (Manchester: Manchester University Press, 2000), 16.
39 Burton and Hofmeyr, 'Introduction', 9, 10.
40 Burton and Hofmeyr, 'Introduction', 6.

and adaptation over time and distance, these books have had unintended and surprising impacts. As a telling example, Christina Twomey shows how Emily Hobhouse's *The Brunt of the War and Where it Fell* (1902) fervently resisted the brutality of British concentration camps during the South African War, only to be put into the service of Afrikaner nationalism, which would underpin the brutal apartheid system in South Africa decades later. The fraught relationship between complicity and resistance, both within texts and in the histories of their reception, is a thread that winds through this volume.

It is also clear that different kinds of books work and move through the world in manifestly different ways. Sally Morgan's confessional memoir *My Place* (1987), for example, operates in a register entirely separate from the *Wake Up, India* lectures of Annie Besant, the literary magazine *Transition* or a work of sociological analysis like W. E. B. Du Bois's *The Souls of Black Folk* (1903). The world-shaping efforts of these books vary greatly. The question of genre is one that the following chapters repeatedly address both explicitly and implicitly, but by juxtaposing these fifteen books that shaped the postcolonial world in diverse ways and at different geohistorical scales we invite readers to track the similarities, as well as differences, between their movements, effects and affects.

With these nuances and complications in mind, it is necessary to state that the chapters collected here, like the soapbox pitches that inspired them, openly foreground the anticolonial and anti-imperial resistance that these books have variously mobilized, and we acknowledge our own agenda in bringing this collection together from the outset. While we do not wish to reduce the world to a set of geopolitical or cultural binaries, it is important to understand the oppositional and antagonistic duality of colonial or neocolonial versus anticolonial or decolonial relations as a structuring device through which the many nuances of different geohistorical contexts and struggles can be refracted. As Benita Parry reminds us, 'it was the writings of liberation movements that inaugurated the interrogation of colonialism and imperialism' in the first place.[41]

---

41 Benita Parry, *Postcolonial Studies: A Materialist Critique* (New York: Routledge, 2004), 6.

Introduction

The project of *Fighting Words* – returning to an archive of anticolonial books to rekindle their resistance and emphasize the extent to which they shaped the postcolonial world – is ultimately motivated by reasons similar to those that moved Said to write *Culture and Imperialism*. For Said, the colonial-anticolonial 'conflict continues in an impoverished and for that reason all the more dangerous form, thanks to an uncritical alignment between intellectuals and institutions of power which reproduces the pattern of an earlier imperialist history' in the present.[42] Other postcolonial critics have more recently rehearsed Said's concerns, perhaps most notably Paul Gilroy, who 'warns against the revisionist accounts of imperial and colonial life that have proliferated in recent years'. These accounts 'fail to recognise that the ambiguities and defects of past colonial relations persist', and that 'those enduring consequences of empire can be implicated in creating and amplifying current problems'.[43] Following Gilroy, Said and Derek Gregory (who draws on Said's notion of 'imaginative geographies'), amongst others, these fifteen case studies are intended as 'contributions to a collective project of resistance and as stepping-stones toward a more humane geography'.[44] The books mapped here shaped the postcolonial world not least to the extent that, as Gregory characterizes the term 'postcolonial', they all remained committed 'to a future free of colonial power and disposition', a stance informed by 'a critique of the continuities between the colonial past and the colonial present'.[45] By proclaiming these books 'fighting words', then, our book must necessarily emphasize that this 'fight' is still ongoing.

---

42 Said, *Culture and Imperialism*, 44.
43 Paul Gilroy, *After Empire: Melancholia or Convivial Culture?* (London: Routledge, 2004), 2.
44 Derek Gregory, *The Colonial Present: Afghanistan, Palestine, Iraq* (Oxford: Blackwell, 2004), xv, 4.
45 Gregory, *The Colonial Present*, 7.

Fighting Words: A Postcolonial Reading List

Fighting Words appears at a moment in which the project of decolonization has once again come notably to the fore not only within academia but also in popular social and political discourse. Movements such as Rhodes Must Fall (RMF) and Black Lives Matter adopt a 'decolonial gaze' that 'deliberately remembers the violence of colonialism, the exploitation of extractive settler economies [and] the disfigurement of African communities and culture – all of which are concealed by grand narratives of development and modernisation'.[46] RMF's initial campaign centred on the symbolic currency of the Cecil Rhodes statue, which until April 2015 stood at the heart of the University of Cape Town campus, to foreground the ways, institutional and otherwise, in which white bodies, cultures and ways of knowing are privileged to the economic, psychological and physical detriment of others, particularly those in the Global South.

Books and their legacies are central to these global and transnational debates.[47] Indeed, many of the books studied throughout the chapters collected here laid the groundwork for engagement with these issues, and continue to play active shaping roles in these contemporary resistance movements. The pithy and accessible style of these chapters might further contribute to the curriculum transformation for which these movements call. As a pedagogic project, *Fighting Words* aims to provide not only 'expanded content', but also 'the analytical and methodological tools for debating, challenging and deconstructing inherited canons', foregrounding the work of fifteen books that enhance our understanding of 'colonialism not only as a political and social event, but also as an epistemic event with

---

46   Kathy Luckett, 'Curriculum Contestation in a Post-Colonial Context: A View from the South', *Teaching in Higher Education* 21/4 (2014), 416.
47   Estelle H. Prinsloo, 'The Role of the Humanities in Decolonising the Academy', *Arts & Humanities in Higher Education* 15/1 (2016), 165.

continuing epistemological and ontological effects'.[48] In so doing, we hope to contribute to the development of a 'critical consciousness', as learned from writers such as Cooper, Du Bois, Fanon and Diop, that can be translated into 'real action' and 'change'.[49]

For this reason, too, we seek to bring to the fore a number of books that influenced anti-racist and anti-imperial movements globally, which have nonetheless remained relatively overlooked in critical conversations. While attending to canonical resistance texts such as *The Communist Manifesto*, *The Wretched of the Earth* and *The Souls of Black Folk*, the volume also highlights, for example, the prescient intersectional awareness of Cooper's *A Voice from the South*, the role played by Besant's *Wake Up, India* lectures on the Indian Home Rule movement, and the more oblique influence of Danquah's *The Akan Doctrine of God* on the early history of decolonization in Africa.

Nonetheless, the selection of books for a collection such as this is always open to critique. In some cases, the omission of titles obviously deserving of inclusion has been made easier by the recent publication of dedicated histories. Mao Zedong's Little Red Book, *Quotations From Chairman Mao* (1964), provides one example where we believed the dedicated work of recent scholars required little elaboration. In their ground-breaking *Mao's Little Red Rook: A Global History* (2014), editor Alexander Cook and his contributors offer a wealth of perspectives on the remarkable power and momentum of Mao's Little Red Book, firstly within China, and then across the world. This pioneering global history of the book provides a vivid illustration of the remarkable potency of Mao's book as an agent of anti-imperial resistance. 'Wherever deployed', as Cook convincingly argues, it acted like a 'spiritual atom bomb [...] a powerful fission device, initiating chain reactions of escalating violence that threatened to destroy, for better or worse, the established structures of the world order'.[50]

---

48 Luckett, 'Curriculum Contestation', 424–5.
49 Prinsloo, 'The Role of the Humanities', 166.
50 Alexander Cook, 'Introduction: The Spiritual Atom Bomb and its Global Fallout', in Alexander C. Cook, ed., *Mao's Little Red Book: A Global History* (Cambridge: Cambridge University Press, 2014), 20.

Assembling a collection such as *Fighting Words* also necessarily involves an element of arbitrariness, and we recognize that we might easily have included books by Chinua Achebe and Ngũgĩ wa Thiong'o, for example, or the writings of Amílcar Cabral and Malcolm X – each of which would have spun new thematic webs and trajectories across the volume. We would also acknowledge the marked anglophone bias in the books examined here – a consequence of the collection's origins in an anglophone academic conference, but also a reflection of the increasing global dominance of anglophone publishing (and 'the onward march of the English language') in the twentieth century.[51] Our intention, however, is not exhaustiveness, but stimulation: these absences may be read as an invitation to others to imagine their own supplementary lists, as we ourselves have done.

Now, though, it remains for us to outline our chosen postcolonial reading list as it features in the fifteen chapters collected together as *Fighting Words*. Focusing on a book that is perhaps not intuitively 'postcolonial' at first glance, Dominic Davies begins by tracing the global influence of Karl Marx and Friedrich Engels's *The Communist Manifesto* (1848) through the numerous anticolonial movements that it informed throughout the twentieth century. He concludes by asking whether, in the twenty-first century, the internet and other technological developments might facilitate a post-capitalist society that bears a marked resemblance to communism as Marx and Engels first conceived it. Similarly, discussing a nineteenth-century book that has had an increasing resonance for contemporary decolonial movements and especially for black feminism, Imaobong Umoren then introduces readers to Anna Julia Cooper's *A Voice from the South* (1892). Umoren shows how Cooper's book, which went largely unread for much of the twentieth century, was in fact decades ahead of its time not only for its black feminist arguments but also for its conception of human rights.

Though shifting geographically, Christina Twomey's discussion of Emily Hobhouse's *The Brunt of War and Where it Fell* (1902) in Chapter 3 of this volume shows how the book's attempt to raise global awareness about

---

[51] Alistair McCleery, 'The Book in the Long Twentieth Century', in Leslie Howsam, ed., *The Cambridge Companion to the History of the Book*, 176.

one instance of what would now certainly be thought of as a human rights abuse by the British Empire was largely dismissed in Britain at the time of its writing, before then being appropriated by the apartheid regime in South Africa throughout the twentieth century. But despite these problems, Twomey shows how, as for Davies's and Umoren's arguments, Hobhouse's book has found a new voice post-1994, one praised for its pacifist and anti-militarist critique. Then, returning to the US context once more, Reiland Rabaka assesses the enduring legacy of W. E. B. Du Bois's *The Souls of Black Folk* (1903), drawing out several of the book's most powerful poetic and conceptual devices – including the 'Veil' and 'second sight' – and arguing for a new, cross-disciplinary re-evaluation of this seminal text on race and resistance.

With resonances of the chapters on Cooper and Hobhouse, the collection's fifth chapter turns to South Asia to assess the ways in which Annie Besant's *Wake Up, India: A Plea for Social Reform* (1913) served as a precursor to the anti-imperial politics of figures such as Nehru, who is in turn taken up by Boehmer in Chapter 7 of this collection. Priyasha Mukhopadhyay's discussion of Besant's text, which was comprised of annotated lectures originally delivered in Madras, also expands the collection's notion of the book and the ways in which these resistant texts are both read and *read out*, reaching wider audiences by migrating from page to speech and back again.

In Chapter 6, Janet Remmington takes us back to Africa, and to the importance of an iconic resistance text in challenging Western notions of racial and cultural superiority. In her exploration of Sol Plaatje's *Native Life in South Africa* (1916), Remmington reflects on Plaatje's impassioned critique of the 1913 Natives Land Act and the British Empire's flagrant betrayal of its black subjects to the demands and prejudices of white settler colonialism. Furthermore, Remmington sheds fresh light on Plaatje's ingenuity when using the Empire's networks of communication and information, along with his connections to prominent black thinkers in the US (such as Du Bois, Marcus Garvey and Booker T. Washington) to distribute his critique. The centrality of books to the making of postcolonial national identities is then further explored by Elleke Boehmer in her study of that iconic anticolonial figure Jawaharlal Nehru. In Nehru's autobiographies (*An Autobiography* of 1936 and *The Discovery of India* of 1946, here discussed as one 'book'), Boehmer explains, Indians and (in time) a range of colonized communities beyond the subcontinent were encouraged to think of themselves not as colonial subjects, but as national citizens, and to imagine a world beyond the imperial one they had inherited.

In Chapter 8, Rouven Kunstmann focuses on an important Ghanaian text published as yet another great global war tested the imperial powers: Joseph B. Danquah's *The Akan Doctrine of God* (1944). Important in the framing of a new national identity, anticolonial and yet curiously grounded in a colonial episteme, Danquah's *Akan*, Kunstmann argues, offered up an important cultural and textual model for a postcolonial Ghanaian state. Chapter 9 then returns to the power of *literary* interventions in resisting empire and its legacies in Johanna Richter's study of Miguel Ángel Asturias's 1949 novel, *Hombres de maíz* [*Men of Maize*]. Here Richter reflects on the novel as a particularly valuable medium for illuminating hardship and injustice (in this case the exploitative nature of imperialism) and, in Asturias's case, for encouraging colonial peoples to find unity and resistance in earlier indigenous and inherited cultural traditions. In Chapter 10, Ruth Bush continues this trajectory in relation to more recent scholarship on the Senegalese historian and scientist Cheikh Anta Diop's seminal study, *Nations nègres et culture* (1954). In *Nations*, as Bush explains, Diop set out to illuminate the black African origins of Ancient Egypt – and thereby of European civilization. It was this project, Bush argues, that proved fundamental to challenging contemporaneous Western notions of modernity and progress which had so often depicted Africans on the lower rungs of the ladder of civilization.

The collection's eleventh chapter crosses from West to East Africa, as Asha Rogers examines Rajat Neogy's literary magazine *Transition: A Journal of the Arts, Culture & Society* between 1961 and 1968, whose ambitious project was to foster the creation of an autonomous regional cultural identity after decolonization. Through the case of *Transition* – sponsored by the Congress for Cultural Freedom, which was in turn part-funded by the CIA – Rogers foregrounds the institutional complexities and ambiguities involved in publishing resistant writing. From a small literary magazine to one of the most renowned anticolonial texts of the twentieth century, John Narayan then discusses Frantz Fanon's *The Wretched of the Earth* (1961), a book that critiques the very kinds of institutional structures Rogers explores. Narayan locates the extraordinary travelling capacity of Fanon's book in its rhetorical and analytical immediacy. It is, he argues, a Third World 'manifesto' that was remarkably prescient about both the limitations of the Third World Project and the rise of the neo-imperial neoliberal global order in the wake of empire.

Travelling then across the globe to Australia, Benjamin Mountford explores the case of *The Unlucky Australians* (1968), Frank Hardy's account of the Wave Hill Walk Off, before Michael R. Griffiths turns in his chapter to Sally Morgan's memoir *My Place* (1987), one of the most popular and widely circulated books to come out of Australia. In the volume's thirteenth chapter, Mountford considers the reach and resonance of Hardy's landmark book, which was instrumental in bringing the plight of Indigenous Australians to a national and international audience. In Chapter 14, Griffiths examines Morgan's autobiography as not only an important stimulator of international discussion about Aboriginality, but also a means of thinking through the implications of voicing resistance through a confessional mode. As both chapters show, these two books – whose genres and histories of circulation and reception differ markedly – both remain important documents of the unfinished business between white and black Australia. Their histories offer insights not only into Australia's own postcolonial concerns but also about its place in the broader history of race and resistance in the long twentieth century.

The final chapter of the collection, Chapter 15, returns to Africa to consolidate the collection's geographical trajectories. There, Erica Lombard discusses the legacy of Nelson Mandela's *Long Walk to Freedom* (1994), which she views as the concrete embodiment of Mandela's symbolic power. Tracking the movement of Mandela's story across media, time and distance, Lombard foregrounds the ambivalent consequences of his status as both freedom fighter and postcolonial saint, which have come under increasing critical scrutiny in the twenty-first century.

As these brief chapter summaries indicate, *Fighting Words* seeks to emphasize the continuities between the extremely diverse and truly global historical and geographic contexts of a group of books that shaped the postcolonial world. Acknowledging that this is of course once again a necessarily narrow connection, we nevertheless hope that the examples of fighting words documented across these fifteen chapters foreground the importance of the book not only in constituting the 'imperial commons', but in stimulating, discussing and rethinking anti-imperial resistance from the nineteenth century through to the twenty-first.

Bibliography

Barnes, A. A. S., *On Active Service with the Chinese Regiment: A Record of the Operations of the First Chinese Regiment in North China from March to October 1900* (London: Grant Richards, 1902).
Bayly, Chris, *The Birth of the Modern World* (Malden, MA: Blackwell, 2004).
Bickers, Robert, *Britain in China: Community, Culture and Colonialism, 1900–1949* (Manchester: Manchester University Press, 1999).
——, 'Introduction', in Robert Bickers and R. G. Tiedemann, eds, *The Boxers, China and the World* (Plymouth: Rowman & Littlefield, 2001), xv–xvii.
——, 'Paul Cohen, the Boxers, and Alfred, Lord Tennyson', *The Chinese Historical Review* 14/2 (2007), 192–5.
Boehmer, Elleke, *Colonial & Postcolonial Literature: Migrant Metaphors* (Oxford: Oxford University Press, 1995).
——, *Empire, the National and the Postcolonial, 1890–1920: Resistance in Interaction* (Oxford: Oxford University Press, 1998).
Brooke, George Cecil, diary for 1900, George Cecil Brooke Papers, National Army Museum, 2004-09-244-1.
Burton, Antoinette, and Isabel Hofmeyr, 'Introduction: The Spine of Empire? Books and the Making of an Imperial Commons', in Antoinette Burton and Isabel Hofmeyr, eds, *Ten Books That Shaped the British Empire: Creating an Imperial Commons* (Durham, NC and London: Duke University Press, 2014).
Chatterjee, Rimi B., *Empires of the Mind: A History of the Oxford University Press in India under the Raj* (New Delhi: Oxford University Press, 2006).
Cook, Alexander C., ed., *Mao's Little Red Book: A Global History* (Cambridge: Cambridge University Press, 2014).
Crosby, Alfred W., *Ecological Imperialism: The Biological Expansion of Europe, 900–1900* (Cambridge: Cambridge University Press, 1986).
Darwin, John, *After Tamerlane: The Rise & Fall of Global Empires, 1400–2000* (London: Penguin, 2008).

Dirks, Nicholas B., ed., *Colonialism and Culture* (Ann Arbor: University of Michigan Press, 1992).
Finkelstein, David, and Alistair McCleery, *An Introduction to Book History* (New York: Routledge, 2005).
Fitchett, W. H., *Deeds That Won the Empire: Historical Battle Scenes* (New York: Charles Scribner's Sons, 1898).
Gilroy, Paul, *After Empire: Melancholia or Convivial Culture?* (London: Routledge, 2004).
Gregory, Derek, *The Colonial Present: Afghanistan, Palestine, Iraq* (Oxford: Blackwell, 2004).
Hall, Catherine, 'Introduction: Thinking the Postcolonial, Thinking the Empire', in Catherine Hall, ed., *Cultures of Empire: A Reader* (Manchester: Manchester University Press, 2000), 1–33.
Hevia, James, *English Lessons: The Pedagogy of Imperialism in Nineteenth-Century China* (Durham, NC and London: Duke University Press, 2003).
—— , 'Regulating the Facts of Asia: Military Reports and Handbooks', in *The Imperial Security State: British Colonial Knowledge and Empire-Building in Asia* (Cambridge: Cambridge University Press), 107–51.
Hobsbawm, Eric, *The Age of Empire, 1875–1914* (London: Abacus, 2007).
Hofmeyr, Isabel, *The Portable Bunyan: A Transnational History of* The Pilgrim's Progress (Princeton, NJ: Princeton University Press, 2004).
Howsam, Leslie, ed., *The Cambridge Companion to the History of the Book* (Cambridge: Cambridge University Press, 2014).
—— , 'The Study of Book History', in Leslie Howsam, ed., *The Cambridge Companion to the History of the Book*, 1–13.
Luckett, Kathy, 'Curriculum Contestation in a Post-Colonial Context: A View from the South', *Teaching in Higher Education* 21/4 (2014), 415–28.
Lyons, Martin, and John Arnold, eds, *A History of the Book in Australia, 1891–1945: A National Culture in a Colonised Market* (Brisbane: University of Queensland Press, 2001).
McCleery, Alistair, 'The Book in the Long Twentieth Century', in Leslie Howsam, ed., *The Cambridge Companion to the History of the Book*, 162–80.
Ostler, Nicholas, *Empires of the Word: A Language History of the World* (London: HarperCollins, 2005).
Packenham, Thomas, *The Scramble for Africa, 1876–1912* (London: Abacus Books, 2009).
Parry, Benita, *Postcolonial Studies: A Materialist Critique* (New York: Routledge, 2004).
Potter, Simon J., *News and the British World: The Emergence of an Imperial Press System* (Oxford: Oxford University Press, 2003).

Prinsloo, Estelle H., 'The Role of the Humanities in Decolonising the Academy', *Arts & Humanities in Higher Education* 15/1 (2016), 164–8.

Said, Edward, *Culture and Imperialism* (London: Chatto & Windus, 1993).

Secord, James A., *Victorian Sensation: The Extraordinary Publication, Reception, and Secret Authorship of* Vestiges of the Natural History of Creation (Chicago and London: Chicago University Press, 2000).

Shep, Sydney, 'Books in Global Perspectives', in Leslie Howsam, ed., *The Cambridge Companion to the History of the Book*, 53–70.

Thomson Zainu'ddin, A. G., 'Fitchett, William Henry', *Australian Dictionary of Biography* <http://adb.anu.edu.au/biography/fitchett-william-henry-6179> accessed 30 October 2016.

Trivedi, Harish, 'The "Book" in India: Orality, Manu-Script, Print (Post)Colonialism', in Robert Fraser and Mary Hammond, eds, *Books Without Borders: Volume 2, Perspectives from South Asia* (Basingstoke: Palgrave MacMillan, 2008), 12–33.

DOMINIC DAVIES

1   From Communism to Postcapitalism:
    Karl Marx and Friedrich Engels's
    The Communist Manifesto (1848)

ABSTRACT
History bears testament to the *Manifesto*'s planetary circulation, global readership and material impact. Interpretations of this short document have affected the lives of millions globally, particularly in the second half of the twentieth century. The text is somehow able to outline the complex theoretical foundations for the world's most enduring critique of capitalism in a comprehensible and persuasive language, and as such, readers of all classes, professions, nations and ethnicities have drawn on – and in many cases warped and manipulated – its valuable insights. Whilst arguing for the importance of the *Manifesto* as an anti-imperial book and exploring the reasons for its viral circulation, this chapter will also show that it is a self-reflexive text that predicts its own historic impact. It is the formal and generic – or, in fact, 'literary' – qualities of this astonishing document that have given it such primacy in the canon of anti-imperial and anti-capitalist writing.

> A spectre is haunting Europe – the spectre of Communism.
>
> The history of all hitherto existing society is the history of class struggles.
>
> All that is solid melts into air.
>
> [T]he free development of each is the condition for the free development of all.
>
> The proletarians have nothing to lose but their chains [...] WORKING MEN OF ALL COUNTRIES, UNITE![1]

1   Karl Marx and Friedrich Engels, *The Communist Manifesto* (London: Penguin Books, 2002 [1848]), 218, 219, 223, 244, 258. Throughout I use the Penguin edition, with an introduction and comprehensive notes by Gareth Stedman Jones, and which includes the numerous prefaces and other paratexts that Marx and Engels wrote for the *Manifesto*'s various editions. The chapter addresses this complex history of the *Manifesto*'s multiple editions and translations below.

That most readers will recognize at least one of these now (in)famous phrases is testament to the global impact of *The Communist Manifesto*. First drafted by Friedrich Engels (1820–95) in October 1847, in December 1847 and January 1848 Karl Marx (1818–83) added the rhetorical force that launched its words into the world's imagination. Perhaps of all the books included in this volume, *The Communist Manifesto*'s planetary influence is the least contested. The critics included in this chapter's bibliography – by no means a comprehensive list of the thinkers to have reflected on this short document – are generally in consensus: 'It is said that the Bible and the Quran are the only two books that have been printed in more editions and disseminated more widely than *The Communist Manifesto*', remarks postcolonial theorist Aijaz Ahmad; 'the Manifesto conquered the world', observes historian Eric Hobsbawm; '[m]illions of people all around the world – peasants, soldiers, intellectuals as well as professionals of all sorts, have over the years, been touched and inspired by it', comments geographer David Harvey; philosopher Martin Puchner argues that, '[t]he *Communist Manifesto* influenced the course of history more directly and lastingly than almost any other text'; and literary theorist Terry Eagleton claims that '[v]ery few [texts] have changed the course of actual history as decisively' as the *Manifesto*.[2]

Eagleton is not wrong. Interpretations of the *Manifesto* have affected the material lives of millions of the world's inhabitants. As Gareth Stedman Jones writes, the *Manifesto*'s importance is undeniable 'not because of its intrinsic merits, but because of the brute facts of world politics' – after the Second World War, 'millions in the Soviet Union, China, Cuba and Eastern Europe lived under communist rule', whilst millions more in Southern

---

2 Aijaz Ahmad, '*The Communist Manifesto* in its Own Time, and in Ours', in Prakash Karat, ed., *A World to Win: Essays on The Communist Manifesto* (New Delhi: Leftword Books, 1999), 14; Eric Hobsbawm, introduction in *The Communist Manifesto: A Modern Edition* (London and New York: Verso, 2012), 8; David Harvey, introduction in *The Communist Manifesto* (London: Pluto Press, 2008), 1; Martin Puchner, *Poetry of the Revolution: Marx, Manifestos, and the Avant-Gardes* (Princeton, NJ: Princeton University Press, 2006), 11; Terry Eagleton, *Why Marx Was Right* (New Haven, CT and London: Yale University Press, 2011), x.

Figure 1.1: A stamp of the Soviet Union, issued in 1948 to mark the hundredth anniversary of the first publication of *The Communist Manifesto* in 1848, and bearing the now iconic portraits of Marx and Engels.

Africa, Latin America and South East Asia were caught up in anti-imperial movements and civil wars fuelled by the communist ideals Marx and Engels outlined one hundred years earlier.³ The appearance of Marx and Engels's portraits on stamps in the Soviet Union, issued in the case of the above image to mark the centenary of the *Manifesto*'s publication, bear testament to the text's virality and socio-political weight. But separating the *Manifesto*'s 'intrinsic merits' from the 'brute facts of world politics' is a mistake: that the text outlines the theoretical foundations of the world's most enduring critique of capitalism in remarkably accessible language has allowed readers of all classes, nations and ethnicities to draw on – and in many cases to manipulate – its valuable insights.

Whilst emphasizing the importance of the *Manifesto* as a set of fighting words, this chapter will also demonstrate that the book self-reflexively predicted its own historic impact. It is the *Manifesto*'s formal and generic innovations that have given it such primacy in the canon of anti-imperial and anti-capitalist writing. Despite recent claims by neoliberal economists that we have reached 'the End of History', the *Manifesto*'s influence, and the history it has both described and created, is far from over.⁴ In 2005 the *Manifesto* was listed as the most 'harmful' book in recent history by the American Conservative Journal *Human Events*, while in the same year a BBC Radio Four poll voted Karl Marx the 'Greatest Philosopher of All Time'.⁵ After the global financial crisis in 2008, there was a surge in 'Marx-mania' – capitalism now appears to be on the brink of the collapse that the *Manifesto* predicted so long ago, and new kinds of information networks and collaborative production increasingly resemble the vision of communism first espoused by Marx and Engels.⁶

---

3   Gareth Stedman Jones, introduction in *The Communist Manifesto* (London: Penguin Books, 2002), 3.
4   Francis Fukuyama, 'The End of History?', *The National Interest* (1989) <https://ps321.community.uaf.edu/files/2012/10/Fukuyama-End-of-history-article.pdf> accessed 5 June 2015.
5   Jeffrey C. Isaac, ed., *Rethinking the Western Tradition: The Communist Manifesto* (New Haven, CT and London: Yale University Press, 2012), 1.
6   Paul Mason, *PostCapitalism: A Guide to Our Future* (London: Allen Lane, 2015), 49.

The *Manifesto* as World Literature

To begin, I want to consider *what* that text, *The Communist Manifesto*, actually is. Such a question is not as simple as it seems. The text originally written and published by Marx and Engels in 1848 was in fact entitled *The Manifesto of the Communist League*, 'a nineteenth century political tract [...] written in two months for an unknown and uninfluential group of German émigrés in London'.[7] It was not until the preface to the German Edition of 1872 that Marx and Engels proclaimed that 'the Manifesto has become a historical document which we have no longer any right to alter'.[8] Its content may not have altered significantly in the intervening period, but this preface reshaped the way it was read. It proclaimed the *Manifesto*'s global significance, transforming it from an 'uninfluential' political tract into a 'historical document'. Given the importance of the *Manifesto*'s conception of 'History' (significantly with a capital 'H'), the dialogue within the text between old sections and new reignites the original's revolutionary rhetoric. In the Penguin edition used as the primary text for this chapter, no fewer than seven prefaces precede the actual text of the *Manifesto* itself. Today, critics continue to write introductions that relight the explosive energy lying dormant in the *Manifesto*; as Harvey rhetorically concludes: 'We communists are the persistent spectral presence [...] The struggle continues.'[9]

Though '[n]obody would have predicted a remarkable future for the *Manifesto* in the 1850s and early 1860s', after nine new editions appeared in six languages between 1871 and 1872, the *Manifesto* 'conquered the world'.[10] However, the *Manifesto* is a product of the decade in which it was first written. Throughout the 1840s, social unrest across Europe was so

---

[7] Geoff Dow and George Lafferty, eds, *Everlasting Uncertainty: Interrogating The Communist Manifesto, 1848–1998* (Annandale: Pluto Press, 1998), 1. Indeed, 'nowhere is the actual body on whose behalf the *Manifesto* was written, the Communist League, mentioned in it' – from the outset, Marx and Engels emphasized the *Manifesto*'s universal and enduring reach. Hobsbawm, ed., *The Communist Manifesto*, 15.
[8] Marx and Engels, *The Communist Manifesto*, 194.
[9] Harvey, introduction in *The Communist Manifesto*, 30.
[10] Hobsbawm, introduction in *The Communist Manifesto: A Modern Edition*, 6–7.

pervasive that 'the idea of revolution, of one kind or another, seemed [...] as natural as the prospect that the sun would set in the evening and rise in the morning'.[11] It was 'the age of revolution', a 'twin upheaval' of 'political revolution' in France and 'industrial revolution' in Britain, culminating in the revolutions of 1848 that swept across Europe just weeks after the *Manifesto*'s first publication.[12] Furthermore, its diagnosis of capitalism was rooted in Engels's first-hand experience. His 1847 document, 'Principles of Communism', on which much of the book's first section is based, was a political response to his experience of Manchester in the early 1840s, recorded in detail in his *Condition of the Working Class in England* (1845). Suffering from the depression of 1841–2, the Lancashire cotton industry offered a 'classic example of technological unemployment' and the resulting exacerbation of class relations between an impoverished working class and a small bourgeois elite were conditions that would become symptomatic of industrial capitalism globally.[13]

Language similarly complicates the text of the *Manifesto*. As Marx and Engels admitted in 1872, their document was published first in German, then quickly in French in 1848 and English in 1850.[14] The 544 editions of the *Manifesto* published prior to the Russian Revolution in 1917 spanned thirty-five different languages and though, as Ahmad observes, these were predominantly 'European languages', there were also 'three editions in Japanese and one in Chinese'.[15] In the following years, it furthered its geographical and linguistic reach as 'the two Russian revolutions helped catapult the *Manifesto* to the position of being the primary revolutionary text'.[16]

---

11 Aijaz Ahmad, 'The Communist Manifesto and "World Literature"', *Social Scientist* 29/7–8 (2000), 3.
12 Eric Hobsbawm, *The Age of Revolution* (New York: Vintage Books, 1996), 1–2.
13 George R. Boyer, 'The Historical Background of *The Communist Manifesto*', *The Journal of Economic Perspectives*, 12/4 (1998), 152–62.
14 Marx and Engels, *The Communist Manifesto*, 193.
15 Ahmad, '*The Communist Manifesto* in its Own Time, and in Ours', 14; Hobsbawm, ed., *The Communist Manifesto*, 8.
16 Puchner, *Poetry of the Revolution*, 38.

For example, it arrived in India in 1922 and was first published in Bengali in 1926; by 1933 it had also been translated into Urdu, Marathi, Tamil and Hindi.[17] At no point did Marx and Engels feel that the reader of the translated text was distanced from the political content of the German original, nor did this concern the many twentieth-century revolutionary movements inspired by the *Manifesto*'s words. 'What emerges', writes Puchner, is 'the dream of a new world literature: all editions of the *Manifesto* in all languages are equivalent so that the conception of an original language no longer matters'.[18]

However, reading the *Manifesto* as a world literary text, S. S. Prawer identifies the proliferation of 'metaphors [and] images, from oral and written literature, from publishing, and from theatrical performance' present in the original German.[19] For German readers, the *Manifesto* is a literary palimpsest: 'beneath the utterances of Marx and Engels they detect those of German poets', most notably that of Goethe, whose poem 'The Sorcerer's Apprentice' (made famous by Walt Disney's 1940 film, *Fantasia*) informs the *Manifesto*'s theory of class history.[20] In Goethe's poem, the apprentice 'calls up spirits he cannot, in the end, subdue'; for Marx and Engels, the bourgeoisie may have transformed a feudalist society into a capitalist one, but they cannot 'subdue' the proletariat they have created. Throughout, the *Manifesto* 'heightens or varies a well-known quotation', using 'the words of great writers to confirm and sanction [its] own'.[21] If these references are

17 Karat, ed., *A World to Win*, 131–2.
18 Puchner, *Poetry of the Revolution*, 52.
19 S. S. Prawer, *Karl Marx and World Literature* (Oxford: Oxford University Press, 1978), 138.
20 Prawer, *Karl Marx and World Literature*, 140. Critics have also pointed out the *Manifesto*'s allusion to Shakespeare's *Hamlet*, Dickens's 'A Christmas Carol' and Mary Shelley's *Frankenstein*. See respectively Jacques Derrida, *Spectres of Marx* (New York and London: Routledge, 2006); Coral Lansbury, 'Melodrama, Pantomime, and the Communist Manifesto', *Browning Institute Studies* 14 (1985), 2–6; Marshall Berman, *All That Is Solid Melts Into Air* (London: Penguin Books, 1988), 101.
21 Prawer, *Karl Marx and World Literature*, 158, 164.

lost on non-German readers, the *Manifesto*'s self-conscious reflections on translation still develop 'a new understanding of international literature that resonates in various ways with current discourses on literature and globalisation'.[22] It actively predicts its own transcendence of linguistic, cultural and geographical barriers.

Somewhat contrarily, the *Manifesto*'s focus is not the blueprint for a communist utopia, but rather the celebration of bourgeois capitalism and the unified global culture it facilitates. Marx and Engels praise the bourgeoisie's 'infinite horizons, its revolutionary energy and audacity, its dynamic creativity, its adventurousness and romance', so that 'next to the *Communist Manifesto*, the whole body of capitalist apologetics, from Adam Ferguson to Milton Friedman, is remarkably pale and empty of life'.[23] If, as Puchner continues, it is 'nowhere clearer how much Marx and Engels admire the bourgeoisie than in [their] remark about bourgeois world literature', this is because the potential for communist revolution is rooted in the international solidarities built through a globalizing culture.[24] The *Manifesto* emphasizes that the global economy and culture created by bourgeois capitalism is a necessary predicate for the international communism that it advocates – it is the 'WORKING MEN OF ALL COUNTRIES', not of one region or nation, that must 'UNITE!' It then creates that global audience by overcoming the problem of its own translatability. The *Manifesto* anticipates 'the world-wide dissemination and mingling of "national and local" literatures' that defines contemporary global culture, as critics such as David Damrosch and Franco Moretti have subsequently explored.[25]

---

22 Puchner, *Poetry of Revolution*, 3.
23 Berman, *All That Is Solid*, 98.
24 Puchner, *Poetry of Revolution*, 49.
25 Prawer, *Karl Marx and World Literature*, 146; David Damrosch, *What is World Literature?* (Princeton, NJ: Princeton University Press, 2003). Franco Moretti, 'Conjectures on World Literature', *New Left Review* 1 (2000), 54–68.

The *Manifesto* and Anticolonialism

The *Manifesto*'s prediction of a global culture is exemplified by its own history of publication, translation and dissemination. Throughout the twentieth century, it not only informed the revolutions in Russia and China, but became 'the most zealous advocate of the world's anticolonialist movements'; after all, though Marx was European, it would be 'in Asia that his ideas first took root, and in the so-called Third World that they flourished most vigorously'.[26] It influenced numerous anticolonial leaders and organizations, from Fidel Castro in Cuba to Frantz Fanon in Algeria, from Kwame Nkrumah in Ghana to Julius Nyerere in Tanzania, and from the Indian National Congress in India to the African National Congress in South Africa. Proliferating translations allowed the *Manifesto* to fuse 'with local traditions and [create] new versions of world literature and new visions of internationalism', a flexibility embedded within its formal structure and rhetorical techniques.[27] It offered a concise and lucid critique of capitalism before, almost immediately, predicting that system's disintegration; the *Manifesto* spoke to political movements of the twentieth century because they were as much anti-capitalist as they were anti-imperial or anticolonial.

It was Lenin's reflections on the *Manifesto* that realized the text's full anticolonial weight. Regardless of what Lenin 'effectively did' in Russia, argues Slavoj Žižek, 'the field of possibilities he opened up' have rightly made Leninist-Marxism the most dominant form of Marxism, both historically and today.[28] Lenin's two pamphlets, *What is to be Done?* (1902) and *Imperialism, the Highest Stage of Capitalism* (1917), updated the *Manifesto*'s critique for the 'Age of Empire', a period that saw 'the triumph and

---

26 Eagleton, *Why Marx Was Right*, 215–25.
27 Puchner, *Poetry of Revolution*, 63.
28 Slavoj Žižek, 'Have Michael Hardt and Antonio Negri Rewritten the Communist Manifesto for the Twenty-first Century?', *Rethinking Marxism: A Journal of Economics, Culture & Society* 13/3–4 (2001), 198.

transformation of capitalism in the historically specific forms of bourgeois society in its liberal vision'.[29] Lenin's bridging of theoretical analysis and the enactment of political change is a 'lesson' inscribed into, and 'learned' from, the *Manifesto*'s form, genre and rhetoric.[30] As Thomas Kemple argues in his close-reading of the *Manifesto*'s final line ('WORKING MEN OF ALL COUNTRIES, UNITE!'), the gap that separates these capitalized words from the rest of the written prose 'open[s] space for action' by calling 'a specific class' into existence: the *Manifesto* 'proposes not simply a *theory of history*, but also a *'thesis about the historicization of theory'*.[31] Formally, it connects the written word to historical and material revolution, developing an intimate relationship between theory and action. The *Manifesto* is a book that not only shaped the postcolonial world, but actually theorized the processes of its own revolutionary shaping.

Despite its global uptake, the fall of the Berlin Wall and then the Soviet Union in the 1980s suggested that 'the communist hypothesis' had 'failed'.[32] However, these societies and states departed from the *Manifesto*'s quite specific formulation of communism in fundamental ways, not least in the size of the state (virtually non-existent in the *Manifesto*'s account) and in the centrality of individualism (an ideology to which many of the so-called 'communist' states were opposed, but that the *Manifesto*'s version harnesses for the greater social good). This is not to detach the kinds of political governance of the Soviet Union and Mao's China, say, from 'communism' as it is outlined in the *Manifesto*. Such an effort would risk repeating arguments that, in their attempts to defend Marx and Engels, begin to look like apologies for those murderous regimes – though Eagleton's point that capitalism has only 'brought untold prosperity to some sectors of the world […] as did Stalin and Mao, at staggering

---

29 Eric Hobsbawm, *The Age of Empire* (New York: Vintage Books, 1989), 8–9.
30 Puchner, *Poetry of Revolution*, 40.
31 Thomas Kemple, 'Post-Marx: Temporal Rhetoric and Textual Action in the *Communist Manifesto*', *Rethinking Marxism: A Journal of Economics, Culture & Society* 12/2 (2000), 57–8.
32 Alain Badiou, *The Communist Hypothesis*, trans. David Macey and Steve Corcoran (London and New York: Verso, 2010), 2.

human cost', is a convincing one.[33] Nevertheless, I want to conclude that, despite communism's apparent 'failure', the *Manifesto* is still relevant in the twenty-first century. Indeed, 'the horizon that conditions our experience', more than ever before, is communism as Marx and Engels originally conceived it.[34]

The *Manifesto* and Postcapitalism

Marshall Berman emphasizes the 'individualism' that underpins the *Manifesto*'s 'vision of communism', pointing out that 'Marx is closer to some of his bourgeois and liberal enemies than he is to traditional exponents of communism'.[35] The *Manifesto* celebrates the social and economic conditions brought about by bourgeois capitalism because they lay the material foundations for the next stage in 'History': communism. As the *Manifesto* famously puts it, 'What the bourgeoisie, therefore, produces, above all, is its own grave-diggers'.[36] Bourgeois capitalism, or today's neoliberalism, is a necessary prerequisite to communism as Marx and Engels envisage it. The enormous wealth generated by capitalist society, no matter how unevenly distributed, is essential: 'Marx himself never imagined that socialism could be achieved in impoverished conditions', such as those of revolutionary Russia or China.[37] To do so would, and did, require an authoritarian state to impose industrial revolution at huge human cost. Despite the historical association of communism with big government, the *Manifesto*'s vision of communism in fact promotes the eradication of the state entirely. It draws

---

33   Eagleton, *Why Marx Was Right*, 15. See also Badiou, *The Communist Hypothesis*, 3.
34   Jodi Dean, *The Communist Horizon* (London and New York: Verso, 2012), 2.
35   Berman, *All That Is Solid*, 98.
36   Marx and Engels, *The Communist Manifesto*, 233.
37   Eagleton, *Why Marx Was Right*, 16.

on liberal individualism, but transforms it, ever so slightly, to benefit not *capitalism* itself, but rather other individuals:

> In bourgeois society, living labour is but a means to increase accumulated labour. In Communist society, accumulated labour is but a means to widen, to enrich, to promote the existence of the labourer. [...] By freedom is meant, under the present bourgeois conditions of production, free trade, free selling and buying. [...] In place of the old bourgeois society, with its classes and class antagonisms, we shall have an association, in which the free development of each is the condition for the free development of all.[38]

As Hannah Arendt argues, 'it was not Karl Marx but the liberal economists themselves who had to introduce "the communist fiction"'; but it *is* the *Manifesto* that is 'courageous' enough to 'conclude that the "socialization" of man would produce automatically a harmony of all interests'.[39] Paradoxically, in 1989 the neoliberal economist Francis Fukuyama drew directly on the *Manifesto* to proclaim that the world had reached 'The End of History'. He claimed that the 'two major challenges to liberalism, those of fascism and of communism', had been defeated, and that the 'class issue' – the antagonism that for Marx and Engels had been '[t]he history of all hitherto existing society' – had 'actually been successfully resolved in the West'.[40] 'History', used in the 'Hegelian-Marxist sense of the progressive evolution of human political and economic institutions', had for Fukuyama 'culminated not in socialism but in democracy and a market economy'.[41]

Peculiarly enough, as Li Xing points out, Fukuyama's argument, along with other defences of neoliberalism, actually returns 'to the most essential basis of the Marxian world-view – *the material foundations of society*, in

---

38 Marx and Engels, *The Communist Manifesto*, 236–7, 244.
39 Hannah Arendt, *The Human Condition* (Chicago: University of Chicago Press, 1998), 43–4.
40 Marx and Engels, *The Communist Manifesto*, 219, and Fukuyama, 'The End of History?'.
41 Francis Fukuyama, 'Second Thoughts: The End of History 10 Years Later', *New Perspectives Quarterly* 16/4 (1999), 40.

other words, *the materialist conception of history*.⁴² Fukuyama assumes that 'the egalitarianism of modern America represents the essential achievement of the classless society envisioned by Marx', blaming issues such as 'black poverty' not on 'liberalism' but rather on 'the "legacy" of slavery and racism'; as though those two historical phenomena were somehow unrelated.⁴³ A quarter century later, during which time neoliberalism has tightened its grip, Fukuyama's argument that 'class' is no longer an ongoing social and economic contradiction sounds absurd.⁴⁴ As Thomas Piketty's recent study has shown, in the past decade capitalism has generated 'arbitrary and unsustainable inequalities that radically undermine the meritocratic values on which democratic societies are based'.⁴⁵ Just as Marx and Engels predicted over 150 years ago, capitalism is 'unsustainable', sowing the seeds of its own destruction.

If 'History' is not over, where might the beginnings of the communist society that Marx and Engels predicted would succeed capitalism be found today? Badiou, who recently proclaimed 'the rebirth of history', argues that the 2011 riots in London and the recent revolutions in the Arab world resemble 'the first working-class insurrections of the nineteenth century'.⁴⁶ But it is also manifesting in other, less obvious ways. Paul Mason, echoing the *Manifesto*, argues that 'capitalism, a complex, adaptive system [...] has reached the limits of its capacity to adapt'.⁴⁷ In its place, he identifies the 'rise of collaborative production': collective organizations such as Wikipedia that provide the 'biggest information product in the world' for free, creating '[n]ew forms of ownership, new forms of lending [and] new legal contracts'.⁴⁸

---

42   Li Xing, 'Capitalism and Globalisation in the Light of the *Communist Manifesto*', *Economic and Political Weekly* 33/33–4 (1998), 2227.
43   Fukuyama, 'The End of History?'.
44   David Harvey, *A Brief History of Neoliberalism* (New York: Oxford University Press, 2005), 2.
45   Thomas Piketty, *Capital in the Twenty-First Century*, trans. Arthur Goldhammer (London: Harvard University Press, 2014), 1.
46   Alain Badiou, *The Rebirth of History: Times of Riots and Uprisings*, trans. Gregory Elliott (London and New York: Verso, 2012), 5.
47   Mason, *PostCapitalism*, xiii (emphasis in original).
48   Mason, *PostCapitalism*, xv.

Whilst Mason does not specifically use the word 'communist', other commentators argue that 'Wikipedia's mode of production [...] bears strong resemblance with what Marx and Engels described as communism', and that 'the classic demands of the left – for less work, for an end to scarcity, for economic democracy, for the production of socially useful goods, and for the liberation of humanity – are materially more achievable than at any other point in history'.[49]

This is not the communism of Stalin and Mao, but rather the kind of 'participatory democracy' that the *Manifesto* first propagated in the 1840s. Just as the 'steam and machinery' that had 'revolutionized industrial production' was a crucial technological development that would make communism possible for Marx and Engels, new technologies such as the internet are making 'communist production practices' realizable today.[50] Though these microcosms of communist production are still 'antagonistically entangled into capitalist class relations', they might yet 'be developed, extended, and intensified' into other spheres of society.[51] As Srinicek and Williams argue, the 'utopian potentials inherent in twenty-first-century technology cannot remain bound to a parochial capitalist imagination; they must be liberated by an ambitious left alternative'.[52] The world literary and social commons that *The Communist Manifesto* drew on and created, in both content and form, and which informed many of the twentieth century's anti-imperial movements, may also be fundamental to the realization of a postcapitalist society in the twenty-first.

---

49   Sylvain Firer-Blaess and Christian Fuchs, 'Wikipedia: An Info-Communist Manifesto', *Television & New Media* 15/2 (2014), 88; Nick Srinicek and Alex Williams, *Inventing the Future: Postcapitalism and a World Without Work* (London and New York: Verso, 2015), 1–3.
50   Marx and Engels, *The Communist Manifesto*, 220; Firer-Blaess and Fuchs, 'Wikipedia', 90.
51   Firer-Blaess and Fuchs, 'Wikipedia', 90, 99.
52   Srinicek and Williams, *Inventing the Future*, 1–3.

Bibliography

Ahmad, Aijaz, 'The Communist Manifesto and "World Literature"', *Social Scientist* 29/7–8 (2000), 3–30.
——, '*The Communist Manifesto* in its Own Time, and in Ours', in Prakash Karat, ed., *A World to Win: Essays on* The Communist Manifesto (New Delhi: Leftword Books, 1999), 14–18.
Arendt, Hannah, *The Human Condition* (Chicago: University of Chicago Press, 1998).
Badiou, Alain, *The Communist Hypothesis*, trans. David Macey and Steve Corcoran (London and New York: Verso, 2010).
——, *The Rebirth of History: Times of Riots and Uprisings*, trans. Gregory Elliott (London and New York: Verso, 2012).
Berman, Marshall, *All That Is Solid Melts Into Air: The Experience of Modernity* (London: Penguin Books, 1988).
Boyer, George R., 'The Historical Background of *The Communist Manifesto*', *The Journal of Economic Perspectives* 12/4 (1998), 151–74.
Damrosch, David, *What is World Literature?* (Princeton, NJ: Princeton University Press, 2003).
Dean, Jodi, *The Communist Horizon* (London and New York: Verso, 2012).
Derrida, Jacques, *Spectres of Marx: The State of the Debt, the Work of Mourning and the New International* (New York and London: Routledge, 2006).
Dow, Geoff, and George Lafferty, eds, *Everlasting Uncertainty: Interrogating The Communist Manifesto, 1848–1998* (Annandale: Pluto Press, 1998).
Eagleton, Terry, *Why Marx Was Right* (New Haven, CT and London: Yale University Press, 2011).
Engels, Friedrich, *Condition of the Working Class in England* (Oxford: Oxford University Press, 2009).
Firer-Blaess, Sylvain, and Christian Fuchs, 'Wikipedia: An Info-Communist Manifesto', *Television & New Media* 15/2 (2014), 87–103.
Fukuyama, Francis, 'The End of History?', *The National Interest* (1989) <https://ps321.community.uaf.edu/files/2012/10/Fukuyama-End-of-history-article.pdf> accessed 5 June 2015.
——, 'Second Thoughts: The End of History 10 Years Later', *New Perspectives Quarterly* 16/4 (1999), 40–2.
Harvey, David, *A Brief History of Neoliberalism* (New York: Oxford University Press, 2005).
Hobsbawm, Eric, *The Age of Empire* (New York: Vintage Books, 1989).
——, *The Age of Revolution* (New York: Vintage Books, 1996).

Isaac, Jeffrey C., ed., *Rethinking the Western Tradition: The Communist Manifesto* (New Haven, CT and London: Yale University Press, 2012).

Karat, Prakash, ed., *A World to Win: Essays on* The Communist Manifesto (New Delhi: LeftWord Books, 1999).

Kemple, Thomas M., 'Post-Marx: Temporal Rhetoric and Textual Action in the *Communist Manifesto*', *Rethinking Marxism: A Journal of Economics, Culture & Society* 12/2 (2000), 44–60.

Lansbury, Coral, 'Melodrama, Pantomime, and the Communist Manifesto', *Browning Institute Studies* 14 (1985), 1–10.

Marx, Karl, and Friedrich Engels, *The Communist Manifesto*, with introduction and notes by Gareth Stedman Jones (London: Penguin Books, 2002 [1848]).

——, *The Communist Manifesto*, with introduction by David Harvey (London: Pluto Press, 2008).

——, *The Communist Manifesto: A Modern Edition*, with introduction by Eric Hobsbawm (London and New York: Verso, 2012).

Mason, Paul, *PostCapitalism: A Guide to Our Future* (London: Allen Lane, 2015).

Moretti, Franco, 'Conjectures on World Literature', *New Left Review* 1 (2000), 54–68.

Piketty, Thomas, *Capital in the Twenty-First Century*, trans. Arthur Goldhammer (London: Harvard University Press, 2014).

Prawer, S. S., *Karl Marx and World Literature* (Oxford: Oxford University Press, 1978).

Puchner, Martin, *Poetry of the Revolution: Marx, Manifestos, and the Avant-Gardes* (Princeton, NJ: Princeton University Press, 2006).

Srinicek, Nick, and Alex Williams, *Inventing the Future: Postcapitalism and a World Without Work* (London and New York: Verso, 2015).

Stedman Jones, Gareth, 'Introduction', in Karl Marx and Friedrich Engels, *The Communist Manifesto* (London: Penguin Books, 2002), 1–187.

Xing, Li, 'Capitalism and Globalisation in the Light of the *Communist Manifesto*', *Economic and Political Weekly* 33/33-4 (1998), 2223–7.

Žižek, Slavoj, 'Have Michael Hardt and Antonio Negri Rewritten the *Communist Manifesto* for the Twenty-First Century?', *Rethinking Marxism: A Journal of Economics, Culture & Society* 13/3-4 (2001), 190–8.

IMAOBONG UMOREN

2 Anna Julia Cooper's *A Voice from the South* (1892): Black Feminism and Human Rights

ABSTRACT

Born in Raleigh, North Carolina, the daughter of an enslaved black woman and her white master, Anna Julia Cooper broke the conventions of her day to become a prominent educator, orator and author. In 1892, she published her black feminist magnum opus, *A Voice from the South*. The text, however, is not only important for its black feminism. It is also significant for Cooper's reflections and ideas relating to imperialism, race, rights, slavery and suffrage in the Americas, Europe, Asia and Africa. This chapter explores the many ways in which it occupies a unique position as not only a piece of black feminism but also a text that promoted human rights.

Born in Raleigh, North Carolina in 1858, Anna Julia Cooper (1858–1964) was the daughter of an enslaved black woman and her white master. A product of the peculiar institution of transatlantic slavery, Cooper broke the conventions of her day to become a prominent educator, orator and author. In 1892 her magnum opus, *A Voice from the South* was published. In the opening chapter Cooper famously declared: 'Only the BLACK WOMAN can say "when and where I enter, in the quiet, undisputed dignity of my womanhood, without violence and without suing or special patronage, then and there the whole *Negro race enters with me*".[1] The collection of essays and speeches that comprises *A Voice from the South* delves deep into the complexities of being black, female and middle class. Literary scholar Mary Helen Washington describes it as 'the most precise, forceful, well-argued

---

1 Anna Julia Cooper, *A Voice from the South* (New York: Oxford University Press, 1988 [1892]), 31.

statement of black feminist thought to come out of the nineteenth century'.[2] As such, it is now widely recognized as *the* black feminist bible.

However, *A Voice from the South* is not only important for its black feminism. The text is also significant for Cooper's reflections on imperialism, race, rights, slavery and suffrage in the Americas, Europe, Asia and Africa. Cooper linked the struggle that African Americans and women were facing for full equality with the plight of other oppressed groups. She was a committed coalition builder who sought to strengthen the position of minorities across the world. This chapter explores the ways in which *A Voice from the South* occupies a unique position as a black feminist text that also promoted what would today be understood as human rights, through Cooper's constant assertion of the humanity of all people. This included people of African descent, whose humanity continued to be debated within the private and public sphere. The chapter begins by exploring Cooper's biography, which was central to her intellectual thought and activism, before moving on to examine the context in which *A Voice from the South* was first published. Finally, it turns to the book itself, closely analysing the text in order to consider why it gained more popularity in the final decades of the twentieth century.

Anna Julia Cooper: The Early Years

Cooper, a highly educated woman, began her formal schooling in the wake of the American Civil War. In 1868, she received a scholarship to study at St Augustine's Normal School in North Carolina, an institution founded to train teachers to educate those who were formerly enslaved and to instruct men for entry into the ministry. While there, Cooper was

---

2   Mary Helen Washington, 'Introduction', in Anna Julia Cooper, *A Voice from the South*, li.

vocal in her critique of the sexism that prevented her from taking classes in Greek, which were reserved for male students.[3] At the age of nineteen, Cooper married the Bahamian-born George A. Cooper, a theology student who moved to Raleigh in June 1879. Like his wife, George Cooper also made history: he was the second black man to be ordained in the Episcopal Church in North Carolina. Though he sadly died within two years of their marriage, his death enabled Cooper to continue to study and teach as a respectable widow. In 1884, she graduated from Oberlin College, one of the first liberal arts colleges to admit women and black students, with a BA in Mathematics. Next, she moved to Wilberforce Institute in Ohio where she became Chair in Languages and Science. A year later, Cooper moved back to St Augustine's and taught German, Latin, Mathematics and Greek. Due to her work at Wilberforce and St Augustine, Oberlin awarded Cooper an MA in Mathematics in 1887.

In the same year, Cooper started teaching Mathematics and Science at M Street School in Washington DC, the nation's first black public school, and in 1901, she was promoted to principal. Her tenure was, however, plagued by constant racism and sexism. After being falsely accused of having an affair with a pupil, Cooper was forced to leave the school, and from 1906 to 1910 she taught at Lincoln University in Kansas City in Missouri.[4] Following the appointment of new leadership at M Street, Cooper returned in 1910 and stayed for twenty years teaching Latin.[5] During her career as a teacher, Cooper continued to study. In the 1920s, she made history as the fourth African American woman to gain a PhD at the prestigious Sorbonne in France, writing her thesis on the topic of 'The Attitude of France regarding slavery during the revolution'. She retired from M Street

---

3   Beverly Guy-Sheftall, ed., *Words of Fire: An Anthology of African-American Feminist Thought* (New York: New Press, 1995), 43.
4   Vivian M. May, *Anna Julia Cooper: Visionary Black Feminist, A Critical Introduction* (New York: Routledge, 2007), 26–7.
5   May, *Anna Julia Cooper*, 27.

School in 1930 and took up the presidency of Frelinghuysen University in Washington DC until 1940.[6]

A Voice from the South was written while Cooper was teaching, and at the height of the Women's Era, a time when she was heavily involved in establishing a range of African American women's organizations that were part of the club movement, which was determined to help uplift the position of black Americans through strategies of self-help.[7] Alongside other black women educators and activists like Mary Church Terrell, who studied at Oberlin College around the same time as Cooper and Mary Jane Patterson, she established the Colored Women's League of Washington DC, a group that would later lead to the formation of the National Association of Colored Women (NACW) in 1896.[8] The NACW was an influential organization that unified local groups. Its motto, 'Lifting as We Climb', galvanized thousands of black women throughout the country to join different groups and by 1916, around 1,500 clubs were under its umbrella.[9] Cooper had deep religious convictions as an Episcopalian, and supported the Women's Christian Temperance Union. In 1905, Cooper also cofounded the Colored Women's Young Women's Christian Association.[10] As an active club woman and activist Cooper practised and preached the idea that black women, especially middle-class women, had a role to play in race leadership within the public sphere.

Cooper's activism not only centred on attempting to tackle the race and gender problem in the US, but was also concerned with the internationalization of these struggles. In 1893, she was invited as one of only three

---

6   May, *Anna Julia Cooper*, 34.
7   Deborah Gray White, *Too Heavy a Load: Black Women in Defense of Themselves, 1894–1994* (New York: W. W. Norton & Company, 1999), 27. For more on African American women and the club movement see Kate Dossett, *Bridging Race Divides: Black Nationalism, Feminism, and Integration in the United States 1896–1935* (Gainesville: University of Florida Press, 2008).
8   White, *Too Heavy a Load*, 27.
9   Stephen Tuck, *We ain't what we ought to be: The Black Freedom Struggle from Emancipation to Obama* (Cambridge, MA: Harvard University Press, 2010), 114.
10 Joy James, *Transcending the Talented Tenth: Black Leaders and American Intellectuals* (New York: Routledge, 1997), 43.

black American women to speak at the World's Congress of Representative Women in Chicago.[11] Additionally, she helped to organize the first Pan-African Congress in London in 1900 alongside W. E. B. Du Bois, where she also delivered a speech on 'The Negro Problem in America'. Cooper's work as educator, activist and intellectual placed her as a leading figure alongside contemporary figures such as Terrell, Du Bois (whose work Reiland Rabaka explores in Chapter 4) and Booker T. Washington. However, Cooper had complicated relationships with these figures. For instance, as scholar Joy James has revealed, Du Bois often failed to credit Cooper for many of her ideas that he used in his own work and that were central to the development of his intellectual thought.[12]

The Text

A Voice from the South was published at a seminal moment. The 1890s was a period that literary scholar Hazel V. Carby describes as a 'ferment of black female intellectual activity'.[13] Other significant works published in 1892 included anti-lynch crusader Ida B. Wells-Barnett's *Southern Horrors: Lynch Law in All Its Phases* and Frances Ellen Watkins Harper's novel *Iola Leroy*. These texts appeared amidst growing racial tensions, as lynchings reached record highs, and just four years before *Plessy v. Ferguson* enshrined Jim Crow segregation as the law of the land.[14] It is unsurprising, then, that a sense of urgency underpins Cooper's text. This fraught context also underscores the significance of *A Voice from the South*. At a time when the country was experiencing a nadir, Cooper and others argued that it was

---

11   James, *Transcending the Talented Tenth*, 43.
12   James, *Transcending the Talented Tenth*, 35–59.
13   Hazel V. Carby, *Reconstructing Womanhood: The Emergence of the Afro-American Woman Novelist* (New York: Oxford University Press, 1987), 96.
14   The landmark 1896 *Plessy v. Ferguson* Supreme Court case upheld segregation in public facilities under the doctrine of 'separate but equal'.

Figure 2.1: Anna Julia Cooper. Courtesy of the Moorland-Spingarn Research Center, Manuscript Division Howard University, Washington, DC.

black women – typically stereotyped as docile mammies, overly sexualized or mannish – and black feminism, that would help the country overcome the twin tyrannies of racism and sexism. When it was published, *A Voice from the South* was well received and popular across the US especially among African American middle-class professionals, cementing Cooper's stature as a leading black woman intellectual.[15]

A Voice from the South is divided into two sections and consists of eight chapters, throughout which Cooper interweaves different styles of writing. Historian Vivian M. May comments that 'Cooper's methodology is interdisciplinary, comparative, flexible, nonlinear, plurivocal, multilevel, coded, dialogic and unruly', while literary scholar Elizabeth Alexander notes that '[t]he essays are at once allegory, autobiography, history, oratory, poetry and literary criticism with traces of other forms of address'.[16] The diverse style of *A Voice from the South* showcases the varied rhetorical strategies in Cooper's writing and reflects the breadth of her elite education. She demonstrates her wide knowledge by citing and critiquing leading, mostly male writers and intellectuals from Thackeray, Voltaire, Macaulay and Ovid, to Emerson, Carlyle, Fenelon and Lowell, to name just a few.[17] But she also cites the important work of black women intellectuals and activists who had paved the way for her, including Frances Watkins Harper, Sojourner Truth, Amanda Berry Smith, Sarah Woodson Early, Martha Briggs, Charlotte Grimke, Hallie Quinn Brown and Fannie Jackson Coppin.[18] Furthermore, in the text Cooper frequently draws on her personal experiences and situates herself within the narrative. According to Alexander, this ensures that 'the book reads not like a moldering tome but as work in the process of being written with a definite sense of source and agency'.[19] Moreover, it adds to the multidisciplinary nature of *A Voice from the South*, demonstrating the

---

15 May, *Anna Julia Cooper*, 20.
16 May, *Anna Julia Cooper*, 106; Elizabeth Alexander, '"We must be about our Father's business": Anna Julia Cooper and the In-Corporation of the Nineteenth-Century African American Woman Intellectual', *Signs* 20/2 (1995), 337.
17 Alexander, 'We must be about our Father's business', 348.
18 Cooper, *A Voice from the South*.
19 Alexander, 'We must be about our Father's business', 345.

diversity within African American women's intellectual traditions and history, which is increasingly becoming a recognized field of scholarship.[20]

Asserting the significance of black women in the struggle for racial and gender emancipation is central to the project of *A Voice from the South*. In the preface, Cooper argues that attention needs to be paid to the 'hitherto voiceless Black Woman of America'.[21] She embodies and speaks as a representative of black women, and identifies their complex intersectional identities, writing that: 'The colored woman of to-day occupies, one may say, a unique position in this country [...] she is confronted by both a woman question and a race problem, and is as yet an unknown or an unacknowledged factor in both'.[22] In this comment, as in other parts of the text, Cooper criticizes the sexism of black men who argue that black women should remain within the domestic realm and not concern themselves with the struggle for racial equality. She dedicated a chapter to stressing the importance of women gaining higher education in order to play a role in public and political life alongside men. Yet, Cooper did not believe that the development of women's rights, especially their access to education, excused them from their domestic duties. And, like many women of her day, she argued that women did not need to hold political office to wield political power. Instead, women could use the soft power of persuasion to shape the political actions of their husbands, if they were married, or could also be involved in local club activities. Nevertheless, she reprimanded black men who claimed to speak on behalf of the race without considering the experiences of black women.

In addition to attacking sexism, Cooper also criticized white women, especially southern white women, for their racism. She took to task the cult of true womanhood that was associated with southern white women

---

20 See for instance essays in Kristin Waters and Carol B. Conaway, eds, *Black Women's Intellectual Traditions: Speaking Their Minds* (Vermont: University of Vermont Press, 2007) and Mia Bay, Farah J. Griffin, Martha S. Jones and Barbara D. Savage, eds, *Toward an Intellectual History of Black Women* (Chapel Hill: University of North Carolina Press, 2015).
21 Cooper, *A Voice from the South*, 2.
22 Cooper, *A Voice from the South*, 134.

by stating that '[t]he black race constitutes one-seventh the known population of the globe; and there are representatives of it here as elsewhere who were never in bondage at any time to any man, – whose blood is as blue and lineage as noble as any, even that of the white lady of the South'.[23] Although Cooper was well aware of the racial tensions amongst women, she warned against fuelling them, saying, 'It is not the intelligent woman vs. the ignorant woman; nor the white woman vs. the black, the brown and the red, – it is not even the cause of woman vs. man. Nay, 'tis woman's strongest vindication for speaking that *the world needs to hear her voice*'.[24] Cooper believed that continuing divisions between women and men would detract from the full and equal role that both sexes should play in society, reasoning that '[i]t would be subversive of every human interest that the cry of one-half the human family be stifled'.[25]

In order to challenge racism and sexism, Cooper employed what historian Evelyn Brooks Higginbotham has since called 'the politics of respectability', arguing that if African Americans presented only positive attributes then this would change white attitudes and lead to equality.[26] As Cooper stressed,

> If we represent the ignorance and poverty, the vice and destructiveness, the vagabondism and parasitism, in the world's economy, no amount of philanthropy and benevolent sentiment can win for us esteem: and if we contribute a positive value in those things the world prizes, no amount of negrophobia can ultimately prevent its recognition.[27]

Cooper was not alone in thinking that if blacks exhibited irreproachable behaviours and practices this would limit the violence they faced. The politics of respectability was a tool used by others like Du Bois, Terrell, and

---

23   Cooper, *A Voice from the South*, 109.
24   Cooper, *A Voice from the South*, 121.
25   Cooper, *A Voice from the South*, 121.
26   Evelyn Brooks Higginbotham, *Righteous Discontent: The Women's Movement in the Black Baptist Church, 1880–1920* (Cambridge, MA: Harvard University Press, 1993), 14.
27   Cooper, *A Voice from the South*, 284–5.

Washington, but it ultimately failed to achieve its aim. It put the onus on blacks to change rather than address the racism of white Americans, and did little in the end to undermine the entrenched nature of white supremacy.

Cooper's strong Christian beliefs permeate throughout *A Voice from the South*. Although she criticized the church for its sexism, she believed that Christian values could transform individuals and lead to equality. These ideals meant that unlike other middle-class African American women, such as Terrell, who had an ambivalent relationship to the black poor, Cooper was more sympathetic to their struggles.

A Voice from the South is also notable for the way in which Cooper expresses the importance of human rights. Cooper argued that 'My "people" are just like other people – indeed, too like for their own good. They hate, they love, they attract and repel, they climb or they grovel, struggle or drift, aspire or despair, endure in hope or curse in vexation, exactly like all the rest of unregenerate humanity'.[28] She asserted that 'what the dark man wants then is merely to live his own life, in his own world, with his own chosen companions, in whatever of comfort, luxury or emoluments his talent or his money can in an impartial market secure'.[29] These comments demonstrate how Cooper repeatedly stressed the similarities blacks shared with others, undermining racist arguments that blacks were subhuman.

Cooper emphasized that human rights could not be prescribed to one racial group but ought to be predicated on the liberation and freedom of all. She argued that 'the cause of freedom is not the cause of a race or a sect, a party or a class, – it is the cause of human kind, the very birthright of humanity'.[30] She continued by asserting that there were links between the movement for human rights and women's equality: 'Now unless we are greatly mistaken the Reform of our day, known as the Woman's Movement, is essentially such an embodiment, if its pioneers could only realize it, of the universal good.'[31] Although she was aware of the limits of the women's movement, feminism for Cooper was undeniably liberating, as it freed men

---

28   Cooper, *A Voice from the South*, 112.
29   Cooper, *A Voice from the South*, 112.
30   Cooper, *A Voice from the South*, 120–1.
31   Cooper, *A Voice from the South*, 121.

and women from gender inequalities. In her opinion, human rights and equality for all would lead to 'equilibrium, not repression among conflicting forces', which 'is the condition of natural harmony, of permanent progress, and of universal freedom'.[32]

The Post-1960s Reception of *A Voice from the South*

The numerous ideas that Cooper expressed in *A Voice from the South* began to gain greater recognition in the wake of the Civil Rights and women's liberation movement in the 1970s and 1980s. This period saw the birth of black studies and women's studies in colleges and universities across the US. It also witnessed the rise in popularity of black women writers like Alice Walker, Toni Morrison and Maya Angelou, amongst others, who wrote stories and autobiographies that foregrounded the experiences of black women and girls. This in turn influenced the increase in scholarship on black women's history and black feminism by historians and literary scholars including Gerda Lerna, Hazel V. Carby, Patricia Hill Collins, Paula Giddings, Kimberlé Crenshaw, Mary Helen Washington and Darlene Clark Hine, to name just a few. These scholars were crucial to the rediscovery not only of Cooper but also of many of her forgotten contemporaries, including figures such as Maria Stewart and Sojourner Truth, who were then placed at the centre of American, African American and global histories. This historical, political and academic context served as the backdrop to renewed interest in Cooper following the republication of *A Voice from the South* in 1988.

In the following decades, more scholarship on Cooper has coincided with the rise of black feminism within the academy. Scholars and scholar-activists have used Cooper's work to show the long history of black feminism that placed intersectionality at its core, which has evolved since the

---

32   Cooper, *A Voice from the South*, 160.

nineteenth century. In 1995, Beverly Guy Sheftall's edited collection *Words of Fire: An Anthology of African-American Feminist Thought* described *A Voice from the South* as promoting a 'cultural feminist position which posits that women, because of their inherent moral superiority, have the responsibility and capacity to reform the human race'.[33] LaRese Hubbard has argued that Cooper is an Africana Womanist, a term coined by Clenora Hudson-Weems that describes women of African descent 'grounded in African culture', and that therefore 'necessarily focuses on the unique experiences, struggles, needs, and desires of Africana women'.[34] The varied scholarly works on Cooper continue to show how much of a visionary she was and how this shone through in her writings and activism.

Although *A Voice from the South* was published over 120 years ago, it remains relevant today. Cooper was an insightful intellectual who challenged racism, sexism and imperialism at a time when black women in the US were on the bottom rung of society and the least likely to transform it. She anticipated a future where black women played a role in improving not only the US but the world as a whole. In a context of growing inequality, old and new forms of xenophobia, racism, sexism and imperialism, *A Voice from the South* is a reminder of the revolutionary potential of black feminism to liberate men and women from oppression, and to promote human rights as central to the security, safety and freedom of all.

Bibliography

Alexander, Elizabeth, '"We must be about our Father's business": Anna Julia Cooper and the In-Corporation of the Nineteenth-Century African American Woman Intellectual', *Signs* 20/2 (1995), 336–56.

---

[33] Guy-Sheftall, *Words of Fire*, 43.
[34] LaRese Hubbard, 'Anna Julia Cooper and Africana Womanism: Some Early Conceptual Contributions', *Black Women, Gender and Families* 4/2 (2010), 31–53; Clenora Hudson-Weems, *Africana Womanism: Reclaiming Ourselves* (Troy, MI: Bedford Publishing, 1994), 24.

Bay, Mia, Farah. J. Griffin, Martha S. Jones and Barbara D. Savage, eds, *Toward an Intellectual History of Black Women* (Chapel Hill: University of North Carolina Press, 2015).
Carby, Hazel V., *Reconstructing Womanhood: The Emergence of the Afro-American Woman Novelist* (New York: Oxford University Press, 1987).
Cooper, Anna Julia, *A Voice from the South* (New York: Oxford University Press, 1988 [1892]).
Dossett, Kate, *Bridging Race Divides: Black Nationalism, Feminism, and Integration in the United States 1896–1935* (Gainesville: University of Florida Press, 2008).
Guy-Sheftall, Beverly, ed., *Words of Fire: An Anthology of African-American Feminist Thought* (New York: The New Press, 1995).
Higginbotham, Evelyn Brooks, *Righteous Discontent: The Women's Movement in the Black Baptist Church, 1880–1920* (Cambridge, MA: Harvard University Press 1993).
Hubbard, LaRese, 'Anna Julia Cooper and Africana Womanism: Some Early Conceptual Contributions', *Black Women, Gender and Families* 4/2 (2010), 31–53.
Hudson-Weems, Clenora, *Africana Womanism: Reclaiming Ourselves* (Troy, MI: Bedford Publishing, 1994).
James, Joy, *Transcending the Talented Tenth: Black Leaders and American Intellectuals* (New York: Routledge, 1997).
May, Vivian M., *Anna Julia Cooper: Visionary Black Feminist, A Critical Introduction* (New York: Routledge, 2007).
Tuck, Stephen, *We ain't what we ought to be: The Black Freedom Struggle from Emancipation to Obama* (Cambridge, MA: Harvard University Press, 2010).
Washington, Mary Helen, 'Introduction', in Anna Julia Cooper, *A Voice from the South* (New York: Oxford University Press, 1988 [1892]), xxvii–liv.
Waters, Kristin, and Carol B. Conaway, eds, *Black Women's Intellectual Traditions: Speaking Their Minds* (Vermont: University of Vermont Press, 2007).
White, Deborah Gray, *Too Heavy a Load: Black Women in Defense of Themselves, 1894–1994* (New York: W. W. Norton & Company, 1999).

CHRISTINA TWOMEY

3 Ambivalence, Admiration and Empire: Emily Hobhouse's *The Brunt of the War and Where it Fell* (1902)

ABSTRACT
The ambivalent response in Britain to Emily Hobhouse's *The Brunt of the War and Where it Fell* (1902) contrasted with a long-standing admiration for its author in South Africa. Despite its influence in the interwar pacifist movement, the book's legacy was ultimately overshadowed by the Afrikaner nationalist movement's appropriation of the memory of Hobhouse's work in the South African War. In the 1990s, the end of the apartheid regime and increased humanitarian interventions around the world, combined with new academic work on empire and the politics of memory, renewed interest in the career of Emily Hobhouse and her anti-militarist book.

Emily Hobhouse (1860–1926) was reviled and revered in equal measure. She first came to public notice during the South African War (1899–1902), as a prominent critic of Britain's use of concentration camps. Hobhouse's work led to accusations of disloyalty in Britain, but won her the gratitude of the Afrikaans population in South Africa. In 1902, she published *The Brunt of the War and Where it Fell* to demonstrate the vileness of war and its impact on women and children in particular. The ambivalent response to the book in Britain belied its later influence in the interwar internationalist pacifist movement. By the mid-century period, largely owing to Hobhouse's associations with the white South African political elite responsible for apartheid, the book was almost forgotten. It regained traction in feminist peace activist circles from the 1980s. By the mid-2000s, *The Brunt of the War* was subject to renewed attention, largely owing to increased humanitarian interventions around the globe and a concomitant interest in their history.

Emily Hobhouse's personal experiences, family connections and immersion in Christian philanthropic endeavours drove her interest in the South African War. The unmarried daughter of an Anglican minister, Hobhouse lived in Cornwall until her mid-thirties, undertaking parish work. She later described that period of her life as one of virtual incarceration with her widowed father, a man disinterested in modern life.[1] Hobhouse moved to London after his death in 1895. There she joined her brother, the sociologist and journalist Leonard Hobhouse, and his network of progressive thinkers. Hobhouse ultimately befriended her neighbours, Leonard and Kate Courtney, a couple with liberal political leanings and an interest in contemporary social problems. When the conflict in South Africa broke out, the Courtneys founded the South African Conciliation Committee. Hobhouse was soon deeply involved and replaced her earlier focus on the Women's Industrial Council with the cause.[2] The Committee was concerned to promote a peaceful settlement to the bitter struggle in South Africa over the right to control land rich in gold and diamonds. After British annexation of the Boer Republics (sited on this territory) in 1900, the war entered a guerrilla phase. The British Army adopted tactics of farm burning and concentration camps to deprive Boer commandos of support.[3]

Hobhouse developed an abiding interest in the fate of Boer women and children confined in the camps, and she emerged as a major figure in the South African Women's and Children's Distress Fund. By late 1900, the fund had raised enough money for Hobhouse to travel to South Africa personally to distribute relief. Leonard Hobhouse, who was by then writing for the famous journalist, editor and critic of the war, W. T. Stead, suggested that his sister's vibrant writing style would make good copy for the anti-war cause. Emily Hobhouse may have been relatively unknown when she arrived in London, but her family and social connections, and natural fluency with words, ensured that her reporting on the fate of Boer women and children from South Africa would not go unnoticed.

1   Emily Hobhouse, *Emily Hobhouse: A Memoir*, comp. A. Ruth Fry (London: Jonathan Cape, 1929), 33–4.
2   Eliza Riedi, 'The Women Pro-Boers: Gender, Peace and the Critique of Empire in the South African War', *Historical Research* 86/231 (2013), 92–115.
3   S. B. Spies, *Methods of Barbarism: Roberts, Kitchener and Civilians in the Boer Republics, January 1900–May 1902* (Cape Town: Human & Rousseau, 1977).

Emily Hobhouse's The Brunt of the War and Where it Fell *(1902)*

Figure 3.1: Emily Hobhouse in England: St Ives, Cornwall. Courtesy of the Free State Provincial Archives, VA1435.

The Brunt of the War and Where it Fell

Hobhouse returned to England from South Africa in 1901, determined to publicize the plight of Boer women and children through speeches, letters to newspapers and the publication of a pamphlet. In its use of Boer women's letters and testimony, and Hobhouse's eyewitness accounts, the pamphlet was effectively a blueprint for *The Brunt of the War*.[4] Hobhouse detailed how British troops evicted Boer women and children from their

---

4 Emily Hobhouse, *Report of a Visit to the Camps of Women and Children in the Cape and Orange River Colonies* (London: The Friars Printing Association, 1901).

farms, then razed their homes to the ground. Further ignominy awaited: transportation to a concentration camp in open trucks and train carriages, or hauling whatever remained of their possessions in wagons across the veld. Hobhouse's concerns were not misplaced – before they were transferred from military to civil administration, mortality rates in the camps were alarmingly high as sanitation problems and confinement exacerbated the spread of infections and disease. By the time they began to be dismantled in 1902, over 25,000 deaths had occurred within the white camps and there were an equal, if not greater, number of deaths in the 'native camps'.[5]

Despite Hobhouse's awareness that there were separate camps for black Africans, her central concern remained with Boer women and children. As she put it on the opening page of her book: 'On them fell the brunt of the war'.[6] Hobhouse chose to give precedence to the suffering of white women and children, and always maintained that it was not her responsibility to investigate conditions in the black camps. 'It is a new departure in our own history to have placed 93,000 white women (besides 24,000 natives) in camps', Hobhouse insisted, the parentheses indicative of the secondary importance she accorded to African inmates.[7] In her 1901 pamphlet, Hobhouse had remarked: 'I do wish someone would come out and take up the question of Native Camps'.[8] Later, Hobhouse claimed that she had been 'unable myself, from lack of time and strength, to investigate conditions or personally carry relief to the native camps'.[9] Still, the decision to prioritize Boer women and children did not relieve Hobhouse of a troubled conscience. Critical that a government-appointed Commission of Inquiry into the camps in 1901 'had not touched this important branch of the concentration system', Hobhouse raised the matter with Henry Fox

---

5 Stowell Kessler, 'The Black Concentration Camps of the Anglo-Boer War 1899–1902: Shifting the Paradigm from Sole Martyrdom to Mutual Suffering', *Historia* 44/1 (1999), 110–47; Elizabeth van Heyningen, *The Concentration Camps of the Anglo-Boer War: A Social History* (Auckland Park: Jacana, 2013).
6 Emily Hobhouse, *The Brunt of the War and Where it Fell* (London: Methuen & Co., 1902), xv.
7 Emily Hobhouse, 'Concentration Camps', *Contemporary Review* (1 July 1901), 531.
8 Hobhouse, *Report of a Visit*, 8.
9 Hobhouse, *The Brunt of the War*, 350.

Bourne, Secretary of the Aborigines Protection Society. In early 1902, Fox Bourne complained to the government, expressing alarm that there were over 43,000 'coloured persons' in concentration camps, that the death rates therein were 'appalling' and calling for an immediate inquiry. The platitudinous response, claiming that 'Lord Milner will not fail to exercise all proper care in dealing with the Natives', typified the low priority accorded to black lives in the conflict.[10]

Hobhouse thought that the creation of concentration camps had fundamentally undermined Britain's claim to sit at the table of civilized nations, though not primarily because it had been so careless with the lives of Africans. 'Never before have women and children been so warred against', she wrote.[11] *The Brunt of the War* was, in part, a plea to prevent the recurrence of such barbarism in war: 'It ought to become a fixed principle with the English people that no General acting in their name should ever again resort to measures of such a nature'.[12] This was a variation on the theme of 'Why am I fit to rule?', a question which Antoinette Burton and Isabel Hofmeyr have argued was a key concern of books that shaped the British Empire.[13] Hobhouse modified its terms by contemplating how an imperial power had come to such a pass. For her, the lesson was that 'all war is barbarous, varying only in degree'.[14] The solution was pacifism: 'None of us can claim to be wholly civilized until we have drawn the line above war itself and established universal arbitration in place of universal armaments'.[15]

Hobhouse was conscious that despite her pacifist motivations, the book would be interpreted as either slandering British troops or 'aggravating a controversy amongst the Boers by its publication'.[16] She was fully aware of

---

10   Hobhouse, 'Appendix D: Native Camps', in *The Brunt of the War*, 350–3.
11   Hobhouse, *The Brunt of the War*, 317.
12   Hobhouse, *The Brunt of the War*, 318.
13   Antoinette Burton and Isabel Hofmeyr, 'Introduction: The Spine of Empire? Books and the Making of an Imperial Commons', in Antoinette Burton and Isabel Hofmeyr, eds, *Ten Books That Shaped the British Empire: Creating an Imperial Commons* (Durham, NC and London: Duke University Press, 2014), 10.
14   Hobhouse, *The Brunt of the War*, xvi.
15   Hobhouse, *The Brunt of the War*, xvi.
16   Hobhouse, *The Brunt of the War*, xv.

her vilification in the pro-war British press, the antipathy in which she was held by key figures in the Colonial and War Offices, and the ways she had been derided by military men such as Herbert Kitchener, the Commander in Chief of British forces in South Africa. Consequently, Hobhouse was careful to distinguish her work from the genre of polemical pamphlet by downplaying her own authorial voice and basing the text to a large degree on the letters of Boer women 'and their friends', official proclamations and correspondence, newspaper reports and first-person observations. Constructing the text in this way was a conscious decision, derived from the methodologies implicit in other contemporary publications that were designed to expose and overcome social ills, and to 'portray the sufferings of the weak and the young with truth and moderation.'[17]

Hobhouse was also determined to use photographic evidence to support her analysis of the war, but here met the resistance of her publisher. Hobhouse's annotations on her own copy of the book, as well as her in-text references, make clear the contest over visual images.[18] *The Brunt of the War* included nine photographs, accompanied by text designed to enhance their impact. Hobhouse claimed that her publisher truncated the original caption on 'Occupants and furniture of one bell tent soon after arrival from the farm, November 1900'. 'The condition of this overcrowded family six weeks later was pitiable in the extreme (Words omitted by publisher)', is a hand-written annotation scrawled across Hobhouse's own copy in the University of Cape Town library.[19] The publisher also rebuffed as 'too painful for reproduction' a photograph of the extremely emaciated child Lizzie van Zyl.[20] Yet, as Hobhouse herself pointed out, 'pictures of the famine-stricken Indian children' had been widely circulated as part of relief campaigns since the late nineteenth century.[21] While it is tempting to see the whiteness of the child as too taboo for publication, it was in fact

---

17 Hobhouse, *The Brunt of the War*, xvi.
18 Michael Godby, 'Confronting Horror: Emily Hobhouse and the Concentration Camp Photographs of the South African War', *Kronos* 32 (2006), 34–48.
19 Godby, 'Confronting Horror', 46.
20 Hobhouse, *The Brunt of the War*, 215 n. 2.
21 Emily Hobhouse to the Editor, *Westminster Gazette* (27 January 1901).

another controversy that proved a greater stumbling block. The question of whether or not Lizzie van Zyl was in such a condition as a result of maternal neglect, or starvation and disease acquired within the camp, was the subject of extensive debate in 1901.[22] In *The Brunt of the War*, Hobhouse explicitly contested Sir Arthur Conan Doyle's view that the photograph was 'characteristic of the unscrupulous tactics which have been used from the beginning to poison the mind of the world against Great Britain'.[23] Conan Doyle repeated a charge that the photograph had been originally taken to institute criminal proceedings against Lizzie's mother. Countering this argument, Hobhouse insisted that the mortality statistics spoke for themselves and 'the great body of Boer women have come finely out of the ordeal to which we have subjected them'.[24]

The Reception of *The Brunt of the War*

The Brunt of the War's pacifist sentiments, while winning favour in small reformist circles, were out of step with the majority view of the war in South Africa.[25] Most commentators vilified Hobhouse as a 'pro-Boer' (the contemporary term for those against the war) who had besmirched the reputation of British soldiers simply doing their job when faced with a backwards and inscrutable enemy.[26] Although *The Brunt of the War* appeared within six months of the war's end, and employed contemporary best practice for social investigation, it did not sell well. Most major daily papers merely

22 National Archives of South Africa (NASA), VAB, CO Volume 49, 4492/01, Lizzie van Zyl.
23 Arthur Conan Doyle, *The War in South Africa: Its Cause and Conduct* (New York: McClure, Phillips and Co., 1902), 92.
24 Hobhouse, *The Brunt of the War*, 317.
25 Jennifer Hobhouse Balme, *To Love One's Enemies: The Work and Life of Emily Hobhouse Compiled from Letters and Writings, Newspaper Cuttings and Official Documents* (Cobble Hill: Hobhouse Trust, 1994), 477.
26 For instance: *St James Gazette* (24 June 1901), 3–4.

noted its publication, rather than running a full review.²⁷ *The Times*, the conservative and influential newspaper that had supported the British government position throughout the war, ignored its existence altogether. In Britain, railway booksellers refused to carry the title. *The Brunt of the War* was less widely reviewed than the Quaker Ruth Fry's memoir of Hobhouse, published in 1929, three years after Hobhouse's death. The *Spectator*'s review of Fry's biography summed up the establishment view of Hobhouse, which contributed to the ongoing poor reception of *The Brunt of the War*: 'Emily was a rebel always, a bitter, useful, effective rebel, during the best years of her life. She did undoubtedly desire her country's righteousness, and would have sacrificed her life for the honour of her countrymen, but she was eager to shame them into that honour, and such eagerness is hard to forgive'.²⁸

Despite her somewhat compromised reputation in Britain, in South Africa Hobhouse was the people's princess. In 1913 Hobhouse travelled to South Africa to deliver a speech at the unveiling of the Nasionale Vrouemonument [National Women's Memorial], a 35-metre obelisk erected to commemorate the white women and children who died in the concentration camps. Although Hobhouse was too unwell to attend, an edited version of her speech was read at the ceremony attended by 20,000 people. The omitted text cohered around the question of race and women's rights: Hobhouse insisted that black Africans had also died in the camps, criticized the Boers for 'withholding from others in your control, the very liberties and rights you have valued and won for yourselves', and insisted that 'liberty is the equal right and heritage of every child of man, without distinction of race, colour or sex'.²⁹ In 1923, as the memory of the concentration camps was utilized in the service of white South African nationalism, *The*

---

27 For example: 'The Book Market', *Daily News* (19 November 1902), 8; 'New Books', *St James Gazette* (19 November 1902), 17.
28 'An Heroic Malcontent', *Spectator* (2 March 1929), 42.
29 Emily Hobhouse, 'Commemoration Speech by Miss Hobhouse', in *Emily Hobhouse: Boer War Letters*, ed. Rykie van Reenen (Cape Town: Human & Rousseau, 1984), 401–8, 515–16.

Brunt of the War was translated and published in Afrikaans.[30] This time it included the much-discussed photograph of the emaciated child Lizzie van Zyl. Upon Hobhouse's death in 1926, the South African Prime Minister Jan Smuts declared that while Hobhouse was a 'stormy petrel to her own people, she was a great healing influence in South Africa'.[31] It is indicative of the affection in which she was held there that Hobhouse's ashes were brought from England and buried alongside two male war heroes at the Nasionale Vrouemonument in Bloemfontein.

Hobhouse's books, including *The Brunt of the War* and *War Without Glamour* (1924), helped to shape the memory of the war in South Africa.[32] They also cemented her connections with prominent South Africans and brought her to the attention of local reformers such as Mohandas Gandhi. Betty Molteno, daughter of the first Prime Minister of the Cape, worked with Hobhouse on concentration camp relief efforts during the war. In subsequent years, Hobhouse and Molteno shared disillusionment about the hardening racial policies in South Africa. Molteno built alliances with South African residents who were critical of segregation and discrimination, including Gandhi. In 1913, Gandhi's final South African *satyagraha* campaign to reverse discrimination against Indians coincided with Hobhouse's visit to South Africa and her failed effort to attend the unveiling ceremony of the Vrouemonument. While recuperating at the house of Prime Minister Louis Botha, Hobhouse acted as a go-between for Gandhi, Botha and Smuts, then a key government minister, to resolve the political stand-off.[33] 'It was during the Boer war that I came to admire your selfless devotion to

30 Emily Hobhouse, *Die Smarte van die Oorlog en Wie Dit Gely Het*, trans. N. J. van der Merwe (Cape Town: Nasionale Pers, 1923); Johan Snyman, 'Ways of Remembering', in Charles Villa Vicencio, ed., *Transcending a Century of Injustice* (Cape Town: Institute of Justice and Reconciliation, 2000), 22–37.
31 General Smuts, 'Foreword', in *Emily Hobhouse: A Memoir*, 9–10.
32 Emily Hobhouse, *War Without Glamour* (Bloemfontein: Nasionale Pers Beperk, 1924).
33 Catherine Cordner and Martin Plaut, 'Gandhi's decisive South African 1913 Campaign: A Personal Perspective from the Letters of Betty Molteno', *South African Historical Journal* 66/1 (2014), 22–54.

Truth', Gandhi told Hobhouse in response to her overture to him in 1913.[34] Gandhi's gratitude to Hobhouse remained life-long: 'she made my way smooth among [the Boers] by throwing in the whole weight of her influence with the Indian cause'. On Hobhouse's death, Gandhi commented that despite her 'weak and diseased body, she had a soul that could defy the might of kings and emperors with their armies'.[35]

European internationalists also took note of *The Brunt of the War* in the interwar period. Stanford University's copy of the book was bequeathed from the collection of Alfred Fried, an Austrian internationalist and pacifist active from the late nineteenth century who won the Nobel Peace Prize in 1911.[36] Felix Moscheles, an English painter, peace activist and one-time President of the International Arbitration and Peace Association, annotated Fried's copy with the comment: 'read and realize some of the inevitable consequences of what they call "inevitable" war!'[37]

Despite its circulation among interwar pacifists, *The Brunt of the War* fell from public view thereafter and was not revived again outside of South Africa until the 1980s. The memory of the concentration camps had been used to foment Afrikaner nationalism and eroded public memory of Hobhouse's pacifist commitments. In 1948 the official institution of the apartheid system in South Africa further entrenched the associations between Hobhouse and Afrikaner nationalism. The South African Navy's launch of the submarine *SAS Emily Hobhouse* in 1971 represented the apotheosis of that regime's appropriation of her memory. Hobhouse's esteem in apartheid South Africa accounts, in part, for her relative neglect

---

34 M. K. Gandhi to Miss Hobhouse, 5 January 1914, repr. in 'Appendix: Some Unpublished Letters of Gandhiji' <http://www.sahistory.org.za/archive/some-remarkable-european-women-who-helped-gandhiji-south-africa> accessed 26 March 2016.

35 M. K. Gandhi, 'A Great Heart', *Young India* (15 July 1926), repr. in *The Collected Works of Mahatma Gandhi* (New Delhi: Publications Division Government of India, 1999), 36–7 <http://www.gandhiserve.org/e/cwmg/cwmg.htm> accessed 26 March 2016.

36 Roger Chickering, *Imperial Germany and a World Without War: The Peace Movement and German Society 1892–1914* (Princeton, NJ: Princeton University Press, 1975), 46.

37 Annotation by Felix Moscheles on the Stanford University copy of *The Brunt of the War*.

by women's historians when feminist history emerged as a key conceptual innovation of the 1970s. In an era in which white feminists were coming under increasing criticism for the colour-blindness of their own political project, a figure so heartily embraced by a nation that was an international pariah for its policies on race and rights was unlikely to gain attention.

Yet in the thawing Cold War context of the early 1980s, as British women organized in opposition to the installation of nuclear missiles at the Royal Air Force base Greenham Common, a new generation rediscovered Hobhouse's work. Inspired to research the history of the women's peace movement and antimilitarism in Britain, historian Jill Liddington focused on the South African War as a watershed moment. Liddington argued that Hobhouse, inspired by international peace and arbitration movements, pioneered the study of the gendered implications of war.[38]

Other feminist historians, in keeping with the growing influence of postcolonial theory in the academy, developed an interest in gender, race and empire by the 1990s. Paula Krebs's work, published in that period, considered anew the role of Emily Hobhouse in the public debate over concentration camps. Reflecting the impact of poststructuralism on cultural history, Krebs was especially alert to the discursive construction of the concentration camps issue and to how Victorian ideologies about gender and race cohered in Hobhouse's writing. Hobhouse, unpopular for her criticism of British imperialism, nevertheless deployed some of its central narrative tenets about white women's need for protection and the sexual savagery of black men. Krebs paid particular attention to the figure of the 'Kaffir' in *The Brunt of the War* – most often presented as male, and as an intimidating sexual and physical threat to white women – as a textual strategy designed to foster empathy for Boer women. In keeping with contemporary feminist critiques, Krebs postulated that the marked absence in *The Brunt of the War* was the fate of black women.[39] This emphasis on textual analysis certainly revealed how ideologies of race overdetermined

---

38 Jill Liddington, *The Road to Greenham Common: Feminism and Anti-Militarism in Britain since 1820* (New York: Syracuse University Press, 1991), 57.
39 Paula M. Krebs, *Gender, Race and the Writing of Empire: Public Discourse and the Boer War* (Cambridge: Cambridge University Press, 1999), 55–79.

Hobhouse's representations of Africans, though it does not allow for the admittedly piecemeal efforts Hobhouse made on their behalf, as evidenced in her approaches to Fox Bourne and the excised sections of her speech at the unveiling of the Vrouemonument.

Several political and historiographical developments account for renewed attention to *The Brunt of the War* since the 1990s. The end of apartheid in South Africa in 1994, coupled with the 'memory boom' in Western liberal democracies of preceding decades that had focused attention on events deemed difficult for the individual or the nation, made the text a fascinating case study for the politics of memory. The deployment of Hobhouse's work in the commemoration and memory of the concentration camps in South Africa, and its intersection with white nationalism, was the subject of feminist sociologist Liz Stanley's work in the 2000s.[40] The coming of democracy in South Africa also coincided with the end of the Cold War, and the reinvigorated role of the United Nations in its wake led to a renewed focus on human rights abuses and efforts to conduct international humanitarian interventions.[41] A wave of historical work on humanitarianism, which often intersected with new imperial histories that sought to break out of parochial national contexts and to explore the networks that influenced the form and shape of the British world, also reconsidered the role of early activists such as Hobhouse.[42] With the co-option of Hobhouse's name by white nationalism now firmly re-evaluated in the critical scholarly literature, and her reputation as a pacifist and internationalist restored in a postcolonial and post-imperial world, *The Brunt of the War* was reprinted in 2008, the first time in more than a century.

---

40 Liz Stanley, *Mourning Becomes: Post-Memory, Commemoration and the Concentration Camps of the South African War* (Manchester: Manchester University Press, 2006).
41 See Samuel Moyn, *The Last Utopia: Human Rights in History* (Boston, MA: Belknap Press, 2012).
42 See, for example, Rebecca Gill, *Calculating Compassion: Humanity and Relief in War, Britain 1870–1914* (Manchester: Manchester University Press, 2013).

When Emily Hobhouse died in 1926, one of the few sympathetic notices appeared in the *Manchester Guardian*, a newspaper considered 'pro-Boer' during the South African War. According to the obituary, Hobhouse 'was as truly the heroine of the concentration camps as Florence Nightingale was of the Scutari hospitals in the Crimea. It is to courage and persistence like hers that we owe some memories of the war that are not bitter'.[43] While Nightingale became and remained a household name, after the interwar period Hobhouse slipped into obscurity everywhere in the English-speaking world except South Africa. Hobhouse's fame in South Africa, and the utilization of her memory by white nationalists, militated against a full appreciation of the innovation of *The Brunt of the War* until British women's involvement in protest against nuclear weapons during the 1980s renewed interest in the history of women's peace activism in Britain. In this context, Hobhouse's work and her insistence on the cost of war for non-combatants, and her suggestion that *militarism itself* was the enemy, received new attention. South Africa's transition to a postcolonial state also allowed for a rehabilitation of Hobhouse, as historians interested in the study of memory and commemoration demonstrated how Afrikaner nationalists had provided a very partial account of her thought and work. In *The Brunt of the War*, Hobhouse also insisted on the politicized nature of the provision of humanitarian relief. This insight contained renewed resonance in the post-Cold War world, when humanitarian intervention became more commonplace. The charge long levelled against Hobhouse – that she had besmirched the name of Britain on the world stage – also eventually lost its emotional and political traction. Subsequently, she has been re-embraced by feminists, pacifists and scholars as a significant figure in the international history of anti-militarism and humanitarianism.

---

43   *Manchester Guardian*, clipping, c. 1926, NASA, VAB14, A53 Bestelling.

Bibliography

Balme, Jennifer Hobhouse, *To Love One's Enemies: The Work and Life of Emily Hobhouse Compiled from Letters and Writings, Newspaper Cuttings and Official Documents* (Cobble Hill: Hobhouse Trust, 1994).
'Book Market, The', *Daily News* (19 November 1902), 8.
Burton, Antoinette, and Isabel Hofmeyr, 'Introduction: The Spine of Empire? Books and the Making of an Imperial Commons', in Antoinette Burton and Isabel Hofmeyr, eds, *Ten Books That Shaped the British Empire: Creating an Imperial Commons* (Durham, NC and London: Duke University Press, 2014), 1–28.
Chickering, Roger, *Imperial Germany and a World Without War: The Peace Movement and German Society 1892–1914* (Princeton, NJ: Princeton University Press, 1975).
Cordner, Catherine, and Martin Plaut, 'Gandhi's Decisive South African 1913 Campaign: A Personal Perspective from the Letters of Betty Molteno', *South African Historical Journal* 66/1 (2014), 22–54.
Doyle, Arthur Conan, *The War in South Africa: Its Cause and Conduct* (New York: McClure, Phillips and Co., 1902).
Gandhi, M. K., 'A Great Heart', *Young India* (15 July 1926), repr. in *The Collected Works of Mahatma Gandhi* 36 (New Delhi: Publications Division Government of India, 1999), 36–7 <http://www.gandhiserve.org/e/cwmg/cwmg.htm> accessed 26 March 2016.
——, Letter to Miss Hobhouse, 5 January 1914, repr. in 'Appendix: Some Unpublished Letters of Gandhiji' <http://www.sahistory.org.za/archive/some-remarkable-european-women-who-helped-gandhiji-south-africa> accessed 26 March 2016.
Gill, Rebecca, *Calculating Compassion: Humanity and Relief in War, Britain 1870–1914* (Manchester: Manchester University Press, 2013).
Godby, Michael, 'Confronting Horror: Emily Hobhouse and the Concentration Camp Photographs of the South African War', *Kronos* 32 (2006), 34–48.
'Heroic Malcontent, An', *Spectator* (2 March 1929), 42.
Hobhouse, Emily, *The Brunt of the War and Where it Fell* (London: Methuen & Co., 1902).
——, 'Concentration Camps', *Contemporary Review* (1 July 1901), 528–37.
——, *Emily Hobhouse: Boer War Letters*, ed. Rykie van Reenen (Cape Town: Human & Rousseau, 1984).
——, *Emily Hobhouse: A Memoir*, comp. A. Ruth Fry (London: Jonathan Cape, 1929).
——, Letter to the Editor, *Westminster Gazette* (27 January 1901).
——, *Report of a Visit to the Camps of Women and Children in the Cape and Orange River Colonies* (London: The Friars Printing Association, 1901).

——, *Die Smarte van die Oorlog en Wie Dit Gely Het*, trans. N. J. van der Merwe (Cape Town: Nasionale Pers, 1923).

——, *War Without Glamour* (Bloemfontein: Nasionale Pers Beperk, 1924).

Kessler, Stowell, 'The Black Concentration Camps of the Anglo-Boer War 1899–1902: Shifting the Paradigm from Sole Martyrdom to Mutual Suffering', *Historia* 44/1 (1999), 110–47.

Krebs, Paula M., *Gender, Race and the Writing of Empire: Public Discourse and the Boer War* (Cambridge: Cambridge University Press, 1999).

Liddington, Jill, *The Road to Greenham Common: Feminism and Anti-Militarism in Britain since 1820* (New York: Syracuse University Press, 1991), 57.

Manchester Guardian, c. 1926, National Archives of South Africa, VAB14, A53 Bestelling.

Moyn, Samuel, *The Last Utopia: Human Rights in History* (Boston, MA: Belknap Press, 2012).

National Archives of South Africa, VAB, CO Volume 49, 4492/01, Lizzie van Zyl.

'New Books', *St James Gazette* (19 November 1902), 17.

Riedi, Eliza, 'The Women Pro-Boers: Gender, Peace and the Critique of Empire in the South African War', *Historical Research* 86/231 (2013), 92–115.

St James Gazette (24 June 1901), 3–4.

Snyman, Johan, 'Ways of Remembering', in Charles Villa Vicencio, ed., *Transcending a Century of Injustice* (Cape Town: Institute of Justice and Reconciliation, 2000), 22–37.

Spies, S. B., *Methods of Barbarism: Roberts, Kitchener and Civilians in the Boer Republics, January 1900–May 1902* (Cape Town: Human & Rousseau, 1977).

Stanley, Liz, *Mourning Becomes: Post-Memory, Commemoration and the Concentration Camps of the South African War* (Manchester: Manchester University Press, 2006).

Van Heyningen, Elizabeth, *The Concentration Camps of the Anglo-Boer War: A Social History* (Auckland Park: Jacana, 2013).

REILAND RABAKA

4   W. E. B. Du Bois's *The Souls of Black Folk*
    (1903): Of the Veil and the Color-Line, Of
    Double-Consciousness and Second-Sight

ABSTRACT
This chapter will survey W. E. B. Du Bois's immortal *The Souls of Black Folk* with an eye on the ways in which he created discursive devices, such as the Veil, second-sight, double-consciousness and the color-line, to capture the conundrums and complexities of what it means to be black in a white world. The concepts of race and critiques of racism Du Bois advanced in the book complemented his ongoing efforts at the turn of the twentieth century to establish the social scientific study of race. Intellectually interconnected and intersecting, they offer several of his most enduring contributions to the history, sociology, politics and economics of race. This chapter will ultimately help readers comprehend why *The Souls of Black Folk*, widely considered one of Du Bois's greatest works, remains relevant, and why it is considered a classic and conceptual cornerstone in fields as wide and varied as American studies, African American studies, ethnic studies, cultural studies, critical race studies, subaltern studies, decolonial studies and postcolonial studies.

Of the Souls of Black Folk

W. E. B. Du Bois's (1868–1963) contributions to intellectual history and culture emerging from his 1903 classic, *The Souls of Black Folk*, revolve around the conundrums and complexities of what it means to be black in a white world. In *The Souls of Black Folk* he created several seminal concepts of race and critiques of racism that complement his earlier efforts to establish the social scientific study of race in ground-breaking works such as 'The Conservation of Races', 'The Negroes of Farmville, Virginia', 'The Study of the Negro Problems', *The Philadelphia Negro*, 'The Negroes of Dougherty County, Georgia', 'The Relation of the Negroes to the Whites of the South' and 'The Spawn of Slavery: The Convict Lease-System in the South', among others.[1] Many of the concepts of racial lived-experience that Du Bois articulated in *The Souls of Black Folk* are intellectually interconnected and endlessly intersect. Ultimately, these concepts offer several of his most enduring contributions to both the humanistic and social scientific study of race and racism. Undoubtedly his concepts of 'double-consciousness' and the 'color-line' are significant.[2] However, his theory of blacks' 'Veiled' visibility and invisibility, as well as his emphasis on blacks' unique 'second-sight' in the white world are equally relevant with regard to the study of race and racism.

1 I offer more detailed discussion of each of the aforementioned works in *Against Epistemic Apartheid: W. E. B. Du Bois and the Disciplinary Decadence of Sociology* (Lanham, MD: Rowman & Littlefield, 2010). Consequently, please see the first chapter of *Against Epistemic Apartheid*, which is entitled, 'Du Bois and the Early Development of Urban and Rural Sociology: *The Philadelphia Negro* and the Souls of Black Farming Folk' (47–106). With regard to Du Bois's work prior and leading up to *The Souls of Black Folk*, see also Shamoon Zamir, *Dark Voices: W. E. B. Du Bois and American Thought, 1888–1903* (Chicago: University of Chicago Press, 1995); Reiland Rabaka, *Du Bois's Dialectics: Black Radical Politics and the Reconstruction of Critical Social Theory* (Lanham, MD: Rowman & Littlefield, 2008); Reiland Rabaka, ed., *W. E. B. Du Bois: A Critical Reader* (London: Ashgate, 2010); Aldon D. Morris, *The Scholar Denied: W. E. B. Du Bois and the Birth of Modern Sociology* (Berkeley: University of California Press, 2015); W. E. B. Du Bois, *The Problem of the Color-Line at the Turn of the Twentieth Century: The Essential Early Essays*, ed. Nahum Dimitri Chandler (New York: Fordham University Press, 2015); and Earl Wright, *The First American School of Sociology: W. E. B. Du Bois and the Atlanta Sociological Laboratory* (Burlington, VT: Ashgate, 2016).
2 Given the iconic status of the concept, the original US spelling of 'color-line' is retained throughout this collection.

Of the Veil and the Color-Line

Literary theorists have frequently commented on the 'Veil' and 'second-sight' in *The Souls of Black Folk*. However, few social scientists have offered nuanced interpretations of the ways in which Du Bois's vision of the Veil, along with its corollary concept of the color-line, was 'prophetic' in the sense that it continues to capture the conundrums of the trajectory and transmutation of American apartheid: from late nineteenth-century Black Codes and Jim Crow laws, to the twentieth-century rabid racial segregation which led to the Civil Rights movement and ultimately the new forms of twenty-first-century racism. Where the color-line calls to mind the racially segregated, Jim Crowed separate and unequal (as opposed to 'separate, but equal') white and black worlds of the late nineteenth and early twentieth centuries, Du Bois's discourse on the Veil points to the ways in which racial colonization does not render the racially oppressed completely devoid of human agency and cultural creativity. In fact, in some ways Du Bois's work here suggests that the Veiled quality of the color-line at best *blurs*, and at worst *blinds* whites to blacks' human agency and capacity for cultural creation. Consequently, the Veil's discursive significance is dual or, rather, *doubled*, and although both whites' and blacks' life-worlds and lived-experiences revolve around the very same color-line, it is their divergent relationships to the Veil, and the ways in which the Veil racially (re)structures their psychological, social and cultural worlds that determines their self-conceptions and, quite literally, the quality of their *soul-lives*.

Du Bois's discourse on the Veil accentuates not only African Americans' agency, but also their ability to create an anti-racist culture of resistance and human redemption in the midst of the mayhem of the white supremacist capitalist colonial world. The Veil has been, and can continue to be used by the racially oppressed to *conceal*. However, the Veil can also be used by the racially oppressed to *reveal*, if – and this is an extremely important 'if' – an earnest opportunity presents itself, as Du Bois deemed it did in *The Souls of Black Folk*, where he stated in 'The Forethought': 'Herein lie buried many things which if read with patience may show the strange meaning of being black here at the dawning of the Twentieth Century [...] I have sketched in swift outline the two worlds within and without the Veil'.³ Du Bois's theory of the Veil, consequently, is essentially a trope that sociologically symbolizes *white (hyper)visibility* and *black (hyper)invisibility*, white humanity and black subhumanity in a white supremacist capitalist colonial world.

The 'strange meaning of being black', Du Bois declared, 'is not without interest to you, Gentle Reader', referring to both black and white 'Gentle Reader[s]', because 'the problem of the Twentieth Century', he prophesied with words that continue to resonate and ring true, 'is the problem of the color-line'.⁴ *The Souls of Black Folk*, therefore, was written with 'Gentle Reader[s]' from both the world 'within' and the world 'without the Veil' in mind. That is to say, for those blacks who unceasingly searched for the 'strange meaning of being black' in a white world, and for those whites who had consciously or unconsciously drawn the color-line after the collapse of Reconstruction and the rising tidal wave of anti-black racial violence that rolled across the United States as the twentieth century dawned.

Du Bois's discourse on the Veil and the color-line are significant for contemporary scholars of race and racism because they represent one of the first times a bona fide social scientist endeavoured to articulate a *critical social theory of racial oppression, racial exploitation, and racial violence.* That is to say, a critical social theory of the ways in which racial oppression, racial exploitation and racial violence: first, racially divides and socially separates (the color-line); second, distorts cultural communications and human relations between those it racially divides along the color-line (the Veil); and, third, as a result of each of the aforementioned, causes blacks to suffer from a severe inferiority complex that insidiously induces them to constantly view themselves from whites' supposed 'superior' points of view (double-consciousness). The Veil's processes and practices of concealment racially (re)organizes, literally, everything that crosses the color-line, every interaction between 'the two worlds within and without the Veil', thus *blurring* or, more frequently, *blinding* those who are white and who negligently and nonchalantly wish not to view non-whites – which is to say, non-whites' humanity, history and culture.

3 W. E. B. Du Bois, *The Souls of Black Folk: Essays and Sketches* (Chicago: A. C. McClurg, 1903), vii.
4 Du Bois, *The Souls of Black Folk*, vii.

In *The Souls of Black Folk* Du Bois deployed the vivid and oft-times lyrical language of the Veil, as well as its conceptual complement, the color-line, to make his race-centred social science accessible to as wide an audience as possible. Du Bois's biographer David Levering Lewis revealingly wrote in 1993: 'Three years into yet another century of seeming unassailable European supremacy, *Souls* countered with the voices of the dark submerged and unheard'.[5] The marvellous meaning of *The Souls of Black Folk* was (or, at the least, should have been) crystal clear, according to Lewis. Until Du Bois's 'Gentle Reader[s]' 'appreciated the message of the songs sung in bondage by black people', which was one of the only ways enslaved African Americans could meaningfully express themselves during the antebellum era, then, 'Du Bois was saying, the words written in freedom by white people would remain hollow and counterfeit'.[6]

Certain scholars may have overlooked the social scientific significance of *The Souls of Black Folk* on account of its remarkable lyricism. However, their visceral reaction to the volume unequivocally reinforces precisely why Du Bois's discourse on the Veil has resonated with so many, both within and without academe. The theory of the Veil is interconnected with the concept of the color-line, but they should not be, as they frequently have been, collapsed into one and the same thing. Du Bois uses the metaphor of the Veil to expatiate racially colonized and racially divided life along the color-line. He also uses the metaphor of the Veil to explain the ways in which an invisible social construction such as the color-line actually becomes highly visible when viewed from the long-veiled perspective of blacks in a white supremacist world. Because blacks are veiled in invisibility in a white supremacist world, Du Bois brought whites' tendency to approach blacks more as problems than as human persons to his readers' attention at the outset of *The Souls of Black Folk*, thereby innovatively inverting whites' pathological approach to black humanity, history and culture. In other words, Du Bois problematized whites' problematic conceptions or, rather, *misconceptions* of blacks by audaciously asserting blacks' humanity

5   David Levering Lewis, *W. E. B. Du Bois: Biography of a Race, 1868–1919* (New York: Henry Holt, 1993), 278.
6   Lewis, *W. E. B. Du Bois*, 278.

and autonomous agency. Cautiously lifting the Veil so that whites might have a window into the black world, he wryly wrote:

> Between me and the other world there is ever an unasked question: unasked by some through feelings of delicacy; by others through the difficulty of rightly framing it. All, nevertheless, flutter round it. They approach me in a half-hesitant sort of way, eye me curiously or compassionately, and then, instead of saying directly, How does it feel to be a problem? they say, I know an excellent colored man in my town; or, I fought at Mechanicsville; or, Do not these Southern outrages make your blood boil? At these I smile, or am interested, or reduce the boiling to a simmer, as the occasion may require. To the real question, How does it feel to be a problem? I answer seldom a word.[7]

Although Du Bois deceptively claims that he seldom answers a word in response to the often unasked and insulting question, 'How does it feel to be a problem?', *The Souls of Black Folk* should be seen as part of his everevolving and often intricate answer to this nagging question. Both the Veil and the color-line are invisibly (to most whites) and visibly (to most blacks) present in each and every one of their interactions; in all of the cracks and crevices of the crucial questions that could have, and indeed should have been earnestly asked of one another; in the many millions of racial myths and cultural stereotypes that the media produces for mass consumption and, as far as one can see, for mass confusion. Du Bois's vision of the Veil, then, is also a critical theory of wilful white blindness to black humanity, history and culture. By this, I wish to emphasize whites' ability, theoretically and technically speaking, to see blacks and their humanity, history, and culture if – and, again I say, this is an extremely important 'if' – they *choose* to do so. At the same time (and here is the real rub) whites' tendency to intentionally turn a blind-eye to black humanity, history and culture – or, further, whites' custom of selectively seeing certain 'exceptional' blacks (usually black entertainers and black athletes), coincides with their apparent inability to authentically see the ongoing suffering and social misery of the black masses, who continue to live within the world of the Veil and whose lives are cruelly quarantined to the color-line.

---

7   Du Bois, *The Souls of Black Folk*, 1–2.

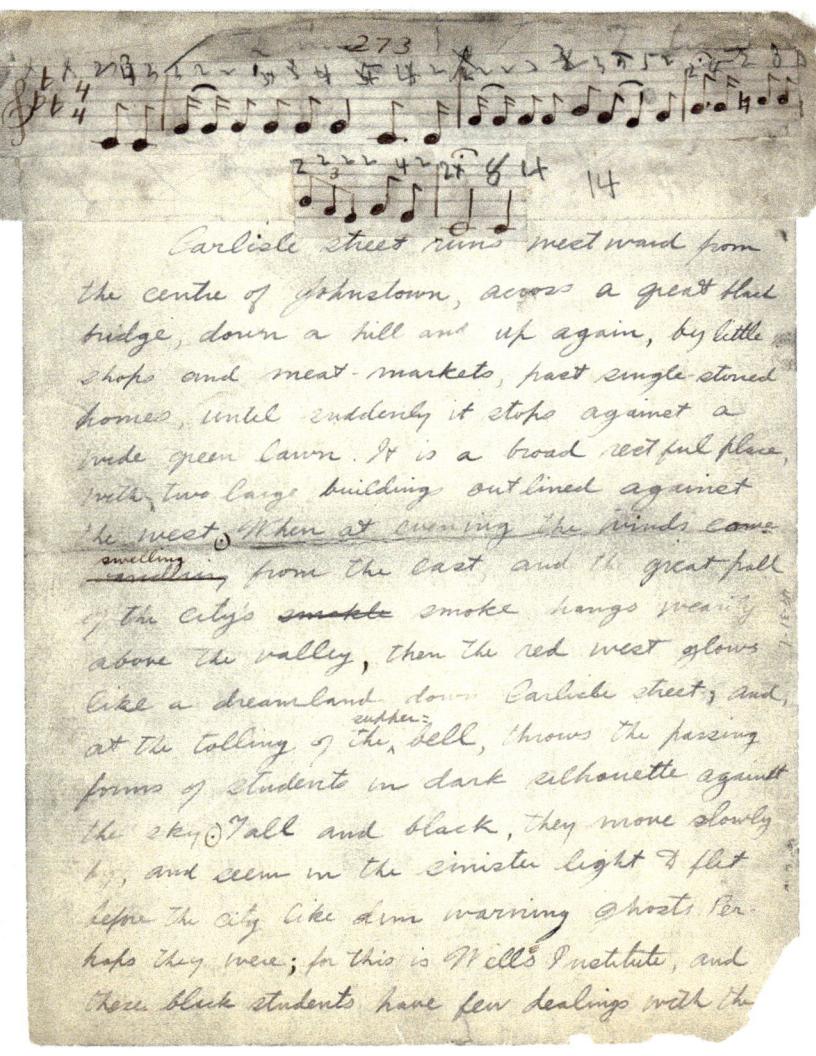

Figure 4.1: The first page of W. E. B. Du Bois's handwritten draft of Chapter 13, 'Of the Coming of John'. Courtesy of the University of Massachusetts Amherst Libraries, with the permission of The Permissions Company, Inc., on behalf of the David Graham Du Bois Trust.

Of Double-Consciousness and Second-Sight

Du Bois, as *The Souls of Black Folk* undoubtedly demonstrates, was willing to solemnly raise the Veil and cross the color-line. But, the question remains: how many whites at the turn of the twentieth century were willing to cross with him? It could almost go without saying that there was for the most part a stubborn refusal to cross the color-line on the part of most early twentieth-century whites. Perceptively anticipating that this would be the case, Du Bois developed his concept of double-consciousness to capture the excruciating anguish that the diabolical dialectic of white superiority and black inferiority inflicted on blacks.

Du Bois's discourse on the Veil dovetails with his concept of double-consciousness insofar as it also seeks to explain that blacks' efforts to gain self-consciousness in a white supremacist world will be, by default, always and everywhere damaged and distorted because the most prevalent and pervasive ideas and images of blacks and blackness in white supremacist societies are those predicated on, and prefabricated by the diabolical dialectic of white superiority and black inferiority. In other words, where the Veil metaphorically represents the ways in which the color-line is constantly cloaked in a dark cloud of misconceptions, miscommunications and misgivings between 'the two worlds within and without the Veil', double-consciousness conceptually captures the often-overlooked fact that blacks not only internalize the diabolical dialectic of white superiority and black inferiority in the white supremacist world, but also the fact that part and parcel of the white supremacist world's 'ideological hegemony' (in the Gramscian sense) is the constant blanketing of the white-dominated black world with anti-black racist and white supremacist (mis)conceptions of blacks and blackness. The concept of double-consciousness, therefore, boldly broaches the taboo topic (among both blacks and whites) of many blacks' intense internalization of white supremacist anti-black racist creations and disseminations of blackness or, as Du Bois said above, 'the strange meaning of being black here in the dawning of the Twentieth Century'.

Even though Du Bois was willing to work with whites in their earnest efforts to transgress their blindness to black humanity, history and culture, he was not willing to do so at the expense of downplaying or diminishing the physical and psychological damage that life within the Veil and life along the color-line, as well as the diabolical dialectic of white superiority and black inferiority and anti-black racist and white supremacist (mis)conceptions of blacks and blackness, had on the 'souls of black folk'. The conceptual culmination of Du Bois's insurgent efforts to make both blacks and whites aware of the physical and psychological damage that life within the Veil and life along the color-line had on the 'souls of black folk' was his intellectual history-making discourse on double-consciousness and its corollary concept of second-sight. He revealingly wrote, in perhaps the most widely commented upon passage in *The Souls of Black Folk*:

> After the Egyptian and Indian, the Greek and Roman, the Teuton and Mongolian, the Negro is a sort of seventh son, born with a veil, and gifted with second-sight in this American world, – a world which yields him no true self-consciousness, but only lets him see himself through the revelation of the other world. It is a peculiar sensation, this double-consciousness, this sense of always looking at one's self through the eyes of others, of measuring one's soul by the tape of a world that looks on in amused contempt and pity. One ever feels his two-ness, – an American, a Negro; two souls, two thoughts, two unreconciled strivings; two warring ideals in one dark body, whose dogged strength alone keeps it from being torn asunder.
>
> The history of the American Negro is the history of this strife, – this longing to attain self-conscious manhood, to merge his double self into a better and truer self. In this merging he wishes neither of the older selves to be lost. He would not Africanize America, for America has too much to teach the world and Africa. He would not bleach his Negro soul in a flood of white Americanism, for he knows that Negro blood has a message for the world. He simply wishes to make it possible for a man to be both a Negro and an American, without being cursed and spit upon by his fellows, without having the doors of Opportunity closed roughly in his face.[8]

Here, with these hallowed words, Du Bois indelibly etched his name into the annals of American intellectual history. Although the Veil and the color-line are central tropes in *The Souls of Black Folk*, Du Bois's concept of double-consciousness and its corollary concept of second-sight are simultaneously essential to understanding *The Souls of Black Folk* and

---

8   Du Bois, *The Souls of Black Folk*, 3–4.

vital to comprehending the conundrums and contradictions of racial colonization and racial segregation in a nation, even more, in a world which pretentiously prides itself on its cultural liberalism and commitment to unfettered democracy. Observe that Du Bois's doubling discourse connected the Veil with second-sight ('the Negro is a sort of seventh son, born with a veil, and gifted with second-sight in this American world'), and America (i.e. the United States), representing the white supremacist capitalist colonial world in deep-seated denial, was to those 'born with a veil', 'a world which yield[ed] [them] no true self-consciousness, but only lets [them] see [themselves] through the revelation of the other world'.

Then, as if faithfully harking back to his stated intention at the book's opening – that is to say, to candidly explore 'the strange meaning of being black here in the dawning of the Twentieth Century' – Du Bois articulated his own homespun ontology of black life-worlds and black life-struggles in a white supremacist capitalist colonial world: 'It is a peculiar sensation, this double-consciousness, this sense of always looking at one's self through the eyes of others'. Black life-worlds, Du Bois correctly assumed, would be 'strange' and 'peculiar' to whites because of the ideology of black invisibility, the diabolical dialectic of white superiority and black inferiority, and anti-black racist and white supremacist (mis)conceptions of blacks and blackness. The concept of double-consciousness asserts that the very color-line that racially divides the white world from the black world simultaneously creates a tortured 'two-ness' in blacks' souls. In fact, the racial fault-lines of the color-line ultimately drive blacks to constantly question whether they are Africans or Americans (and, even whether they are human) to such an excruciating degree that their souls become doubled and divided like the loveless racially colonized world that they are forced to live in. Du Bois's concept of double-consciousness, then, is also a discursive *doppelgänger*, textually representing the consequences of blacks' racial colonization and the ways in which the color-line not only racially divides society but, even more, black souls and black selves.

Du Bois distressingly wrote of 'two souls, two thoughts, two unreconciled strivings; two warring ideals in one dark body, whose dogged strength alone keeps it from being torn asunder'. Against this backdrop, where have blacks found the 'dogged strength' to keep their souls and bodies 'from being torn asunder'? After painting such a bleak picture of the 'souls of black folk', and their trials and tribulations in the white supremacist world, this seems like a fair question and, indeed, it is a query which Du Bois ingeniously answered with his saga of blacks' second-sight.[9] Second-sight symbolizes blacks' ability, even in the face of adversity (i.e. holocaust, enslavement, colonization, segregation and neo-apartheid), to see both Africa's (the black world's) and America's (the white world's) strengths and weaknesses. Moreover, it illuminates the ways in which these two worlds might, and indeed should, educate and support each other. Du Bois described African Americans in the passage above as being 'gifted with second-sight'. It is their experiences in and visions of 'the two worlds within

---

9   I emphasize the epic aspects of Du Bois's theory of second-sight here by referring to it as the '*saga* of second-sight' in an effort to accent the fact that, first, if indeed a saga is a 'story of heroic achievement' and, second, as David Levering Lewis observed, if Du Bois's writings, especially his memoirs, utilized the 'language of the saga', then, it is important for us to make a connection between his autobiography and his African and African American historiography (Lewis, *W. E. B. Du Bois*, 19). In other words, Du Bois's 'saga of second-sight' demonstrates not only that his soul is bound up with those of the 'souls of black folk', but also that he boldly believed that just as he was able to arrive at the critical black consciousness (as opposed to double-consciousness) of second-sight, so too could and would his beloved black folk break free from the gruesome grasp of double-consciousness. In order to wrench themselves free from the clutches of double-consciousness, like Du Bois, black folk would have to systematically and critically study continental and diasporic African history, culture and struggle on their own terms – that is to say, consciously countering the 'ideological hegemony' of anti-black racist capitalism, which is also to say that there are serious implications for what we are currently calling 'Africana studies' scattered throughout Du Bois's oeuvre but especially apparent in his critique of double-consciousness and saga of second-sight. Further commenting on Du Bois's distinct synthesis of his personal history with the nuances of national African American and international Pan-African history, Lewis announced: 'In those lyrical memoirs, whether *Darkwater*, *A Pageant of Seven Decades*, *Dusk of Dawn*, or the *Autobiography* [*of W. E. B. Du Bois*], we are drawn to participate in a chronicle of epic sweep, at once familial, racial, national, global, and prophetic' (19). All of this, then, should be borne in mind in the discussion below concerning second-sight as a possible solution to the problem of double-consciousness.

and without the Veil', that ultimately distinguish their special contributions to American and world culture and civilization. In essence, where the majority of whites suffer from white blindness to blackness, blacks have been 'gifted' with second-sight as an ironic consequence of their having endured racial colonization and other forms of racial oppression at the hands of whites. But blacks, it should solemnly be said, should never take their giftedness for granted, as it is neither automatic nor axiomatic: because double-consciousness constantly makes second-sight dangerously double-edged and always and ever enervating, on account of both the intensity and depth of blacks' internalization of anti-black racist and white supremacist (mis)conceptions of blacks and blackness, and the paradoxes of the trajectory and transmutations of American and global apartheid. It is with this in mind that I argue that at its conceptual core double-consciousness is about double or divided selves in the process of spiritually, psychologically, and socially evolving out of tortured 'two-ness' into 'self-conscious manhood' – which is to say, self-conscious humanhood.

Second-sight provides blacks with a window into the 'two worlds within and without the Veil', and it also enables them to begin the dialectical process(es) of revolutionary decolonization and human liberation by critically calling into question double-consciousness. Once this process is initiated it, literally, gives African Americans second-sight. That is to say, first, the ability to view the world from within and without the Veil; second, to see the special contributions that both the 'souls of black folk' and the 'souls of white folk' have made to America and the wider world; and ultimately, and most importantly, to sift through and synthesize the best of the 'souls of black folk' with the best of the 'souls of white folk' in the interest of creating, as Du Bois said, 'a better and truer self', a 'better and truer' nation and a 'better and truer' world. This was Du Bois's sensational solution to the problem of double-consciousness. The 'Negro', armed with second-sight, would have to 'merge his double self into a better and truer self'. However, he wishes 'neither of the older selves to be lost'. In the end second-sight would enable African Americans not simply to see but also to *synthesize* black and white 'gifts' and 'messages' and, in the fullness of time, to *articulate*. Literally, to speak anew America's special truths to the wider world.

Of the Interdisciplinary Legacy of *The Souls of Black Folk*

For more than a century *The Souls of Black Folk* has been praised and criticized, interpreted and misinterpreted by so many scholars from so many different disciplines that there can be little doubt of its vital place in intellectual history. For instance, *The Souls of Black Folk* has been the subject of entire books of critical commentary, innumerable essays, countless journal articles and stacks of book chapters.[10] Scholars working in diverse disciplines, such as history, philosophy, political science, psychology, anthropology, economics, education, literature and religion, among others, have

10   For example, see William L. Andrews, ed., *Critical Essays on W. E. B. Du Bois* (Boston, MA: G. K. Hall, 1985); Harold Bloom, ed., *W. E. B. Du Bois* (New York: Chelsea House Publishers, 2001); Edward J. Blum and Jason R. Young, eds, *The Souls of W. E. B. Du Bois: New Essays and Reflections* (Macon, GA: Mercer University Press, 2009); Tamara Brown, Ida Jones and Yohuru R. Williams, eds, *The Souls of Black Folk: Centennial Reflections* (Trenton, NJ: Africa World Press, 2004); Rebecca Carroll, ed., *Saving the Race: Conversations on Du Bois from a Collective Memoir of The Souls of Black Folk* (New York: Harlem Moon, 2003); Stanley Crouch and Playthell Benjamin, *Reconsidering The Souls of Black Folk: Thoughts on the Groundbreaking Classic Work of W. E. B. Du Bois* (Philadelphia, PA: Running Press, 2002); Chester J. Fontenot, ed., *W. E. B. Du Bois & Race: Essays Celebrating the Centennial Publication of The Souls of Black Folk* (Macon, GA: Mercer University, 2001); Chester J. Fontenot and Mary Keller, eds, *Re-Cognizing W. E. B. Du Bois in the Twenty-First Century: Essay on W. E. B. Du Bois* (Macon, GA: Mercer University Press, 2007); Robert Gooding-Williams and Dwight A. McBride, eds, *100 Years of The Souls of Black Folk: A Celebration of W. E. B. Du Bois* (Durham, NC: Duke University Press, 2005); Dolan Hubbard, ed., *The Souls of Black Folk: One Hundred Years Later* (Columbia: University of Missouri Press, 2003); Paul C. Mocombe, *The Soul-less Souls of Black Folk: A Sociological Reconsideration of Black Consciousness as Du Boisian Double-Consciousness* (Lanham, MD: University Press of America, 2008); Stephanie J. Shaw, *W. E. B. Du Bois and* The Souls of Black Folk (Chapel Hill: University of North Carolina Press, 2013); E. Victor Wolfenstein, *A Gift of the Spirit: Reading* The Souls of Black Folk (Ithaca, NY: Cornell University Press, 2007); Alford A. Young, ed., *The Souls of W. E. B. Du Bois* (Boulder, CO: Paradigm Publishers, 2006).

hailed it as a timeless tome. *The Souls of Black Folk* has been particularly well received in a number of interdisciplinary disciplines that emerged between the middle of the twentieth century and the early decades of the twenty-first century. It is widely considered a foundational text and major discursive point of departure in American studies, African American studies, ethnic studies, cultural studies, critical race studies, subaltern studies, decolonial studies and, of course, postcolonial studies.

The Souls of Black Folk's interdisciplinary import is easily detected, as revered biographer Arnold Rampersad's tripartite discursive division of the text reveals: Chapters 1 to 3 ('Of Our Spiritual Strivings', 'Of the Dawn of Freedom' and 'Of Mr. Booker T. Washington and Others') hinge on the historical 'strivings' of the 'souls of black folk'; Chapters 4 to 9 ('Of the Meaning of Progress', 'Of the Wings of Atalanta', 'Of the Training of Black Men', 'Of the Black Belt' and 'Of the Quest of the Golden Fleece') symbolize the sociological 'strivings' of the 'souls of black folk'; and, Chapters 10 to 14 ('Of the Sons of Master and Man', 'Of the Faith of the Fathers', 'Of the Passing of the First-Born', 'Of Alexander Crummell' and 'The Sorrow Songs') represent the spiritual and religious 'strivings' of the 'souls of black folk'.[11] Hence, Du Bois's discourse, here and throughout his oeuvre, was much more interdisciplinary than many Du Bois scholars have been willing to concede: partly owing to their monodisciplinary manoeuvres to reclaim and reframe Du Bois for their own respective single subject-focused fields or disciplines, and partly on account of the fact that, truth be told, W. E. B. Du Bois and Du Bois studies continues to be conceptually quarantined because of the ongoing epistemic apartheid of the academy of the twenty-first century. Needless to say, *The Souls of Black Folk*, much like Du Bois's larger legacy, undoubtedly, and even if often clandestinely, continues to influence contemporary intellectual history and culture. Epistemic apartheid be damned!

---

11 Arnold Rampersad, *The Art and Imagination of W. E. B. Du Bois* (New York: Schocken, 1990), 70.

Bibliography

Andrews, William L., ed., *Critical Essays on W. E. B. Du Bois* (Boston, MA: G. K. Hall, 1985).

Bloom, Harold, ed., *W. E. B. Du Bois* (New York: Chelsea House Publishers, 2001).

Blum, Edward J., and Jason R. Young, eds, *The Souls of W. E. B. Du Bois: New Essays and Reflections* (Macon, GA: Mercer University Press, 2009).

Brown, Tamara, Ida Jones and Yohuru R. Williams, eds, *The Souls of Black Folk: Centennial Reflections* (Trenton, NJ: Africa World Press, 2004).

Carroll, Rebecca, ed., *Saving the Race: Conversations on Du Bois from a Collective Memoir of The Souls of Black Folk* (New York: Harlem Moon, 2003).

Crouch, Stanley, and Playthell Benjamin, *Reconsidering The Souls of Black Folk: Thoughts on the Groundbreaking Classic Work of W. E. B. Du Bois* (Philadelphia, PA: Running Press, 2002).

Du Bois, W. E. B., *The Problem of the Color-Line at the Turn of the Twentieth Century: The Essential Early Essays*, ed. Nahum Dimitri Chandler (New York: Fordham University Press, 2015).

——, *The Souls of Black Folk: Essays and Sketches* (Chicago: A. C. McClurg, 1903).

Fontenot, Chester J., ed., *W. E. B. Du Bois & Race: Essays Celebrating the Centennial Publication of The Souls of Black Folk* (Macon, GA: Mercer University, 2001).

——, and Mary Keller, eds, *Re-Cognizing W. E. B. Du Bois in the Twenty-First Century: Essay on W. E. B. Du Bois* (Macon, GA: Mercer University Press, 2007).

Gooding-Williams, Robert, and Dwight A. McBride, eds, *100 Years of The Souls of Black Folk: A Celebration of W. E. B. Du Bois* (Durham, NC: Duke University Press, 2005).

Hubbard, Dolan, ed., *The Souls of Black Folk: One Hundred Years Later* (Columbia: University of Missouri Press, 2003).

Lewis, David Levering, *W. E. B. Du Bois: Biography of a Race, 1868–1919* (New York: Henry Holt, 1993).

Mocombe, Paul C., *The Soul-less Souls of Black Folk: A Sociological Reconsideration of Black Consciousness as Du Boisian Double-Consciousness* (Lanham, MD: University Press of America, 2008).

Morris, Aldon D., *The Scholar Denied: W. E. B. Du Bois and the Birth of Modern Sociology* (Berkeley: University of California Press, 2015).

Rabaka, Reiland, *Against Epistemic Apartheid: W. E. B. Du Bois and the Disciplinary Decadence of Sociology* (Lanham, MD: Rowman & Littlefield, 2010).

——, *Du Bois's Dialectics: Black Radical Politics and the Reconstruction of Critical Social Theory* (Lanham, MD: Rowman & Littlefield, 2008).

———, ed., *W. E. B. Du Bois: A Critical Reader* (London: Ashgate, 2010).
Rampersad, Arnold, *The Art and Imagination of W. E. B. Du Bois* (New York: Schocken, 1990).
Shaw, Stephanie J., *W. E. B. Du Bois and* The Souls of Black Folk (Chapel Hill: University of North Carolina Press, 2013).
Wolfenstein, E. Victor, *A Gift of the Spirit: Reading* The Souls of Black Folk (Ithaca, NY: Cornell University Press, 2007).
Wright, Earl, *The First American School of Sociology: W. E. B. Du Bois and the Atlanta Sociological Laboratory* (Burlington, VT: Ashgate, 2016).
Young, Alford A., ed., *The Souls of W. E. B. Du Bois* (Boulder, CO: Paradigm Publishers, 2006).
Zamir, Shamoon, *Dark Voices: W. E. B. Du Bois and American Thought, 1888–1903* (Chicago: University of Chicago Press, 1995).

PRIYASHA MUKHOPADHYAY

5   *Wake Up, India: A Plea for Social Reform* (1913): Annie Besant's Anticolonial Networks

ABSTRACT

Annie Besant's *Wake Up, India: A Plea for Social Reform* was a series of eight lectures delivered in Madras in 1913 and published later that year. Besant's lectures focused on a range of subjects, including mass education in India, women's work, industries and foreign travel. While the lectures may not have had the level of circulation or influence that Besant's *Why I Became a Theosophist* (1889) did, this chapter makes a claim for their role as a precursor to anti-imperial politics in early twentieth-century India. To that end, it focuses on Besant as a public intellectual and her text as one designed to have an impact on its listeners and readers, leading to subsequent social reform efforts, with the ultimate goal of Home Rule for India.

In October and November 1913, Annie Besant (1847–1933) delivered a series of eight lectures in Madras to 'mark the beginning of an earnest concerted movement for the uplifting of India'.[1] The city was (and still is) the headquarters of the Theosophical Society, the occult scientific and spiritual movement that brought Besant to India in the first place, and so she would have been a familiar face to many of its inhabitants. It is not surprising then, that the lectures were exceedingly well attended. By all accounts 'wet and gloomy' and 'terrible' weather proved no deterrent and the venue was packed to capacity at every meeting.[2] The series was published as *Wake Up, India: A Plea for Social Reform* by the Theosophical Publishing House later that year.

1   Annie Besant, *Wake Up, India: A Plea for Social Reform* (Madras: Theosophical Publishing House, 1913).
2   Besant, *Wake Up, India*, 108, 198.

While Besant's broader contribution to the Indian Nationalist Movement of the early twentieth century is well known, *Wake Up, India* has been barely visible in historical and literary scholarship. Relegated at best to one-off mentions and footnotes, it has been eclipsed by the flashier reception histories of Besant's other works. Unlike *Why I Became a Theosophist* (1889) or her translation of the *Bhagavad Gita* (1895), *Wake Up, India* has next to no claim to a transnational reputation.³ There are few references to the lectures or their publication in the international Theosophical periodical press.⁴ And while the Theosophical Society's wide network of libraries, reading rooms, and lodges ensured that the book in its material form must have travelled across the anglophone world, the absence of library lending records makes it impossible to determine who was reading Besant's lectures and, if they were, how they were reading them.⁵ Nonetheless, *Wake Up, India* remains an important postcolonial text, particularly in regard to its investment in the *local* as a means of serving the interests of a larger and more dispersed *global* community. For example, the editor of *The Vahan*, the magazine of the Theosophical Society in England and Wales, noted that members of the society needed to 'put [their] shoulder also to the great wheel of the world's progress since similar though not identical problems are coming inevitably to the fore in every nation'.⁶

3   Annie Besant, *Why I Became a Theosophist* (London: Freethought Publishing, 1889); Annie Besant, trans., *The Bhagavad Gita, or the Lord's Song* (London, Benares and Madras: Theosophical Publishing Society, 1895).
4   Two exceptions include: the editorial note to the November 1913 issue of *The Vahan* containing references to the lectures being delivered, and a review of the published lectures in the April 1914 issue of *The Theosophist*. See: 'Editorial Note', *The Vahan* 23/4 (1913), 67–8; and A non-Theosophist, 'Review of *Wake Up, India: A Plea for Social Reform*', *The Theosophist* 35/7 (1914), 127–9. Besant occasionally references the lecture series in her writings, but in no sustained manner.
5   A copy of the lectures, for one, appeared in the 1929 catalogue of the Society's London Library as *Wake Up! India*. See The Theosophical Society in England, Lending Library Catalogue (London: n. p., 1929), 8. The O.E. Library League in Washington D.C. held copies that could be borrowed for $0.65, but given that later announcements by the League offer the book at a reduced rate ($0.30) and state that it was out of print, its popularity among its contemporary readers remains dubious. See 'List No. 2: Theosophy', *The O.E. Library Critic* 5/3 (1915), n.pag.; 'Besant and Leadbeater Books at Half-Price!', *The O.E. Library Critic* 28/9 (1929), n.pag.
6   'Editorial Note', 67.

While child marriage or the caste system may not have been problems the British public had to face on an everyday basis, they were symptomatic for the Theosophists of a wider and universal malaise: spiritual degeneration.

Besant's sensitivity to the connection between the local and the global provided inspiration to the movement for Home Rule between 1916 and 1917, even though her efforts were later displaced by the mass appeal of Mohandas Gandhi's call for *satyagraha* [civil disobedience]. This chapter explores the influence of *Wake Up, India* while also considering the crucial, but often overlooked, limits to Besant's programme of resistance. As we shall see, although Besant's lectures appealed to a language of freedom, she still envisioned India as part of a world empire with Britain at the helm. On the one hand, then, this chapter will examine the ways in which *Wake Up, India* sought to mobilize various religious and nationalist discourses in the aid of a higher empire. On the other, it will move away from simply attempting to find causal connections between the circulation of Besant's lectures and events in Indian history, and seek instead to address the question of the text's genre. How did the published lecture, as a rhetorical mode specifically designed to persuade listeners (and in this case, readers as well), help to rouse the Indian public to political action? Or to frame this question another way, how were Besant's fighting words put to use?

Wake Up, India and the Theosophical Anti-Empire

The ostensible reason for the *Wake Up, India* lectures was to introduce a new reformist group, The Brothers of Service. The work of such organizations, as Besant pointed out in her preface to the published book, was 'the hardest and the most thankless of all'.[7] By highlighting in her lectures the different religious and social reforms for which such groups laboured, Besant hoped to channel their efforts more efficiently, making them 'more public and more effective'.[8] To this end, each of the eight lectures that comprised *Wake Up, India* focused

7   Besant, *Wake Up, India*, n.pag.
8   Besant, *Wake Up, India,* n.pag.

on a different aspect of Hindu religious reform, elaborating the reasons for change and the progress made. Their subjects ranged from explaining that Indians should travel abroad to expand their minds and horizons, and the need for education across all sections of society (particularly women and the working classes); to the problems of child marriage, untouchability, and colonial racism; and the importance of encouraging local industries and businesses.[9]

Throughout the lectures Besant referred to several reform organizations, though the rallying cry of *Wake Up, India* drew its strength primarily from the somewhat esoteric, late nineteenth-century movement, Theosophy. Besant discovered Theosophy in 1889 when W. T. Stead gave her a copy of Helena Blavatsky's *The Secret Doctrine* (1888) to review for the *Pall Mall Gazette*. Given that one of the primary aims of the Theosophical movement was 'to promote the study of Aryan and other Eastern literatures, religions, and sciences', it was not surprising that India, the birthplace of Hinduism, was a natural pilgrimage site for Blavatsky and her followers.[10] As early as 1879, just four years after the establishment of the Theosophical Society in New York, the organization had forged considerable connections with Hindu reformist groups such as the Arya Samaj and the Brahmo Samaj.[11] *Wake Up, India*'s engagement with questions that were being debated in traditional Hindu society drew strength from this intellectual lineage, responding to and capitalizing on an already well-established Theosophical presence in late nineteenth- and early twentieth-century India.

The association between the Theosophists and Hindu reformist groups was very much a two-way exchange. The Theosophists needed

---

9   The lectures and the dates on which they were delivered are as follows: (1) Foreign Travel: Why Indians should go Abroad (10 October); (2) Child-Marriage and its Results (17 October); (3) Our Duty to the Depressed Classes (24 October); (4) Indian Industries as related to Self-Government (31 October); (5) Mass education (7 November); (6) The Education of Indian Girls (9 November); (7) The Colour Bar in England, the Colonies, and India (14 November); (8) The Passing of the Caste System (16 November).

10   Besant, *Why I Became a Theosophist*, 12.

11   On the Theosophical Society's links with the Arya Samaj, see, for example, Mark Bevir, 'Theosophy and the Origins of the Indian National Congress', *International Journal of Hindu Studies* 7/1–3 (2003), 99–115.

support from Indians to claim authenticity for their own doctrines and, given that the influence of the Arya Samaj and Brahmo Samaj was regionally bound, integration with Theosophy promised to enhance that influence via a much wider network of people and institutions.[12] Like the shared space of the lecture hall (to which I will return later in this chapter), Theosophy brought together Indians and Britons alike in bonds of collaborative friendship. To borrow from Leela Gandhi's study of late Victorian radicalism and empire, it created interracial and transnational affective communities.[13] More importantly, perhaps, Theosophy also provided Indian Hindus with a new lens through which to view their religious culture. Since the publication of Edward Said's *Orientalism* (1978), postcolonial studies has focused on the ways in which Western representations of Eastern cultures not only reduced them to exotic stereotypes, but also provided grounds for colonial domination.[14] Theosophy, however, stands as a curious exception. By insisting on the primacy of Hinduism and Buddhism, the movement destabilized the moral authority that accompanied Christianity and, by extension, the divinely sanctioned prerogative of British imperial rule.[15] By doing this, it created a new religious and racial hierarchy that placed Indian civilization at the apex of the social order.

While Theosophy worked to re-emphasize the importance of Hinduism to the colonial Indian public, *Wake Up, India* took this endeavour a step further, providing the colonized with a paradigm for anti-imperial resistance. Central was the Theosophical movement's commitment to becoming 'the nucleus of a universal brotherhood'.[16] As Besant declared in *Why I Became a Theosophist*: 'Atheist and Theist, Christian and Hindu, Mahommedan and Secularist, all can meet on this one broad platform [of the Theosophical brotherhood], and none has the right to look askance at another'.[17] The

---

12   See Peter van der Veer, *Imperial Encounters: Religion and Modernity in India and Britain* (Princeton, NJ: Princeton University Press, 2001); Bevir, 'Theosophy and the Origins of the Indian National Congress', 99–115.
13   Leela Gandhi, *Affective Communities: Anticolonial Thought and the Politics of Friendship* (Ranikhet: Permanent Black, 2006).
14   Edward Said, *Orientalism* (New York: Pantheon Books, 1978).
15   Bevir, 'Theosophy and the Origins of the Indian National Congress', 58, 64.
16   Besant, *Why I Became a Theosophist*, 12.
17   Besant, *Why I Became a Theosophist*, 12.

universal brotherhood thus marked the coming together of diverse and disparate groups of people in the familial bonds of spiritual, rather than merely religious, harmony.

We will return to this concept later, but for now it suffices to say that while the notion of the brotherhood is not unique to *Wake Up, India* (and indeed predates Besant's own conversion to the movement in 1889), the lectures were crucial in suggesting that this community could be created by two levels of resistance working towards the same end. The first was directed towards the practices of orthodox Hinduism. Critics and scholars of Besant's life have been constantly baffled by her seemingly fickle political and ideological commitments; her constantly evolving attitudes towards Hinduism being one example.[18] In line with the Theosophical celebration of Eastern religions, Besant's early years in India saw her speak vociferously in support of returning to a 'purer' form of the religion: one that valued the place of women as participants in public life, for example, but which also argued for the caste system as an efficient model for the social division of labour. Any changes to the contrary, she branded as 'Westernization' and inimical to the very fabric of Indian civilization.[19]

Wake Up, India, by contrast, marked the culmination of Besant's new public stance on Hinduism and religious reform. While a historical past is constantly alluded to, the lectures articulate a more sceptical attitude towards orthodox Hindu practices. Many common religious injunctions (such as the ban on foreign travel) were, according to her, unsupported by religious texts. Likewise, inherent caste and gender inequalities could no longer be ignored. Re-examination and debate, Besant told her audience and readers, could only make Hinduism stronger: 'And I, who would reverence the veda, I would throw it into the furnace of criticism without any fear of doubt, knowing that the fire can only burn the rubbish and

---

18 For a review of Besant's supposedly shifting attitude towards political ideologies, and contemporary reactions to them, see Gauri Viswanathan, *Outside the Fold: Conversion, Modernity, and Belief* (Princeton, NJ: Princeton University Press, 1998), 178–80.

19 For a comprehensive account, see Nancy Fix Anderson, 'Bridging cross-cultural feminisms: Annie Besant and Women's Rights in England and India, 1874–1933', *Women's History Review* 3/4 (1994), 563–80.

that the gold will shine out the purer after that fire is put out'.[20] In doing so, Besant changed her orientation: 'not looking back always to the past but from the past gaining courage for the future, and learning to avoid its errors while [taking] advantage of its wisdom'.[21]

If orthodox Hinduism was the first of Besant's targets in *Wake Up, India*, the second was British Rule in India. The lectures therefore also mark the beginning of a shift in her political commitments. No longer content with promoting spiritual regeneration for its own sake, she had come to see it as the first step towards self-government along the lines of the model adopted in Ireland. Religious reform would, Besant argued, transform Indian subjects into better citizens, capable of making decisions about the future of their nation. To this end, she asked the listeners and readers of her first lecture, 'Foreign Travel: Why Indians should go Abroad':

> What are you looking for in the future, friends? Always to remain as you are, largely aliens in your country? Or are you thinking of the time to which the late reforms are pointing, that gradually you will exercise real authority in your own land, nay, that after a time there will not only be a Parliament in India in which Indians will sit, but an Indian community gathered round the person of the kind in which self-governing India will have her representative, as much as any other country of this vast worldwide Empire.[22]

Besant's rhetorical questions also make clear the oppositional model of governance that she was advocating in direct contradistinction to the top-down violent imposition that characterized British rule in India. It was a model of rule in which the reformed Indian community was to participate. Here she returns to the idea of the universal brotherhood. This commonwealth, as Besant often liked to call it, would be a form of spiritual and ethical assemblage where different groups and communities could meet on an equal plane to pursue common interests. However, as Gauri Viswanathan has pointed out, because of the radical and violent history that surrounds Besant's involvement in Indian nationalist politics,

---

20 Besant, *Wake Up, India*, 15.
21 Besant, *Wake Up, India*, 16–17.
22 Besant, *Wake Up, India*, 39.

the obvious limits and agenda behind the utopic construction of the universal brotherhood has often been obscured. For one, it has largely escaped representation in popular historical accounts, where Besant is often placed on a par with other anticolonial figures such as Gandhi.[23] But the brotherhood, as is clear from the extended passage above, promised only a limited freedom *under* British rule, rather than outright independence; Besant was adamant that Britain and India were 'necessary the one to the other'.[24] Rather than call for a dismantling of empire, she sought to reorient the British government towards enhancing the good of the Indian nation. This, as Viswanathan points out, absorbed Indian political autonomy into another imperial plan: that of a hierarchized system of race, with the Aryan Indians restored to their rightful place in the world's dominant nations.[25] In short, *Wake Up, India* and Besant's subsequent political trajectory point not to a wholesale overhaul but to a 'revision of empire', replacing an economically skewed construct with an organized spiritual – and racially inverted – one.[26]

Falling on Deaf Ears?

While *Wake Up, India*'s status as a text inspiring widespread resistance needs to be qualified and placed in the frame of Theosophy's investment in an alternative vision of empire, it cannot be denied that Besant's lectures nevertheless held the potential to 'stir the impressionable youths of India to revolt', as Governor Lawley observed in 1910.[27] Besant and

---

23   Viswanathan, *Outside the Fold*, 189.
24   Besant, *Wake Up, India*, 39.
25   Viswanathan, *Outside the Fold*, 186–203.
26   Viswanathan, *Outside the Fold*, 186.
27   Letter from Sir A. Lawley to Annie Besant, 20 February 1910, Adyar Archives, SN6, quoted in Anne Taylor, *Annie Besant: A Biography* (Oxford and New York: Oxford University Press, 1992), 288.

her supporters were well aware of the power of both the spoken and the written word, and she had enjoyed a successful career as a political and religious lecturer in England and the United States before arriving in India in 1893. Once in the country she embarked on a similarly hectic series of public-speaking events which, as her biographer Anne Taylor writes, were accompanied by opulent fanfare: 'What Annie always called "tom-toms" [small percussion instruments] and flaring lights, and popular religious symbols greeted her wherever she went. Elephants saluted her by throwing up their trunks, and sacred bulls guarded the flower-bedecked platforms from which she spoke'.[28]

Needless to say, the orientalist spectacle associated with many of Besant's lectures was not included in the experience of readers of the published version of *Wake Up, India*, and a distinction needs to be made between the histories of the lectures as they were delivered, and the printed forms in which they circulated. Moving from content to form, this chapter will now focus on the manner in which, through publication, Besant's lectures continued to develop as a tool for resisting empire.

For Besant, what part then did the genre of the lecture play in social and religious reform? *Wake Up, India* is a particularly good example of her thoughts on this subject, as it presents a self-reflexive account of the lecture form as a means of instigating widespread resistance. The use of the lecture as a means of propagating anticolonial feeling across the world was not, of course, new. Its use in a domestic context, however, was more unorthodox. Besant was credited as being among the first in India to address large audiences at political gatherings in urban and rural contexts alike.[29] Reputedly a very charismatic speaker, for her the lecture was first and

---

28 Taylor, *Annie Besant*, 268.
29 Taylor, *Annie Besant*, 294. That said, it is worth paying attention to Bernard Bate's reminder that the elite anglophone circles of the Theosophists could not have had the political impact that vernacular lecturing after 1918 did. Nevertheless, the Theosophists did provide a model – and the instrument of the lecture – for what it meant to address publics as political entities. See Bernard Bate, '"To Persuade Them into Speech and Action": Oratory and the Tamil Political, Madras, 1905–1919', *Comparative Studies in Society and History* 55/1 (2013), 145, 152–3.

foremost a means of 'inducing [people] to think'.[30] In 'Child-Marriage and its Problems', the second lecture in *Wake Up, India*, she cogently outlines the work of the lecturer:

> A lecturer ought not to do the study for the hearer, much less to give out cut-and-dried opinions which the hearer is expected to adopt. The lecturer's work is to stimulate thought, rather than to do the thinking. The lecturer's work is to win the hearers to study, rather than to give out cut-and-dried opinions. And so I shall take my favourite position as a lecturer, of acting as a signpost to show you the road along which your own feet must carry you, to induce you to think; for if you think, the case for which I plead is won.[31]

It was thus thought and dialogue, rather than simple agreement, that the lectures hoped to initiate. As Besant told the audience of 'Foreign Travel: Why Indians should go Abroad': 'it is better that we should not all think exactly alike – otherwise the world would never go on'.[32]

It was the quiet stimulation of thought, then, rather than the frenzied excitement of the lecture hall, to which Besant aspired. The latter, she realized time and time again, did not always translate into action. The lecture on foreign travel therefore also came with a stern word of caution:

> [A]bove all, remember that to cheer in a hall of reforms which outside the hall you are not brave enough to carry out is not the way in which India will rise to her place among the nations; for never by a nation of those who are not brave and heroic can the high peak of glory be ascended, nor the place of India in the whole world be made known.[33]

This was what, according to Besant, was 'killing India': 'talk, without action; words, without the courage to live up to them'.[34]

But if the impact of listening to a lecture was, more often than not, ephemeral, and its effect temporary, how did publication serve to counter

---

30 Besant, *Wake Up, India*, 51.
31 Besant, *Wake Up, India*, 51.
32 Besant, *Wake Up, India*, 13.
33 Besant, *Wake Up, India*, 12.
34 Besant, *Wake Up, India*, 53.

this?³⁵ At a fundamental level, publication ensured that the lectures were preserved in a more permanent – and mobile – form for posterity. While the audiences of *Wake Up, India* were Britons and Indians local to Madras, *Wake Up, India* could appeal to readers across the anglophone world. Its transmission was facilitated by a network of Theosophical lodges and libraries spread around the globe. In this manner, distributing the lectures as print objects transformed a *local* event into one that could be debated and considered by a *global* community, connected through the act of reading.

The relationship between collective listening and solitary reading was therefore crucial to Besant's project of social and political reform and was built into the design of *Wake Up, India* in its book form. The published texts were, for the most part, very lightly modified transcripts of the lectures Besant originally delivered. To read *Wake Up, India* may not have been the same as listening to it, but the presence of certain kinds of narrative and textual markers in the book would have allowed the reader to imagine the lecture experience, and by extension, to participate in it. While the rhetorical devices on which Besant frequently relied – cascading rhetorical questions, and the repetitive restatement of her core ideas in each lecture – were present in the print form of the lectures, attempts to reproduce the immediacy of being present and listening were also made through the addition of parenthetical indications of what actually happened in the lecture. We are even told, for example, when 'the lecturer took up a paper' and then read from it while discussing the subject of encouraging local industries.³⁶ As simple as these additions may appear at first glance, they were crucial in that they allowed solitary readers to imagine a shared social reformist public, one that existed in the brackets of the lectures, in the interjections, interruptions and casual gestures.

---

35 I discuss the question of ephemerality, political impact, and listening in the theosophical imagination at greater length in other work. See Priyasha Mukhopadhyay, 'Listening Like a Theosophist', *Political Theology* 19/8 (2018), 719–33.
36 Besant, *Wake Up, India*, 65.

As indicated above, Besant was fearful that the casual listener would forget the lessons of the lecture hall once he or she left the confinement of its four walls. The reader, by contrast, was given the opportunity to engage with the arguments of the lecture in a more sustained fashion and over a longer period of time. Readers could repeatedly consult the volume, whether to refresh their memories of the lectures (if they were part of the audience in Madras), or as a substitute for the act of listening in the first place. If the process of listening was powerful because it took place 'in-the-moment', the book form of *Wake Up, India* gave individuals the added chance to consult the volume repeatedly. Moreover, the published lectures included additional textual apparatus to enhance the propagation of the core ideas of the lectures. Footnotes with suggestions for directed reading recur throughout, while entire appendices of statistics and data corroborating Besant's points about local industries are also included. Modulating between the high charge of political rhetoric and the possibility of sustained, long-term engagement, the position of the reader may not have trumped that of the listener, but it certainly developed as its important and necessary complement.

*

Besant's engagement with Indian politics culminated in the Home Rule movement of 1917 and her election as the first woman president of the Indian National Congress later in the same year. This chapter has situated *Wake Up, India* in her political trajectory, demonstrating how the lectures marked a shift in her perceptions of Hinduism and colonialism that built cumulatively towards this climactic moment.

Given the qualifications to Besant's model of resistance, is *Wake Up, India* less a text of anti-imperial resistance than it has been conventionally considered to be? If nothing else, Besant's lectures and the Home Rule movement with which it was associated marked the beginning of a larger – and more successful – independence movement led by Gandhi and others. *Wake Up, India* was not a meek suggestion. It was a bold imperative.

Bibliography

Anderson, Nancy Fix, 'Bridging Cross-Cultural Feminisms: Annie Besant and Women's Rights in England and India, 1874–1933', *Women's History Review* 3/4 (1994), 563–80.

Bate, Bernard, '"To Persuade Them into Speech and Action": Oratory and the Tamil Political, Madras, 1905–1919', *Comparative Studies in Society and History* 55/1 (2013), 142–66.

Besant, Annie, *Wake Up, India: A Plea for Social Reform* (Madras: Theosophical Publishing House, 1913).

——, *Why I Became a Theosophist* (London: Freethought Publishing, 1889).

——, trans., *The Bhagavad Gita, or the Lord's Song* (London, Benares and Madras: Theosophical Publishing Society, 1895).

Bevir, Mark, 'Theosophy and the Origins of the Indian National Congress', *International Journal of Hindu Studies* 7/1–3 (2003), 99–115.

'Editorial note', *The Vahan* 23/4 (1913), 67–8.

Gandhi, Leela, *Affective Communities: Anticolonial Thought and the Politics of Friendship* (Ranikhet: Permanent Black, 2006).

Mukhopadhyay, Priyasha, 'Listening Like a Theosophist', *Political Theology* 19/8 (2018), 719–33.

A non-Theosophist, 'Review of *Wake Up, India: A Plea for Social Reform*', *The Theosophist* 35/7 (1914), 127–9.

Said, Edward, *Orientalism* (New York: Pantheon Books, 1978).

Taylor, Anne, *Annie Besant: A Biography* (Oxford and New York: Oxford University Press, 1992).

Theosophical Society in England, Lending Library Catalogue (London: n. p., 1929).

Van der Veer, Peter, *Imperial Encounters: Religion and Modernity in India and Britain* (Princeton, NJ: Princeton University Press, 2001).

Viswanathan, Gauri, *Outside the Fold: Conversion, Modernity, and Belief* (Princeton, NJ: Princeton University Press, 1998).

JANET REMMINGTON

6   Sol Plaatje's *Native Life in South Africa* (1916): The Politics of Belonging

ABSTRACT

Published in 1916, Sol Plaatje's *Native Life in South Africa* exposed the grievances and hardships of black South Africans in the wake of the 1913 Natives Land Act, while painting a bigger picture of dispossession under settler colonialism. Addressing the politics of belonging, it criticized the British Empire's neglect of its black subjects, appealed for imperial intervention in the newly consolidated Union of South Africa and warned of the tragic eventualities of exclusionary white politics. Published in London, it both took on the Empire and took up its public discourses and print networks. It travelled trans-imperially, to the United States and beyond, raising awareness of the black South African plight, provoking debate and some censure, while inspiring solidarities. It made a significant impact in South Africa too, but fell into relative obscurity for some decades before re-emerging as a struggle book and, later, as a heritage text. It was a book of its time, but is arguably for all time, opening up an under-acknowledged past, interrogating the present and insisting on a better future.

'Can it be really true that we, too, belong to the British Empire?' This stinging question, objecting to native South Africans being excluded from combat in World War I, signals the central concerns around race, rights and belonging of Solomon ('Sol') Plaatje's (1876–1932) *Native Life in South Africa* (1916).[1] It is at once an indicting commentary on imperial Britain's neglect of its black subjects in a globalizing world, an impassioned entreaty for the metropolitan government to intervene in the self-governing dominion of South Africa with its newly implemented discriminatory Natives

1   Sol T. Plaatje, *Native Life in South Africa* (Johannesburg: Picador Africa, 2016), 257 (hereafter *NLSA*). References are to this edition, unless otherwise indicated.

Land Act, and a stirring account of African assertion. Combining reproach, appeal and warning, *Native Life* conveys this assessment:

> It is surely impossible to admit that Great Britain can do nothing for the mass of the native population, although at the moment it appears to them that though they are subjects of the King he cannot even hear their appeal, and will do nothing for them, and has abandoned them, a state of affairs which is quite incomprehensible to them and leads them to depend solely on themselves to obtain redress – and that way rebellion lies.[2]

Published at a pivotal historical juncture, Plaatje's landmark book critiques the imperial and colonial configurations of power, castigates their ins and outs, and foregrounds the resistant articulations and actions of Africans.

The 'Little Book' and the 'Outer World'

Originating in South Africa's farming heartlands where Plaatje investigated the effects of the Natives Land Act and extending to his lengthy lobbying sojourn in Britain, *Native Life* opens up not only a personal journey, but the larger and deeper experience of black dispossession, endeavour and resistance. The Land Act, which had been rushed through parliament, was the protest focus of the 1914 deputation of the South African Native National Congress (SANNC, in 1923 renamed the African National Congress, ANC). In broad terms, it restricted exclusive black land use to less than 8 per cent of the country's total, largely proscribed black land purchase and induced labour tenancy on white farms. The Act was not so much about segregation as about 'reduction', in Plaatje's estimation.[3] Most hauntingly, as foregrounded in *Native Life*'s powerful opening chapter, it catalysed an acute and tragic sense of alienation for black South Africans: 'Awaking on

---

2   Quoting and endorsing an article from the British press; Plaatje, *NLSA*, 217.
3   Plaatje, *NLSA*, 342.

a Friday morning, June 20, 1913, the South African native found himself, not actually a slave, but a pariah in the land of his birth'.[4]

Native Life's prologue introduced the text as a 'sincere narrative of a melancholy situation' arising from 'personal observations', later developing the description into 'a plea', 'an appeal'.[5] Plaatje's resourceful book might thus be considered a political account or travelogue,[6] intersecting with and being amplified by other storytelling, documentary, petitionary and polemic modes.[7] The question of genre engendered discussion at the time and indeed has since. Yet, its status as a political book has never been in doubt; rather, this status contributed to its prominence upon publication, followed conversely by its near-submergence for five hardened decades, its subsequent re-emergence as a struggle text in late apartheid and then post-transition as a revived heritage title.

In Plaatje's article 'Native Delegation to England', composed mostly on board ship, he referred to his book-in-the-making out at sea. He was writing in his capacity as editor of the trilingual newspaper *Tsala ea Batho* and as SANNC Secretary:

> I am compiling a little book on the Land Act and its operation, which I hope to put through the press immediately after landing in England. It keeps me busy writing in the dining-saloon all forenoons and evenings; the afternoons I spend on deck,

---

4   Plaatje, *NLSA*, 21.
5   Plaatje, *NLSA*, 15, 18.
6   Janet Remmington, 'Going Places: *Native Life in South Africa* and the Politics of Mobility', in Janet Remmington, Brian Willan and Bhekizizwe Peterson, eds, *Sol Plaatje's* Native Life in South Africa: *Past and Present* (Johannesburg: Wits University Press, 2016), 54–80; hereafter *PP*.
7   See Bhekizizwe Peterson, 'Sol Plaatje's *Native Life in South Africa*: Melancholy Narratives, Petitioning Selves and the Ethics of Suffering', *The Journal of Commonwealth Literature* 43 (2008), 79–95; A. E. Voss, 'Sol Plaatje, the Eighteenth Century, and South African Cultural Memory', *English in Africa* 21/1–2 (1994), 59–75; Elleke Boehmer, '"Able to Sing Their Songs": Solomon Plaatje's Many-Tongued Nationalism', in *Empire, the National and the Postcolonial 1890–1920* (New York: Oxford University Press, 2002), 125–67.

making notes etc. With such a regular daily programme I can afford to sympathise with fellow passengers who are always very busy doing nothing.⁸

Intent on publishing his work as a book as soon as possible after arrival, he assiduously generated page after page of his typescript manuscript. *Native Life*'s material and intellectual formation provided a creative measure of black capacity in the face of mostly white and more privileged passengers' relative unproductivity. Political urgency, a regard for the communicative potency of print, and the material opportunity of the journey's uninterrupted time would seem to have combined for this nationalist-cum-newspaperman in committing his words to the more sustained, personalized book form.⁹

The buoyancy of Plaatje's textual productivity at sea, his distance from South Africa's geopolitical fixities, and his experience of the integrated social microcosm of the ship ('over 200 of us, representing divers nations of different colours, and speaking several mother tongues') reinforced imaginaries around an idealized empire to which he would lay claim for peoples of colour.¹⁰ In *Native Life*, he would come to criticize Britain for falling short of the inclusivity enunciated by the Empire in its liberal forms and facades. Rome's downfall, he declared, lay in its 'failure to recognize the duty of welding her subjects together as brothers one and all'.¹¹

---

8   Sol T. Plaatje, 'Native Delegation to England', *Tsala ea Batho* (18 July 1914), published also as 'Native Congress Mission to England', *Diamond Fields Advertiser* (14 July 1914). Excerpted in Brian Willan, ed., *Sol Plaatje: Selected Writings* (Athens and Johannesburg: Ohio University Press; Wits University Press, 1996), 174–84; hereafter *SW*.
9   The intensity of Plaatje's work is reminiscent of Gandhi's 1909 ten-day writing spell at sea. See Tridup Suhrud, '*Hind Swaraj*: Translating Sovereignty', in Antoinette Burton and Isabel Hofmeyr, eds, *Ten Books That Shaped the British Empire: Creating an Imperial Commons* (Durham, NC and London: Duke University Press, 2014), 154.
10 Plaatje, 'Native Congress Mission to England'.
11 Plaatje, *NLSA*, 224.

Figure 6.1: Sol Plaatje during his editorship of *Tsala ea Batho*, c.1913–1914. Courtesy of the Kimberley Africana Library.

Though Plaatje unpretentiously referred to *Native Life* as his 'little book' under construction, he had no shortage of belief in its importance, vitality and potential reach. It might be said his phrasing is reminiscent of Chaucer's injunction, 'Go, litel bok, go, litel myn tragedye'.[12] A substantive book, connoting authority and autonomy, was nothing less than Plaatje's ambition. *Native Life*'s prologue suggests that the 'modest' nature of fellow SANNC leader Richard Msimang's thirty-two-page pamphlet, *Natives' Land Act 1913: Specific Cases of Evictions and Hardships* (1914), published shortly before the deputation, motivated Plaatje to produce a more substantial book of his own making – a greatly expanded account, a corrective of sorts.[13] Msimang's 'list', as Plaatje referred to the booklet, was neither 'full' nor optimally timed in its research.[14] Plaatje's volume, by contrast, would address the pamphlet's 'thinness' in every sense, fleshing out the Land Act's disruptions and deprivations in rural South Africa and the larger picture of black diminishment at the hands of the white minority government.

Plaatje spoke at more than 300 events during his time in Britain (1914–17), but these public addresses and their secondary reporting in the press could only convey so much. 'I address more meetings now and everywhere [but everyone is asking] WHERE IS THE BOOK?', he wrote to a friend. Should the volume not materialize, he asserted, 'the Natives can give up appealing to anybody about their grievances'.[15] Such was his view of the book's potential to out-travel its creator in space, time and influence.

Plaatje had a keenly developed sense of print's reach to the 'outer world' and the circulation of ideas, opinion and knowledge across boundaries of all

---

12   Geoffrey Chaucer, 'Troilus and Criseyde', Book V, in *Riverside Chaucer* (Oxford: Oxford University Press, 2008), 584.
13   R. W. Msimang, *Natives' Land Act 1913: Specific Cases of Evictions and Hardships, etc*, introd. Timothy Keegan (Cape Town: Friends of South African Library, 1996 [1914]).
14   Plaatje, *NLSA*, 16.
15   Letter from Plaatje to Philemon Mosheshoe, 16 June 1915, quoted in Brian Willan, *Sol Plaatje: South African Nationalist, 1876–1932* (Berkeley: University of California Press, 1984), 189; hereafter *SAN*. See also Brian Willan, *Sol Plaatje: A Life of Solomon Tshekisho Plaatje, 1876–1932* (Johannesburg: Jacana, 2018).

kinds.¹⁶ The integrated global news section 'Here, There and Everywhere' in *Tsala ea Batho* was illustrative of Plaatje's appreciation of the syndicated universe of information. Throughout *Native Life*, Plaatje alluded, too, to the capacity of print to travel across generations, emphasizing its value in registering facts and recording voices for future readers. He even invoked the colonial archive to challenge contemporary white views and positions: 'In the face of historical records', he averred, 'this argument [about blacks not being suited to white conflicts] will not hold a drop of water. British archives are overloaded with instances of the valour and tractability of the aboriginal races of South Africa'.¹⁷ He pointed also to the silences, erasures and distortions of those not well represented in the paper archive – lacunae which he aimed to redress with *Native Life*. He condemned the government of the day for publishing 'unreliable native records, for they are mainly based on information obtained from self-styled experts, who, in South Africa, should always be white'.¹⁸

Plaatje demonstrated a heightened consciousness of the value of testimony, the durability of print and bibliographic archiving, and the pervasiveness and persistence of audience. His world-aware, multi-generational orientation is suggestive of what Karin Barber calls the 'presumptive quality' of the modern 'emergence and multiplication of publics'.¹⁹ He was writing a narrative and appeal for the present – and an enduring witness and warning for the future. From the outset, Plaatje intended that the book should go out into the world in order to change it, and remain in the world to testify to this insistence.

16   Plaatje, *NLSA*, 319.
17   Plaatje, *NLSA*, 260.
18   Plaatje, *NLSA*, 340.
19   Karin Barber, *The Anthropology of Texts, Persons and Publics: Oral and Written Culture in Africa and Beyond* (Cambridge: Cambridge University Press, 2007), 138.

Publication, 'Peregrination' and Postcolonial Contours

Despite Plaatje's original intentions, it took an unanticipated and beleaguered two years for *Native Life* to come into being. Detractors, financial difficulties and the advent of the world war combined to frustrate and delay his efforts. After several attempts to secure an arrangement with a publisher, Plaatje came to an agreement with P. S. King, a well-established press specializing in 'Economics, Social Questions, Politics, Local Government'.[20] In May 1916, his volume of over 300 pages was issued in hardback between robust maroon covers. If Msimang's soft-cover pamphlet provided a slim, speedily produced print intervention, then the casebound *Native Life*, published two years later, delivered a weighty contribution in every sense, 'able to stand on its own' both physically and discursively.[21] Brian Willan observes that *Native Life* was unlikely to have materialized had Plaatje headed home as he had been advised, for it was in the imperial capital that a number of factors conjoined to make publication possible.[22] These included the support of fellow intellectuals and campaigners of colour, progressive lobbyists and friends with ties to South Africa and the well-established publishing industry at the fulcrum of imperial and international networks.

Native Life was published – one could say, provocatively – on the doorstep of the imperial government. As Willan suggests, P. S. King, with an office on Great Smith Street adjacent to the Palace of Westminster, featured the Houses of Parliament in its promotional material in an attempt to benefit from associations of authority.[23] The significance of publishing a book that critiqued empire in and from its centre was heightened in light of the British government's hostility towards the SANNC deputation, evident in a dismissive and derisive June 1914 meeting with Lord Harcourt, Secretary of State for the Colonies, who took white

---

20 See Brian Willan, '*Native Life in South Africa*: Writing, Publishing, Reception', in *PP*, 1–17.
21 See Burton and Hofmeyr, 'Introduction: The Spine of Empire?', in Antoinette Burton and Isabel Hofmeyr, eds, *Ten Books That Shaped the British Empire*, 12.
22 Willan, '*Native Life in South Africa*', 2–6.
23 Willan, '*Native Life in South Africa*', 3.

South Africa's reassurances as the final word. This disregard culminated in the parliamentary vote to take no further action in relation to the SANNC appeal. Plaatje and his compatriots found more sympathetic engagement in public arenas, which, though outside official government structures, exerted some influence in Westminster and Pretoria. The deputation's statement, drafted by Plaatje, was widely distributed and formed the basis of interviews and meetings, but it did not cover the whole story – this was the purpose of *Native Life*.[24]

Plaatje's well-connected friend and supporter Georgiana Solomon wasted no time in sending copies of the book to both South African and British Prime Ministers, Louis Botha and David Lloyd George, respectively. In November 1916, half a year after *Native Life*'s publication, Solomon paid towards having Plaatje's scathing thirty-page analysis of the Native Land Commission's Report incorporated into the book's second edition.[25] His analysis of the Report reinforced black suspicions that the Commission served to legitimize the carving up of South Africa's land in favour of the white ruling minority. In this regard, *Native Life*'s epilogue climaxes with an explosive parting address to Westminster:

> you will in the interest of your flag, for the safety of your coloured subjects, the glory of your Empire, and the purity of your religion, grapple with this dark blot on the Imperial emblem, the South African anomaly that compromises the justice of British rule and seems almost to belie the beauty, the sublimity and the sincerity of Christianity. [...] Shall we appeal to you in vain? I HOPE NOT.[26]

Plaatje thus wrote 'back to the centre' in no uncertain terms, reinforcing this act of assertion by travelling to the imperial capital in person, and publishing in and from it. He challenged the grand account of empire and the prevailing anodyne storyline about South African segregation with his own 'melancholy narrative', all the time optimizing the reading, distribution and publicity networks that radiated from London.

---

24   'The Natives' Land Act of South Africa: An Appeal to the Imperial Parliament and Public of Great Britain', cited in *SAN*, 179.
25   Willan, '*Native Life in South Africa*', 9.
26   Plaatje, *NLSA*, 338.

Native Life was reviewed widely in the press in Britain and throughout the Empire, as well as in parts of continental Europe and across the Atlantic. The book's second edition, published only six months after the first, included a dedicated page of review extracts, mostly from British newspapers and journals. 'It is a serious case, well and ably put', wrote the *Birmingham Post*, 'Here at any rate is a book which makes the native agitation intelligible and may conceivably have an influence on future events in South Africa – and at home'.[27] A shared sense of being imperial subjects of colour emerged across a number of reviews, and on the other side of the Atlantic, African Americans expressed race solidarities. Lahore's *The Tribune* commented: 'The author makes an excellent case for the consideration of the Imperial Government. [...] The interest of the book for the Punjabis consists [...] in showing the way for inviting attention to the injustice involved in excluding a large class of Hindus from agriculture'.[28] From West Africa, the *Sierra Leone News* reflected that 'this dazzling Imperialism so much in vogue at present does not as a rule make for or advance the welfare of the subject-races under the Empire'.[29] Most reviews thus commended the book for its bold stance and carefully wrought argument, but there were exceptions. Shockingly, the most acerbic was by John Harris of the Anti-Slavery and Aborigines' Protection Society who took exception to the SANNC's and Plaatje's independence of thought and action. Harris, who had endeavoured to thwart *Native Life*'s publication, denounced the published volume for its 'monstrous' representations.[30]

Few copies of *Native Life* made their way to South Africa until Plaatje's return in early 1917, but those reviews that followed recognized the book's strong case, which featured in debates in South Africa's House of Assembly.

---

27 Included at the back of Sol T. Plaatje, *Native Life in South Africa, Before and Since the European War and the Boer Rebellion* (derived from the 4th edn) <http://www.gutenberg.org/ebooks/1452> accessed 20 August 2016.
28 Plaatje, *Native Life in South Africa* <http://www.gutenberg.org/ebooks/1452> accessed 20 August 2016.
29 'Familiar Talks on Familiar Subjects', *Sierra Leone News* (16 September 1916).
30 John Harris, 'General Botha's Native Land Policy', *Journal of Royal African Society* XVI/LXI (1916), 12.

Native Life's animation of parliamentary discussion generated public interest which translated into book orders. The Central News Agency could not keep up with demand for what was then the third edition.³¹ *Native Life*'s articulation of grievances were generally welcomed by black South Africans who found themselves facing the implications of the 1917 Native Administration Bill, which was followed by a raft of other discriminatory policies, laws and practices. In further rounds of investigative travel around South Africa, Plaatje started on a companion volume to *Native Life*, which arguably came to find imaginative expression in his novel *Mhudi* (written 1917–20; published 1930).

Plaatje led a second SANNC deputation abroad after World War I, seeking to leverage the loyalty his people had shown towards Britain in the conflict, and to utilize his public, political and print networks for the native cause. Although unsuccessful in mobilizing intervention from the imperial government – an outcome that Plaatje himself may not have expected given the entrenched nature of South Africa's self-governing status – he reached the highest seat of imperial power to make his case in an interview with Lloyd George, who had in 1916 received a copy of *Native Life*. The interview made an impression on the British Prime Minister, who followed through by expressing concerns to his South African counterpart, Jan Smuts.³²

Eliciting the cooperation of the non-denominational, multiracial Brotherhood movement in arranging a 1919 visit to Canada, Plaatje eluded South African and British authorities who had colluded in trying to halt his 'peregrination' to the United States, where black activism and various guises of Pan-Africanism were flourishing.³³ *Native Life* allowed Plaatje to introduce his message and credentials to prominent African Americans, such as John W. Cromwell, President of the American Negro Academy, whose platforms and socio-political circles were crucial to Plaatje's touring and further publication ambitions. He visited nineteen US states, making diverse connections, from the prominent intellectual W. E. B. Du

---

31 See *SAN*, 208–9.
32 *SW*, 257–64.
33 *SAN*, 257–8. The term 'peregrination' was used by South Africa's Secretary of Native Affairs.

Bois to the firebrand Marcus Garvey, and visiting the gradualist Booker T. Washington's Tuskegee Institute.³⁴ Through Du Bois's print networks, Plaatje sold copies of *Native Life* and when supplies ran out, he produced an American edition (the fourth edition, 1920) under the auspices of the National Association for the Advancement of Colored People's (NAACP) journal, *The Crisis*; in 1921, a fifth edition would be issued by P. S. King in London. In 1923, by which time Plaatje had returned to South Africa, Garvey's rival *Negro World* was advertising *Native Life* as a 'Great Negro Book' in a special offer for subscribers.³⁵ The book raised his profile among African Americans, making an important contribution to multidirectional black diasporic exchange and activism in the early twentieth century. Nonetheless, as copies became scarcer, and as socio-political and economic circumstances took their own courses in South Africa and the USA, *Native Life* faded into obscurity, though a 1969 Negro Universities Press facsimile edition went some way to reanimate American interest.

In South Africa, during the segregationist and apartheid eras, *Native Life* was held up within African political and intellectual history and ANC memory as a foundational text, even as a *tour de force*, but the texture and make-up of its content was little known, and outside these spheres the book remained relatively obscure. As no local copies were published until the 1980s, copies were in very short supply and Africans had restricted library admittance; additionally, other resistance figures and texts came to the fore, overshadowing earlier pioneers. Ironically, Plaatje's path-breaking book became most difficult to access in the country of its focus and by those who were its abiding concern. Bhekizizwe Peterson's reflection on the book's title is resonant in this regard: '[*Native Life in South Africa*] unsettles because, far from describing "native life", Plaatje addresses himself to its precariousness, denial and fugitive nature.'³⁶ The disturbing sense of black South African alienation, which Plaatje conveys from the outset in

---

34   *SAN*, 250–1.
35   Cited in Khwezi Mkhize, 'African Intellectual History, Black Cosmopolitanism and *Native Life in South Africa*', in *PP*, 106.
36   Bhekizizwe Peterson, 'Modernist at Large: The Aesthetics of *Native Life in South Africa*', in *PP*, 27.

Native Life, is echoed in the disquieting irony of the title and is played out in the relative unattainability of the book itself during the country's most racially oppressed decades.

It was some sixty-six years after its original publication that *Native Life* was finally published in South Africa by the radical independent Ravan Press in 1982. Soon after, Longman produced an abridged African Classic for the British and Commonwealth markets. South Africa's political transition in 1994 presented *Native Life* with opportunities for new meanings and new audiences. Following a free Gutenberg.org eBook edition in 1998, the book was republished in 2007 under Pan Macmillan's Picador Africa imprint, including a foreword by the ANC's Kader Asmal, with an eye on educational use. A 2016 impression of the Picador edition was issued to mark the book's centennial year.

Given an incomplete print and oral history archive – albeit with an array of reviews evidencing the book's impact around publication – our understanding of *Native Life*'s influence on the South African liberation movement and on anticolonial, postcolonial or black rights endeavours elsewhere is limited. One early glimpse into how *Native Life* contributed to black resistance beyond South Africa, specifically in speaking out roundly against Britain, is to be found in the case of the teacher, evangelist and campaigner Abraham Twala. Writing in the isiZulu-English newspaper *Ilanga lase Natal* in 1917 as a member of the Natal Native Teachers Conference, Twala called on fellow members to donate towards a 'hero's bonus' for Plaatje's advocacy and for *Native Life*'s exposé of racial injustice:

> From this book, I learn facts that will put a selfish Colonial to blush [...] [that] will show all the Europeans in South Africa that we are not unawares of all injustices meted out to us, 'the sons and daughters of Africa'. Further, facts that will make a New South Africa by and by.[37]

Two years later, with Twala settled in a mission school north of the Limpopo and having founded the Rhodesian Bantu Voters Association, he strongly

---

37   Abraham Twala, 'A Letter to the Natal Native Teachers', *Ilanga lase Natal* (29 June 1917).

promoted African self-reliance. The 1919 Rhodesian native petition for imperial rather than colonial control over African affairs had been rejected by London. In writing to the press, Twala was unequivocal about Africans navigating their own way in the settler colony: 'Experience has taught us that our salvation does not lie in Downing Street'.[38] The lessons learnt from *Native Life* were clear – Britain would not readily intervene to change the course of black lives already under white rule in the Empire's African periphery.

To what extent does *Native Life* have a place in post-apartheid South Africa? Against the backdrop of the country's varied, deeply felt centennial reflections on the Land Act in 2013, writer Athambile Masola asked: 'If Plaatje were alive in current day South Africa, what would he do?' Masola drew connections between her reading of *Native Life* and contemporary South Africa, with its unacceptably high levels of poverty and inequality, to challenge the relentless persistence of the past in the present.[39] Iconic books of later periods by key postcolonial and Black Consciousness figures such as Frantz Fanon and Steve Biko have featured strongly in South Africa's 'decolonization' student activism since 2015. By contrast, *Native Life* has not as yet been widely drawn upon and is generally less well known. If Plaatje and his generation have been associated in some quarters with moderation, *Native Life*'s forceful case and outraged language may surprise. In the book's opening pages, Plaatje uses the evocative metaphor of a 'racial broom' sweeping Africans out of the mainstream of rights and opportunities.[40] By its conclusion, he is using the far starker imagery of natives being 'herded' into 'camps'. Here, *Native Life* does not hold back in naming the

---

38   Quoted in Terence Ranger, 'Traditional Authorities and the Rise of Modern Politics in Southern Rhodesia, 1898–1930', in Eric Stokes and Richard Brown, eds, *The Zambesian Past: Studies in Central African History* (Manchester: Manchester University Press, 1966), 189.

39   Athambile Masola, 'Native Life in South Africa', *Mail & Guardian* (26 August 2013) <http://thoughtleader.co.za/athambilemasola/2013/08/26/native-life-in-southafrica/> accessed 1 March 2016. See also, Remmington, Willan and Peterson, 'Introduction', in *PP*, xxix–xxx.

40   Plaatje, *NLSA*, 28.

African, for all intents and purposes, as not only a pariah or outcast, but a slave, sounding retributive warnings:

> it never occurred to us that the spread of British dominion in South Africa would culminate in consigning us to our present intolerable position. [...] But when an official Commission asks Parliament to herd us into concentration camps, with the additional recommendation that besides breeding slaves for our masters, we should be made to pay for the upkeep of the camps: in other words, that we should turn the Colonials into slave raiders and slave-drivers (but save them the expense of buying the slaves), the only thing that stands between us and despair is the thought that Heaven has never yet failed us. We remember how African women have at times shed tears under similar injustices; and how when they have been made to leave their fields with their hoes on their shoulders, their tears on evaporation have drawn fire and brimstone from the skies.[41]

Conclusion: The Book and Belonging

While Plaatje denounced the Afrikaner nationalist government for its policies, he held the British Empire ultimately responsible for the dividing, diminishing and demeaning impetus that gathered force in the aftermath of South Africa's Act of Union. On the one hand, *Native Life* powerfully registers the injustice and precariousness of black 'unbelonging' – the book's 'melancholy' exploration of black South Africans' deprivations and its haunting plea for imperial responsibility towards native peoples. On the other, through its determined coming-into-being and enduring presence, *Native Life* claims and demonstrates black belonging. Originally published a stone's throw from Westminster, disseminated far and wide, and re-emerging over time, it assumes an immutable and provocative place in national, imperial and global print cultures, refusing the marginalization and erasure of the black voice. *Native Life* continues to bear witness to early twentieth-century black dispossession and resistance, to indict

---

41   Plaatje, *NLSA*, 365.

oppressive and irresponsible authorities, and to insist upon a better future for South Africa's black citizens. It is both the subject and agent of African self-determination.

Bibliography

Barber, Karin, *The Anthropology of Texts, Persons and Publics: Oral and Written Culture in Africa and Beyond* (Cambridge: Cambridge University Press, 2007).

Boehmer, Elleke, '"Able to Sing Their Songs": Solomon Plaatje's Many-Tongued Nationalism', in *Empire, the National and the Postcolonial 1890–1920* (New York: Oxford University Press, 2002), 125–67.

Burton, Antoinette, and Isabel Hofmeyr, eds, *Ten Books That Shaped the British Empire: Creating an Imperial Commons* (Durham, NC and London: Duke University Press, 2014).

Mkhize, Khwezi, 'African Intellectual History, Black Cosmopolitanism and Native Life in South Africa', in Janet Remmington, Brian Willan and Bhekizizwe Peterson, eds, *Sol Plaatje's Native Life in South Africa: Past and Present* (Johannesburg: Wits University Press, 2016), 95–114.

Msimang, R. W., *Natives' Land Act 1913: Specific Cases of Evictions and Hardships, etc*, introd. Timothy Keegan (Cape Town: Friends of South African Library, 1996 [1914]).

Peterson, Bhekizizwe, 'Modernist at Large: The Aesthetics of *Native Life in South Africa*', in Janet Remmington, Brian Willan and Bhekizizwe Peterson, eds, *Sol Plaatje's Native Life in South Africa: Past and Present* (Johannesburg: Wits University Press, 2016), 18–36.

——, 'Sol Plaatje's Native Life in South Africa: Melancholy Narratives, Petitioning Selves and the Ethics of Suffering', *The Journal of Commonwealth Literature* 43 (2008), 79–95.

Plaatje, Sol T., *Native Life in South Africa*, introd. Brian Willan, foreword Kader Asmal (Johannesburg: Picador Africa, 2016 [1916]).

Remmington, Janet, 'Going Places: Native Life in South Africa and the Politics of Mobility', in Janet Remmington, Brian Willan and Bhekizizwe Peterson, eds, *Sol Plaatje's Native Life in South Africa: Past and Present* (Johannesburg: Wits University Press, 2016), 54–80.

———, '"Through Dustless Tracks" for African Rights: Narrative Currents and Political Imaginaries of Solomon Plaatje's 1914 Sea Voyage', in Charlotte Mathieson, ed., *Sea Narratives: Cultural Responses to the Sea, 1600–Present* (Basingstoke: Palgrave, 2016), 81–110.

———, Brian Willan and Bhekizizwe Peterson, 'Introduction: *Native Life in South Africa* Then and Now', in Janet Remmington, Brian Willan and Bhekizizwe Peterson, eds, *Sol Plaatje's Native Life in South Africa: Past and Present* (Johannesburg: Wits University Press, 2016), xv–xl.

Suhrud, Tridup, 'Hind Swaraj: Translating Sovereignty', in Antoinette Burton and Isabel Hofmeyr, eds, *Ten Books That Shaped the British Empire: Creating an Imperial Commons* (Durham, NC and London: Duke University Press, 2014), 153–7.

Voss, A. E., 'Sol Plaatje, the Eighteenth Century, and South African Cultural Memory', *English in Africa* 21/1–2 (1994), 59–75.

Willan, Brian, 'Native Life in South Africa: Writing, Publishing, Reception', in Janet Remmington, Brian Willan and Bhekizizwe Peterson, eds, *Sol Plaatje's Native Life in South Africa: Past and Present* (Johannesburg: Wits University Press, 2016), 1–17.

———, *Sol Plaatje: A Life of Solomon Tshekisho Plaatje, 1876–1932* (Johannesburg: Jacana, 2018).

———, *Sol Plaatje: South African Nationalist, 1876–1932* (Berkeley: University of California Press, 1984).

———, ed., *Sol Plaatje: Selected Writings* (Athens and Johannesburg: Ohio University Press/Wits University Press, 1996).

ELLEKE BOEHMER

7 Making Freedom: Jawaharlal Nehru's *An Autobiography* (1936) and *The Discovery of India* (1946)

ABSTRACT

This chapter considers Jawaharlal Nehru's autobiographies *An Autobiography* (1936) and *The Discovery of India* (1946) as at once nation- and self-making books. It suggests that the two books worked together to exert a shaping influence on the postcolonial world. In his autobiographies, Nehru (1889–1964) mobilized his readers to think of themselves as citizens and also supplied them with a new independent temporality with which to identify. As such, Nehru's two books became icons and models for the leader's (auto)biography across the postcolonial world.

This chapter considers the first Indian Prime Minister Jawaharlal Nehru's *An Autobiography* (1936) and the later *The Discovery of India* (1946) as 'nation-making' books. Using patterns of interpellation and self-projection these two texts, both of them autobiographies fostered during periods of political imprisonment, in interesting ways call the new postcolonial nation of 'all India' into being. Published in the tumultuous years leading up to the decolonization of the Indian sub-continent in 1947, the autobiographies present alternative histories of India, in situations where official history was seen to underwrite the authorities these books sought to resist and supplant. In many ways, Nehru's two books have become foundational texts not only of postcolonial India but of the postcolonial nation more broadly, as well as of the postcolonial leader's biography. The books have laid down lasting templates for 'making freedom' and, as such, have served as important guiding lights in the struggle for independence in India, and more widely.

Foundational Texts

Jawaharlal Nehru's *An Autobiography* and *The Discovery of India* tell the story of the Indian National Congress leader Jawaharlal Nehru's political *Bildung*: his stage-by-stage involvement in non-cooperation politics in India, and his ascent to power as leader of the independence movement. The two texts are foundational for processes of imagining postcolonial India, and the independent postcolonial nation more generally. This is first because Nehru, the prime minister of India in waiting at the time of writing, himself offered a leading example of postcolonial national leadership. But the two texts are also exemplary and form-giving because of their actual shaping force as books and narratives, especially in the Global South, or what was then called the Third World. The ways in which these autobiographies worked – through forms of interpellation and affective structures – and how these intersect with the reader's sense of the leader's character and reputation, influentially moulded a whole post-war genre of exemplary or heroic writing in the postcolonial world. Through these structures and forms of address, the autobiographical subject and outstanding public figure, in this case Nehru, established what would become a game-changing model for other postcolonial leaders, as this chapter will explore.[1]

When speaking of modern nationalism, it is generally true to say that a nation's integrity is recognized both by its own citizens and a wider community of nations through the medium of a rallying tale recounting the process of its constitution. In South Africa, for example, that pre-eminent story since the fall of apartheid has widely been taken to be Nelson Mandela's narrative, captured in his own *Long Walk to Freedom* (which Erica Lombard discusses in Chapter 15) as well as in several biographies.[2] In India, that story until quite recently was shared by two exemplary figures, Jawaharlal Nehru and M. K. Gandhi, and to a lesser extent Muhammad Ali

---

[1] See Geoffrey Cubitt and Allen Warren, *Heroic Expectations and Exemplary Lives* (Manchester: Manchester University Press, 2000).
[2] See Nelson Mandela, *Long Walk to Freedom* (London: Little, Brown, 1994) and Anthony Sampson, *Mandela: The Authorised Biography* (London: Harper Collins, 2000).

Jinnah. However, it is Nehru's autobiographical work, and not Gandhi's, that explicitly sets out to reflect that story. As in the case of other national heroes – Thomas Jefferson, Napoleon, Churchill – the life-story of the pre-eminent national leader is built up through a variety of media, including (auto)biography, as an icon of national progress, liberty, courage and virtue, and as an example worth following.

In *An Autobiography* and *The Discovery of India* Nehru charts first his process of political education and increasing involvement in the freedom struggle, and then the ways in which that freedom struggle brought him into contact with India and Indians – in short, his national community. *An Autobiography*, subtitled *Toward Freedom*, was published in 1936, some eleven years before Indian independence was achieved; *The Discovery of India* was written during the 1940s, when Nehru was mainly in prison, and builds up to the moment of independence (in 1947) through a series of retrospective reflections. Constituting in effect a two-part autobiography, taken together the books can be seen to usher into being the shape of the non-aligned postcolonial nation – a nation not beholden to the West, but independently forging its selfhood and its place in the modern (and for Nehru, non-aligned) world.

As a testimony to this influence, a significant number of postcolonial political life-stories – Kwame Nkrumah's *Ghana: The Autobiography of Ghana*, Kenyatta's ethnographic *Facing Mount Kenya*, Kenneth Kaunda's *Zambia Shall Be Free* and even Mandela's *Long Walk to Freedom* – take aspects of their narrative shape and their underlying teleology, their geographical imagination and their genealogy of the past, from Nehru's *Autobiography* and *The Discovery of India*.[3] As the Burmese leader Aung San Suu Kyi once commented, '*The Discovery of India* was the discovery of myself' – to which we might add, 'the discovery of myself is the discovery of India'.[4] The book clearly gave a national shape and a national answer to some of the leading questions of postcolonial independence: how do we

---

3   See Elleke Boehmer, *Stories of Women: Gender and Narrative in the Postcolonial Nation* (Manchester: Manchester University Press, 2005), 66–87.
4   Aung San Suu Kyi, Jawaharlal Nehru Memorial Lecture 2012 (14 November 2012), repr. in *Outlook India* (15 November 2012) <http://www.outlookindia.com/article/the-discovery-of-nehru-was-also-a-discovery-of-myself/282997> accessed 2 May 2015.

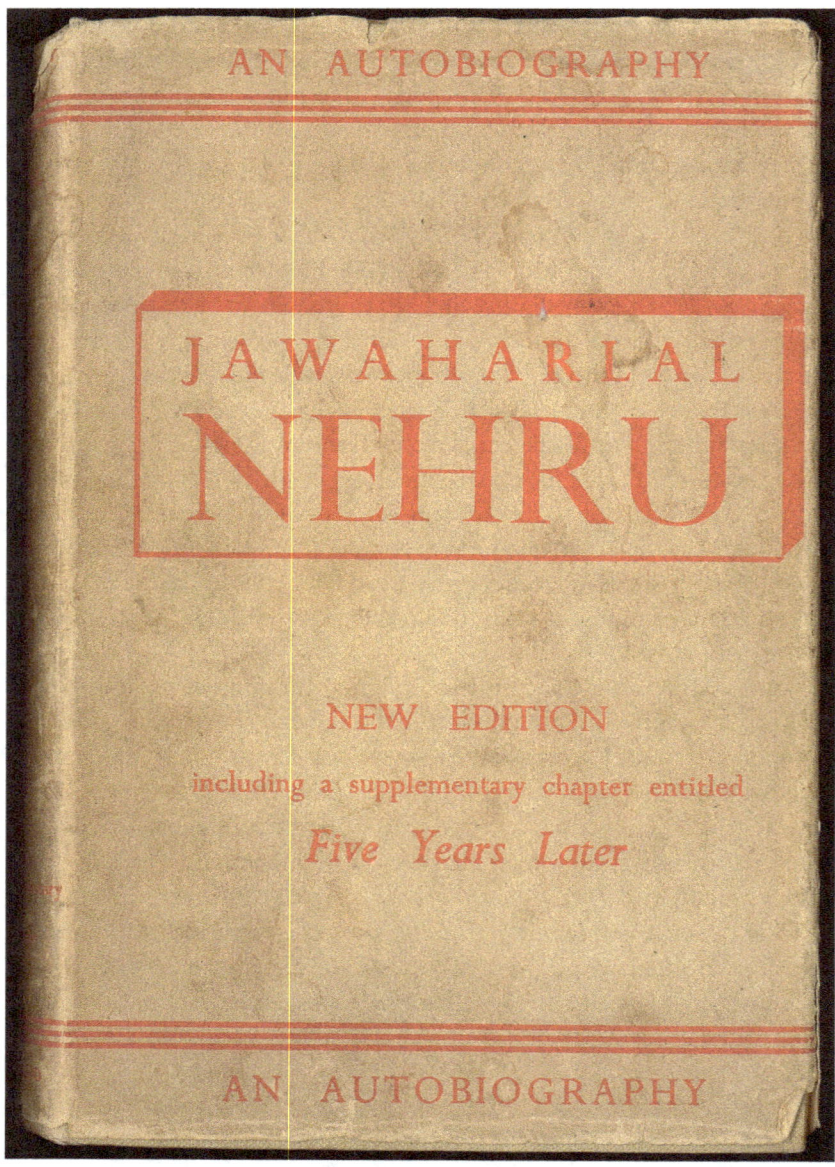

Figure 7.1: The cover of the 1953 edition of *Jawaharlal Nehru: An Autobiography* by Jawaharlal Nehru, published by Bodley Head. Artwork © Random House. Reprinted by permission of The Random House Group Limited.

remake ourselves together after the depredations of colonialism? How does the nation shape identity? How do we give shape to the nation that bestows selfhood upon us? In *Hind Swaraj* (1910), and to an extent in his own *Autobiography* (1927), Gandhi had offered India a philosophy of self-help and soul-making. However, it was not an historical intervention in the same way, a reshaping of the past in order to enter the future, nor an answer to the question of postcolonial belonging within the framework of the nation-state.

The debt to Nehru that marks many postcolonial leader's life-stories is in many cases expressed in structural terms, as if his influence were stamped into the very form of the work. For example, in a number of these (auto)biographical narratives, especially in their opening chapters, the leader-subject is at pains to set himself up in relation to his people or nation, to bridge the divide between himself and his group. So it is noticeable that the more the leader feels separate or separated from his people by education, training, imprisonment or power, the more he appeals to them as his community. Nehru, like Kenyatta and Kaunda, and like Mandela later on, was many times a political prisoner, as he recounts in *An Autobiography*. He was also of an elite background and highly educated, and hence in social terms set apart from the Indian masses, a point to which I will return. Yet his life-story in its two volumes is imbued with the confidence that the very act of addressing the nation through these books will bridge those walls and divides: it will proleptically call the nation into being. It will even, in some sense, spring the leader from gaol and return him to his people. In all cases, therefore, the process of national coming-into-being is seen as end-stopped by success, that is, the achievement of nationhood, and the leader is envisaged as presiding at the moment of victory, embodying the nation. As this suggests, the writer Nehru, like his epigones, pitches his life-writing at once both to his national community and to an international one: by speaking for the first, he feels he has something to say to the second.

From this, it becomes possible to say that the postcolonial leader's (auto)biography, like Nehru's, has history-making effects. If, as Dipesh Chakrabarty has written, people under colonialism are consigned to the waiting room of history, then the story of the leader, or similar representative figure, can come to operate as an alternative history.⁵ For a nation born out of racial or ethnic conflict and repression, the need for such an alternative history is perhaps especially acute. The 'peoples without history' thereby gain much that a formal history might provide: a new genealogy provides access to temporality and so opens out a future. Borrowing terms from Prathama Banerjee, anticolonial narrative in this sense can work as an act of 'taking hold of time' by rejecting the linear time-scale of history, in which the West is always uppermost, and '[reshaping] temporality'.⁶ Banerjee is speaking here mainly in respect of Gandhi's project, but these words could equally be applied to Nehru's autobiographical work: the writing offers citizen-readers a new temporality with which they can freely identify.

It is in this sense of the national leader's (auto)biography rewriting postcolonial time, if not in fact generating it from scratch, that I suggest that life-stories such as Nehru's are central to the process of displacing empire and enabling postcolonial freedom. The individual leader's story projects the nation's story, even if only in virtual terms. Armed with such an alternative history or version of their past, influentially narrated by a prominent actor within that history who, moreover, sets up his life as a national ideal, the readers of the autobiography are encouraged to imagine a new world. In that imagining, they are able to understand themselves as potentially free of colonial history and released from its oppression. It is the practical, formal and rhetorical implications of this idea as they manifest in Nehru's work to which this chapter will turn in its second half. In particular, I will identify certain influential rhetorical devices deployed by Nehru's autobiographies, especially those of interpellation and self-projection.

---

5   Dipesh Chakrabarty, *Provincializing Europe: Postcolonial Thought and Historical Difference* (Princeton, NJ: Princeton University Press, 2000), 8. See also Johannes Fabian, *Time and the Other: How Anthropology Makes Its Object* (New York: Columbia University Press, 2002).
6   Prathama Banerjee, *Politics of Time: 'Primitives' and History-writing in a Colonial Society* (New York: Oxford University Press, 2006).

'Taking Hold of Time': Calling Out and Identification

How the people are 'called out' and invited to identify with the nation as citizens is central to the appeal of the leader's autobiography, especially because, as we have already seen, the leader at once closely associates with, yet stands apart from, the people. In a series of set-piece scenes interspersed across the narrative (that include moments of political awakening, major speeches, political crises and changes of heart), the leader-subject appeals to the nation to identify with him as a representative figure before bringing the nation into being as a community through that very process of interpellation or calling out. His narrative offers and develops unifying emblems for the nation, not least amongst them the structure of a coherently unfolding life, a form of rhetoric through which the leader then offers himself as the ultimate touch-point or symbol of unification.

As this suggests, the life-narrative with its patterns of individual-to-group identification is in many ways perfectly designed to overcome the perceived class or ethnic disconnect that might separate the leader and the people – patterns that are then further reinforced using metaphors of struggle and overcoming. The storyline puts in motion a steady process not just of mutual address but of mutual adjustment, as the nation moving to independence is set up as outlining and modelling the leader's actions, and so in some sense as creating him in its image. At the same time, the leader is represented or self-represents as shaping and reshaping the nation.

His later designation as 'Father of India' notwithstanding, Nehru was in many ways an unlikely candidate to stand as a representative figure for India, as I have already begun to suggest. An exotic product, elite and high-caste by background, the divide separating him from his people was a significant one. His elite education abroad in England, at Harrow and Cambridge (1907–12), had entailed a steady process of Anglicization and an incremental estrangement from himself, of which he was painfully aware. For example, as he writes in the first chapters of the 1936 autobiography, he had read the Victorian classics – Dickens, Thackeray, Kipling, Wells and Conan Doyle – before he ever arrived in England. Therefore, as this might suggest, he was completely without the 'common touch', as his proximity to Gandhi always reminded him.⁷ *The Discovery of India*, perhaps even more so than *An Autobiography*, is unmistakably the book of a man dislocated from his native land by privilege and education, seeking to make it up from the start. Indeed, that *Discovery* is written in English is a clear marker of this alienation. The Indian nation is paradoxically called into being through the medium of simultaneously foreign, yet also malleable nation-making language.

As if to grapple with his self-perceived alienated state, Nehru's autobiographies strive to tell 'big' imaginatively gripping stories (for example, he writes of his 'dark days' in gaol, or, once again, of his national pilgrimages across the length and breadth of India). These stories are also presented as 'everyman stories' that necessarily work through a process of interpellation, with which he calls the nation's citizens to identify. In both of Nehru's texts, this process of interpellation involves a constant restless interchange between experiences of identification and distance: indeed, the identification would not be so urgent if the distance were not so great.

In *Nationalist Thought and the Colonial World: A Derivative Discourse?* (1986) – his account of the transmission of European nationalist thought to India – Partha Chatterjee observes that the transition from colonial to postcolonial nation-states in the Third World can be divided into three phases: the moment of departure, where nationalist consciousness is synonymous with the adoption of European modernity and capitalist production (whilst preserving an 'Eastern' spirituality), as in the Bengal Renaissance; the moment of manoeuvre, associated with Gandhi, where the historical consolidation of the nation decries the modern; and, thirdly, the moment of arrival, embodied in Jawaharlal Nehru, in which nationalist thought combining modern and traditional elements seeks expression in 'the unified life of the [modern] state'.⁸ For Chatterjee, then, concepts of departure, transition and arrival are specifically bound up with the differential

---

7   In recent years, this elitism of Nehru's, and the veiled sectarianism associated with it, has unsurprisingly drawn criticism, in particular from Perry Anderson. See Anderson, *The Indian Ideology* (London: Verso, 2013).
8   Partha Chatterjee, *Nationalist Thought and the Colonial World: A Derivative Discourse?* (London: Zed Press, 1986), 49–53.

stage-by-stage transfer of ideological inputs from West to East. So the idealistic nationalist Nehru on his return to India after an education at Harrow and Cambridge endeavoured to pass off his strong interest in Western science as something that in fact bore close ties to Eastern forms of rationality.[9] Through such stage-by-stage incorporation, Nehru identified by slow increments with an ideal he called India, as his life-story describes, and the Indian public in turn, through reading his story, came by slow increments to identify with him.

Having said this, we must at the same time concede that the life-story does not operate independently of its material contexts in achieving these effects. The book form in which life-stories like Nehru's were until very recently disseminated is also crucial to the process – that is, as a form consumed through the private experience of reading, through that one-on-one identification between reader and subject. Reading the life-story, the different would-be participants in the national future could link in with aspects of the leader's life and of his vision, and so with each other. Through the medium of reading Nehru's *An Autobiography* Indians came to see themselves as inhabiting his space-time, interestingly both *as him*, having entered into his experiences as readers, and *as themselves*, as living national beings involved in their own particular Indian social worlds. The indefinite article in the title, '*An*' *Autobiography*, serves as an interesting pointer to this everyman status, one its subject at once assumed and disavowed.

Benedict Anderson's model of newspaper reading as nation-making further clarifies this understanding of how reading life-writing might operate as a means of postcolonial identification.[10] In all contexts that experienced modernity, as Anderson describes, the newspaper worked in diagnostic ways. With its juxtaposed stories and images, it supplied tools

9   On one level, however, Nehru was not deluded in finding the forms of Western science at work in India, and not in a merely imitative, colonial way. From the 1880s India was treated as a vast laboratory in which to develop not only new educational policies, but also new scientific methods of statistical and population analysis, amongst other innovations. See Nigel Leask, *British Romantic Writers and the East: Anxieties of Empire* (Cambridge: Cambridge University Press, 1992).
10 Benedict Anderson, *Imagined Communities* (London: Verso, 1991).

through which readers could make sense of the rapid social and political changes that marked the world around them. However, the leader's autobiography is not consumed in homogeneous time as is the newspaper, in Anderson's account. Its structures are different, more singular and coherent, based on narrative continuities and consistency, and on the personality of the leader. Arguably, therefore, the identifications it permits and encourages are stronger. The leader's life-story invites readers to 'make up' their own nation as they read, but in a way that is inevitably refracted through the lens of the leader's character and selfhood.

We can now turn to observe how the leader-writer's self-projection operates in textual form and how this involves a concomitant interpellation of the nation. Consider these two linked extracts from *The Discovery of India*:

> But all this while, in a corner of my mind, lay something deeper and more vivid, and elections or the other excitements of the passing day meant little to it. Another and a major excitement had seized me, and I was again on a great voyage of discovery and the land of India and the people of India lay spread out before me. India with all her infinite charm and variety began to grow upon me more and more, and yet the more I saw of her, the more I realised how very difficult it was for me or for anyone else to grasp the ideas she had embodied. It was not her wide spaces that eluded me, or even her diversity, but some depth of soul which I could not fathom, though I had occasional and tantalizing glimpses of it. She was like some ancient palimpsest on which layer upon layer of thought and reverie had been inscribed, and yet no succeeding layer had completely hidden or erased what had been written previously.

And:

> In this and other ways I tried to discover India, the India of the past and of the present, and I made my mood receptive to impressions and to the waves of thought and feeling that came to me from living beings as well as those who had long ceased to be. I tried to identify myself for a while with this unending procession, at the tail end of which I, too, was struggling along. And then I would separate myself and as from a hill-top, apart, look down at the valley below.[11]

---

11   Jawaharlal Nehru, *The Discovery of India* (Oxford: Oxford University Press, 2002), 58–9.

Jawaharlal Nehru's An Autobiography *(1936) and* The Discovery of India *(1946)*   131

Before we comment on how the nation is seen in classic gendered terms, as a winsome and ultimately mysterious woman, there are other significant details worth noticing. In particular, the speaker Nehru's pervasive sense of separation from India relates to his sense that identification with India must involve a ceaseless journeying or voyage of self-discovery. This repeated oscillation between experiences of identification and separation allows Nehru to dramatize both his own internal dividedness and that of India, even as he expresses feelings of affinity to the nation. The independence struggle thus becomes linked with the leader's own process of self-making and self-assertion, expressed in images of uphill climbs, and views from hilltops. National-coming-into-being is cast as a personal journey, a secular pilgrim's progress.

Though it may on one level appear too obvious to highlight, it is worth observing the prevalence of clichés that characterizes Nehru's language of self-assertion, as he traces his gradual embrace of a national identity. He joins with other leader (auto)biographers in partaking in the same standardized rhetorical figures: of repeated overcoming and further hills to climb; of lions in the path; of a sense of inevitable destiny; and, most noticeably perhaps, of the national body as female. The pervasiveness of clichés can be explained in part because such life-narratives are often written imitatively and, as we have seen, with deference. But the fact is also that clichés represent a powerful way of insisting upon concord. Accessible, transnational, migratory, charismatic, they are generic images that, like the newspaper story or boy's own tale, work to appeal to the greatest number and so break down barriers. Through the standard generic patterns imposed by the cliché, the leader's simultaneous mastery over and connection with the nation can be asserted and his difference from the nation bridged. The nation is called into being through the story's power to appeal to the everyman, and the everyman in his or her turn identifies through the book and its charismatic clichés with the leader.

To illustrate, by ascribing a female character to the Indian nation, Nehru gives 'her' the classical shape of a woman, and a flirtatious one at that. Significantly, following the chronology of his story, India as a political and emotional preoccupation rises out of his account of his marital difficulties, which then come to an end with the death of his wife. Therefore, India becomes in some sense a replacement spouse to Nehru, in relation to whom he positions himself as a prime minister husband, as if to make an honest woman of her (given her winsomeness). He gives her respectability and substance by at once embracing her people, yet observing them from a distance: 'India was in my blood and there was much in her that instinctively thrilled me. And yet I approached her almost as an alien critic. To some extent I came at her via the West, and looked at her as a friendly westerner might have done'.[12] As these examples suggest, *An Autobiography* and, perhaps even more emphatically, *The Discovery of India*, operate as performative speech-acts: they call into being what they designate; they invoke and they point. The leader both *is* the national community, representing and embodying it, and yet he also stands outside it, cajoling, beseeching, encouraging and chastising. Throughout, Nehru depicts himself as searching for the meanings of India through travel and discovery, including in libraries and archives. His journeys and related activities are intended not only to demonstrate and justify the values of the nation – resilience, doggedness, a commitment to finding out the truth – but also to carry out the foundational work of tracing out its spatial-temporal dimensions – its continental mass and its borders; its history and its myths.

Conclusion

Jawaharlal Nehru's autobiographies, working together, exerted a shaping influence on the postcolonial world by mobilizing its readers to think of themselves as citizens. It called them out as being in some sense 'after empire' and so, in imaginative terms at least, encouraged them to dislodge the power-systems of the past. Throughout, the two books linked self-making and nation-making, casting both processes as masculine, unidirectional narratives. 'Did I know India?', Nehru repeatedly asks himself in the course of *The Discovery of India*. He did, but only to the extent that he knew himself, and in as far as he was prepared to shape his world in his own image.

---

12 Nehru, *Discovery of India*, 50.

Bibliography

Anderson, Benedict, *Imagined Communities* (London: Verso, 1991).
Anderson, Perry, *The Indian Ideology* (London: Verso, 2013).
Banerjee, Prathama, *Politics of Time: 'Primitives' and History-writing in a Colonial Society* (New York: Oxford University Press, 2006).
Boehmer, Elleke, *Stories of Women: Gender and Narrative in the Postcolonial Nation* (Manchester: Manchester University Press, 2005).
Chakrabarty, Dipesh, *Provincializing Europe: Postcolonial Thought and Historical Difference* (Princeton, NJ: Princeton University Press, 2000).
Chatterjee, Partha, *Nationalist Thought and the Colonial World: A Derivative Discourse?* (London: Zed Press, 1986).
Cubitt, Geoffrey, and Allen Warren, eds, *Heroic Expectations and Exemplary Lives* (Manchester: Manchester University Press, 2000).
Fabian, Johannes, *Time and the Other: How Anthropology Makes Its Object* (New York: Columbia University Press, 2002).
Gandhi, M. K., *An Autobiography; or, the Story of my Experiments with Truth* (Ahmedabad: Navajivan, 1927).
——, *Hind Swaraj*, ed. Anthony J. Parel (Cambridge: Cambridge University Press, 1997).
Hardiman, David, *Gandhi in His Time and Ours: The Global Legacy of His Ideas* (New York: Columbia University Press, 2003).
Leask, Nigel, *British Romantic Writers and the East: Anxieties of Empire* (Cambridge: Cambridge University Press, 1992).
Mandela, Nelson, *Long Walk to Freedom* (London: Little, Brown, 1994).
Nehru, Jawaharlal, *An Autobiography* (London: The Bodley Head, 1942 [1936]).
——, *The Discovery of India* (Oxford: Oxford University Press, 2002 [1946]).
Sampson, Anthony, *Mandela: The Authorised Biography* (London: Harper Collins, 2000).
Suu Kyi, Aung San, Jawaharlal Nehru Memorial Lecture 2012 (14 November 2012), repr. in *Outlook India* (15 November 2012) <http://www.outlookindia.com/article/the-discovery-of-nehru-was-also-a-discovery-of-myself/282997> accessed 2 May 2015.

ROUVEN KUNSTMANN

8 Joseph B. Danquah's *The Akan Doctrine of God* (1944): Anticolonial Fragments?

ABSTRACT

The Akan Doctrine of God: A Fragment of Gold Coast Ethics and Religion, published in 1944 by Joseph B. Danquah, then one of Ghana's leading anticolonial politicians, provided an intellectual blueprint for a unified Akan culture and a foundational theory of the postcolonial Ghanaian state: the 'Ghana hypothesis'. While opposing the colonial idea of African cultural primitivism, the book set monotheism and Greek tradition as the measure of comparison for reinterpreting a precolonial Akan past for the postcolonial future. Hence, it promoted an anticolonialism partially based on a colonial episteme.

Fragments of History

The late 1930s and 1940s saw the emergence of a global 'counter-current to empire's master narrative'.[1] Pamphlets, newspapers, novels and academic books circulated emancipatory thoughts to individuals and organizations around the world. In the Gold Coast, the first sub-Saharan country to gain independence after the Second World War, the expansion of formal

---

1   Antoinette Burton and Isabel Hofmeyr, 'Introduction: The Spine of Empire? Books and the Making of an Imperial Commons', in Antoinette Burton and Isabel Hofmeyr, eds, *Ten Books That Shaped the British Empire: Creating an Imperial Commons* (Durham, NC and London: Duke University Press, 2014), 11.

British-styled education created new reading publics.² Academic books soon reached these new audiences, many of whom had significant grievances due to the increasingly limited employment opportunities available to school graduates in the interwar and post-war periods.³ In this environment of uncertainty and changing social organization, academic books drawing on history, politics and anthropology provided critiques of colonialism that created significant momentum in this 'anticolonial current'.⁴ The reinterpretation of African religion featured notably within these simultaneously decolonizing and modernizing intellectual movements in Africa, as philosopher and cultural theorist Kwame Anthony Appiah summarizes: 'These celebrators of the African race may have spoken of the need to Christianize or Islamize Africa, to modernize, so to speak, its religion'.⁵ *The Akan Doctrine of God* (hereafter *Akan*) was an academic book central to this celebration of African culture and religion, but one that has received little to no attention from prominent scholars of Akan history, such as Tom McCaskie and Ivor Wilks.⁶ Danquah's project and

---

2   John Iliffe, *Africans: The History of a Continent* (Cambridge: Cambridge University Press, 2007), 219–51; Stephanie Newell, 'Entering the Territory of Elites: Literary Activity in Colonial Ghana', in Karin Barber, ed., *Africa's Hidden Histories: Everyday Literacy and Making the Self* (Bloomington: Indiana University Press, 2013), 211–35; Stephanie Newell, *The Power to Name: A History of Anonymity in Colonial West Africa* (Athens: Ohio University Press, 2013), 44–61. According to the official definition of the United Nations, Sudan, which gained independence in 1956, is not part of sub-Saharan Africa. See United Nations Statistics Division, 'Composition of Macro Geographical (Continental) Regions, Geographical Sub-regions, and Selected Economic and Other Groupings', *United Nations Statistics Division* (2016) <http://unstats.un.org/unsd/methods/m49/m49regin.htm> accessed 26 November 2016.
3   James S. Coleman, *Nigeria: Background to Nationalism* (Berkeley: University of California Press, 1971), 125–36.
4   Burton and Hofmeyr, 'Introduction', 11.
5   Kwame Anthony Appiah, *In My Father's House: Africa in the Philosophy of Culture* (Oxford: Oxford University Press, 1992), 24.
6   Thomas McCaskie only references the empirical evidence in *Akan*. Thomas C. McCaskie, *State and Society in Pre-colonial Asante* (Cambridge: Cambridge University Press, 1995), 222, 279. Ivor Wilks focused on the 'material base of Asante

the book's mixed academic and political legacy in the twentieth century form the focus of this chapter.

Akan offers a self-proclaimed philosophical-anthropological approach to understanding Gold Coast society from the most outspoken anticolonial politician of the interwar period, Joseph B. Danquah (1895–1965). The book shaped postcolonial identities in the Gold Coast and reached a global readership in South Africa, Britain, Germany and the United States, provoking passionate discussions amongst African nationalists, missionaries and scholars.[7] In the book, Danquah sought to explain how the Akan shared a coherent monotheistic belief structure that in turn united Ghanaian cultural ethnicity. In so doing, he wrote against the stereotypical colonial image of 'primitive African people whose religion had no discernible system', arguing instead that Akan religion was equivalent to Ancient Greek religious beliefs and Judaism.[8] To justify this claim, Danquah based his understanding of Akan heritage on available scholarship and his own experience. The result was, as renowned scholar of nationalism in Africa Thomas Hodgkin argues, a 'traditionalist' reinterpretation.[9] It was an attempt to modernize Akan religion by reinventing its past through a common religious identity.

---

society' and therefore paid no attention to *Akan*: Ivor Wilks, *Asante in the Nineteenth Century: The Structure and Evolution of a Political Order* (Cambridge: Cambridge University Press, 1989), xx.

[7] The copy of the text referred to in this chapter belonged to the Methodist minister, Geoffrey Parrinder, who acquired it in 1945 while a missionary in what is now the Republic of Benin.

[8] Eva L. R. Meyerowitz, *The Divine Kingship in Ghana and Ancient Egypt* (London: Faber and Faber, 1960), 17.

[9] Thomas Hodgkin, *Nationalism in Colonial Africa* (London: Frederick Muller, 1956), 175.

The Genesis of the Book

The history of Danquah's political involvement provides the context for *Akan*'s origins. Danquah was one of the 'big six' leaders of the pro-independence United Gold Coast Convention Party, then the leading political party in the Gold Coast. He was Kwame Nkrumah's main adversary, and promoted a line of conservative thought which still influences the contemporary politics of the New Patriotic Party, the presidential party from 2001 to 2009.[10] In December 2016, The New Patriotic Party, now led by Danquah's great-nephew, Nana Addo Dankwa Akufo-Addo, won the Ghanaian presidential election. Despite this legacy, however, other authors, such as Nnamdi Azikiwe in Nigeria and Jomo Kenyatta in Kenya, became important politicians in those independent nation-states while Danquah's political career declined. His reputation gradually faded during the 1950s, no doubt due to the repeated imprisonment and censorship he endured after Nkrumah became Leader of Government Business in 1951. When Danquah passed away in detention in the Nsawam Medium Prison on 4 February 1965, his political life had already been shattered for many years. However, the government succeeding Nkrumah's rehabilitated Danquah's legacy posthumously by providing him with a national funeral, establishing the J. B. Danquah Memorial Lecture Series and founding the Danquah Institute. Today, his statue features prominently as a centrepiece on Danquah Circle in Osu, the touristic and commercial centre of Accra, and is well known to locals and visitors alike.

Despite this relatively apolitical memorialization of Danquah in contemporary Ghana, both the text of *Akan* and its legacy are deeply entrenched in local politics. After an education in the Basel Mission schools in the Gold Coast, he studied law and philosophy in London during the 1920s, where he became a member of the West African Students' Union and editor of its newspaper. In 1926 Danquah was called to the bar at the Inner Temple.

---

10   Kwame D. Fordwor, *The Danquah-Busia Tradition in the Politics of Ghana: The Origins, Mission, and Achievements of the New Patriotic Party* (Accra: Unimax Macmillan, 2010), 1–32.

In 1927, he became the first West African to receive a doctorate in philosophy from University College London. That same year, he returned to the Gold Coast to practise law and engage with politics. Law, philosophy and his ancestral heritage then inspired his first publication, *Gold Coast: Akan Laws and Customs and the Akim Abuakwa Constitution*, in 1928.[11] The book combined a description of Akan customs with criticism of the local constitution in Akyem Abuakwa in southeast Ghana, where his brother sat on the throne. His brother, Nana Sir Ofori Atta I, the *Okyenhene* [king] of Akyem Abuakwa, was the head of one of the largest and wealthiest kingdoms in the Gold Coast. As a descendant of the royal family, Danquah saw himself as belonging to the Akan, a *Twi*-speaking cultural group to which other groups, such as the Ashanti, also trace their origin.

For his second book, Danquah planned a three-volume academic project that would develop his intellectual preoccupation with Akan customs, values and religious beliefs and challenge the primitivist image of African religion propagated by colonial missionary education. Danquah intended to 'set forth the Akan idea of the good, or the supreme good, and examine [...] for the purpose, all the anthropological evidence available: the Akan gods, the "fetishes", the customs, the maxims, or proverbs (3,680 of them), the festivals, the religious observances, the calendars, folklore, the family system, the social and moral codes, racial history, racial fears and hopes'.[12] Drawing on a wealth of primary and secondary sources, *Akan* would contribute to religious, anthropological and philosophical scholarship, following in the footsteps of other members of the Gold Coast elite such as Joseph E. Casely Hayford.[13]

---

11   Joseph B. Danquah, *Gold Coast: Akan Laws and Customs and the Akim Abuakwa Constitution* (London: George Routledge, 1928).

12   Joseph B. Danquah, *The Akan Doctrine of God: A Fragment of Gold Coast Ethics and Religion* (London: Lutterworth Press, 1944), ix.

13   See Joseph Ephraim Casely Hayford, *Gold Coast Native Institutions: With Thoughts Upon a Healthy Imperial Policy for the Gold Coast and Ashanti* (London: Sweet and Maxwell, 1903); and Joseph Ephraim Casely Hayford, *Ethiopia Unbound: Studies in Race Emancipation* (London: C. M. Philip, 1911).

Had Danquah's plans come to fruition, his book would have been more widely recognized as a key anticolonial publication. However, events turned out differently than planned. On the evening of 29 January 1941, a defect in an electrical circuit in Danquah's study caused a fire, reducing the manuscripts of the first two volumes 'to a heap of ashes'.[14] This loss rendered the rewriting of these volumes impossible, and so Danquah condensed aspects of the fragments that survived into the third volume, which Lutterworth Press published in England as the 206-page *Akan*.[15] This fragmentation distinguished it from other anticolonial academic books, but also prevented it from becoming a widely recognized anticolonial text, for it contributed to the inconsistency of the book's core arguments.

The Arguments

Danquah's dense and detailed writing style often makes a clear line of argument difficult to determine. However, three overarching contentions are discernible. The first is that Akan deities support a monotheistic metaphysics; the second, that the nuclear and extended family represent the smallest social categories in which God is present – a conclusion Danquah reaches by analysing different concepts of deities such as '*Onyame*, the Akan Deity' and '*Onyankopon Kwaame*, or The God of Saturday'.[16] The third core argument is for the dominant status of a messianic 'nana' figure, a person of high social status whose family has the highest rank, and who exerts social and moral authority over other families.[17] The 'nana' embodies the unevenness in the relationship between different Akan lineages. Combining these

---

14 Danquah, *Akan*, ix.
15 The fire also destroyed rare documents collected for *Gold Coast Ethics and Religion*.
16 Danquah, *Akan*, 30, 43.
17 Danquah, *Akan*, 127.

three argument threads, Danquah deduces a 'universal community' of the Akan – also rooted in the family.[18]

Crucially, the argument relies on a favourable comparison between Akan culture and core tenets in European philosophical traditions. As such, *Akan* suggests that the 'Greek ideal, like the Akan, was one made for human nature'.[19] Danquah frequently draws parallels between the Akan and Ancient Greece: 'At any rate, the Grecian and the Gold Coast answers can, without obvious strain, be reduced to similar terms in one proposition: The practical expansion of patriotic devotion to a personal ideal of dignity that sustains the common life'.[20] In effect, Danquah explicates the sophistication of Akan culture by emphasizing its similarities with Greek political philosophy.

To illustrate that the monotheism of Akan culture was widely practised, Danquah featured Adinkra symbols in the book, which are ubiquitous in pottery, fashion and advertising in Ghana. They represent the in-between of 'the dead and the living, present and the future' and are worn during the day for funeral ceremonies.[21] One of the most used symbols for God is 'GYE NYAME ("Except God")' (see Figure 8.1).[22]

Choosing these symbols, which for Danquah represented 'something intensely native' and 'interpretative of the Akan faith and tradition', he rooted his argument about Akan monotheism in the visual culture of Gold Coast society, thereby claiming for it more credibility.[23]

18 Danquah, *Akan*, xii.
19 Danquah, *Akan*, 123.
20 Danquah, *Akan*, 123–4.
21 Danquah, *Akan*, xix.
22 Danquah, *Akan*, frontispiece. The Adinkra symbols used in the book were illustrated by Spio Garbrah, an art teacher at the Achimota School, and his student Kofi Antubam, who later became a painter and sculptor. Achimota was the most prestigious of secondary schools in Ghana.
23 Danquah, *Akan*, xx.

Figure 8.1: GYE NYAME ('Except God'), featured on the frontispiece of *The Akan Doctrine of God*. Courtesy of the Lutterworth Press.

The Ghana Hypothesis

Representing Akan identity as unified and almost monolithic, *Akan* wholly supported the 'Ghana hypothesis', a theory about the historical, political and cultural origins of the Akan that became a foundational idea of the Ghanaian state.[24] Against endogenous explanations of intensification of labour and the consolidation of the political hierarchies of the Asante Empire, as proposed by historian Ivor Wilks, Danquah, like anthropologist Eva L. Meyerowitz, emphasized the influence of exogenous factors in the emergence of the Akan.[25] According to Danquah's Ghana hypothesis, Akan identity and culture are rooted in a common origin in either the distant Kingdom of Ghana or Ancient Egypt.[26] The Akan, Danquah argued, appropriated core elements of these ancient civilizations' cultural achievements, which had diffused from the Levant to West Africa by migration. As anthropologist Jack Goody notes, 'Danquah adopted the idea of a migration': 'in an appendix [to *Akan*] he writes of Ghana as an Arab corruption of Akane or Akana, and suggests that these should be identified with the "old Babylonian race known as Akkad"'.[27]

The same adoration for the Kingdom of Ghana or Ancient Egypt espoused in Danquah's work became an important trope for African American politics in the Black Power movement. At a local level, moreover, his ideas were so suitable for creating and consolidating a Ghanaian national identity that his political adversaries borrowed them. In particular, Danquah's version of the Ghana hypothesis, which argued further that the Gold Coast is the ancient state of Ghana, proved a concept politically

---

24 Harcourt Fuller, *Building the Ghanaian Nation-State: Kwame Nkrumah's Symbolic Nationalism* (New York: Palgrave Macmillan, 2014), 91.
25 Kwasi Konadu, 'Introduction', in Kwasi Konadu, ed., *Akan Peoples in Africa and the Diaspora: A Historical Reader* (Princeton, NJ: Markus Wiener Publishers, 2015), xi–xix; Eva L. R. Meyerowitz, *The Divine Kingship in Ghana and Ancient Egypt*, 8–34; Ivor Wilks, *Asante in the Nineteenth Century*, 1–79; Ivor Wilks, *One Nation, Many Histories: Ghana Past and Present* (Accra: Ghana University Press, 1996), 13–26.
26 Fuller, *Building the Ghanaian Nation-State*, 91.
27 Jack Goody, 'The Myth of a State', *The Journal of Modern African Studies* 6/4 (1968), 468.

useful to Nkrumah, who adapted related ideas such as 'Ghanaland' when founding the postcolonial Ghanaian nation-state. As Robert C. Scott, an administrator in the colonial government, observed in a despatch to Charles Noble Arden-Clarke, the incumbent Governor of the Gold Coast:

> Even Mr Nkrumah's axial fantasy – Ghanaland – has been cribbed from Dr. Danquah. With some malversation of history and considerable recourse to mystical interpretation, Dr. Danquah demonstrated some time ago that the Gold Coast is the ancient state of Ghana. The romantic notion was enthusiastically received and much elaborated by local bards, but it was Mr. Nkrumah who transformed it into a political conception.[28]

Despite intensifying tensions in the build-up to independence, the Ghana hypothesis as partially formulated by *Akan* rooted the postcolonial nation in a distant past.

The Scholarly Community

Although the Ghana hypothesis was adapted for use in the postcolonial nation-state, scholars have both accepted and criticized the ideas Danquah expressed in *Akan*. Examining this criticism allows for a fuller understanding of how influential the book became in academic circles. There were two phases of reviews by readers from the United States, Europe and Africa: the first occurred immediately after its publication in 1944, and the second after the publication of the second edition in 1968. These reviews were diverse: some were in favour of the book's ideas, others were strongly critical of its overall claims and methods and still others adopted a more moderate position.

An important reader in the first camp was Geoffrey Parrinder, a Methodist minister whose first-edition copy I have consulted for this chapter. According to his notes in *Akan*, Parrinder acquired it in 1945 when he

---

28 National Archives, Kew Gardens, London: CO 537/4638, no. 1, 10 March 1949.

was as a missionary in Dassa-Zoumé, in the French colony of Dahomey (now the Republic of Benin). Parrinder's notes on his personal copy of the book give detailed insights into his engagement with Danquah's thoughts. He highlighted and commented on the text, pointing out contradictions and taking notes on its blank last page. For Parrinder, who became Professor of Comparative Religion at King's College London in 1958, Danquah was a 'writer' and 'sociologist' who argued that 'Akan religion is fundamentally monotheistic despite the lesser gods'.[29] Although Parrinder referenced *Akan* consistently in his own writing as empirical evidence of Akan culture's alleged monotheism and exogenous origin, whether he eventually agreed with Danquah's arguments is uncertain. Another positive reception came from the Professor of Religious Studies at the University of Bristol, Fred Welbourn, who described *Akan* as a 'most illuminating case-study of culture conflict in the realm of one man's ratiocination'.[30] Parrinder and the other favourable reviewers only took issue with some of the book's arguments and pointed out that sources such as interviews could further substantiate Danquah's claims.

Other academics in the 1940s, such as the anthropologist William Bascom and the Reverend Edwin W. Smith, were more critical of Danquah's methods and argument.[31] The Reverend C. J. Braker contended: 'this is a book of importance for all teachers of religion'. He continued, 'Despite hazardous philological arguments, Dr. Danquah's exposition is significant for our understanding of the nature of religion in general'.[32] Braker gave

---

29   Geoffrey Parrinder, *African Traditional Religion* (London: Hutchinson's University Library, 1954), 31; Geoffrey Parrinder, *Religion in Africa* (London: Pall Mall Press, 1969), 8; Geoffrey Parrinder, *West African Religion: Illustrated from the Beliefs and Practices of the Yoruba, Ewe, Akan, and Kindred Peoples* (London: Epworth Press, 1949), 14.

30   Fred B. Welbourn, 'Review: J. B. Danquah, The Akan Doctrine of God', *Journal of Asian and African Studies* 4/4 (1969), 320.

31   William R. Bascom, 'West Africa and the Complexity of Primitive Cultures', *American Anthropologist* 50/1 (1948), 18; Edwin W. Smith, 'Religious Beliefs of the Akan', *Journal of the International African Institute* 15/1 (1945), 28.

32   C. J. Braker, 'Eschatology and Christian Perfection', *Religion in Education* 12/2 (1945), 51.

high praise to Danquah's theological contribution, even though he considered the significance of his philological considerations to be marginal.

Interestingly, Danquah's strongest critics were Ghanaian theologians writing in the 1960s at a time when the post-Nkrumah government was attempting to rehabilitate Danquah's reputation. The second edition of *Akan* was published in 1968, and included a preface written by the Ghanaian theologian Kwesi Abotsia Dickson, who was Professor of Religious Studies at the University of Ghana, Legon. He found *Akan* 'an untrustworthy account of Akan theology, a suggestion that is not completely defensible'. Nevertheless, he also believed that 'there is much that is authentic Akan wisdom; points of light blink through the clouds of speculation and etymologisings'.[33] Dickson disagreed with Danquah's main argument about the monotheist belief structure of the Akan. The theologian C. R. Gaba, another Ghanaian academic, further accused Danquah of being too subjective as an 'auto-ethnographer' who 'unfortunately fell a [sic] victim to fitting his facts to his theory'.[34] Gaba kowtowed to Dickson, his senior in the department, by suggesting that Dickson might provide a more comprehensive account of the Akan religious belief 'as the people themselves know and interpret it'.[35] That *Akan* had been an influential book for the understanding of Akan culture and religion is evident in the fact that Dickson decided to write a long introduction that meticulously refuted Danquah's claims (and worked against the restoration of Danquah's reputation). Nevertheless, in their vocal disagreements with Danquah's argument, his critics paradoxically contributed to the importance of the book: further critiques from eminent scholars such as Feinberg arose in response to Dickson's introduction, and *Akan* was widely discussed in academic circles.[36]

---

33   Kwesi A. Dickson, 'Introduction to the Second Edition', in Joseph B. Danquah, *The Akan Doctrine of God: A Fragment of Gold Coast Ethics and Religion* (London: Routledge, 1968), xxiii–iv.
34   C. R. Gaba, 'Review: The Akan Doctrine of God: A Fragment of Gold Coast Ethics and Religion', *Journal of Religion in Africa* 2/1 (1969), 152.
35   Gaba, 'Review', 152.
36   Harvey M. Feinberg, 'Review: The Akan Doctrine of God', *African Historical Studies* 2/1 (1969), 149.

In addition, *Akan* became an important reference text for Western academics working on societies in Africa. The East German historian Walter Markov noted in 1963 that an African identity should not be based on the belief (and pride) that one's ancestors had come from the Levant.[37] More importantly, like Parrinder, the anthropologist Marc Augé relied heavily on *Akan* as factual evidence of religious beliefs in West Africa in his *Théorie des pouvoirs et idéologie: Étude de cas en Côte-d'Ivoire* published in 1975.[38] Similarly, in 1983, sociologist Shmuel N. Eisenstadt used *Akan* to explain the social organization of the Asante Kingdom.[39] Whether criticized or favourably received, Danquah's interpretation of the past was a seriously influential contribution to the global production of anticolonial academic writing.

Fragments of a Doctrine

Akan represents the emerging postcolonial world through two interrelated but conflicting trajectories. First, the contrasting movement of the book's success and Danquah's decline sets him apart from other influential politicians at the time and asks us to reconsider a common narrative that conflates the simultaneous triumph of postcolonial leaders' rises to power and the influence of their books. Second, *Akan* borrowed from colonial ideas of civilization to advance its version of the Ghana hypothesis, explicating Akan culture through the idea of cultural diffusion from the outside, and justifying its exploration through comparisons with tenets of European religion

---

37   Walter Markov and Fausto Codino, 'Appunti Sulla Storiografia Africana', *Studi Storici* 4/4 (1963), 776.
38   Paulin J. Hountondji, 'Une Pensée Pré-personnelle. Note Sur "Ethnophilosophie et Idéo-logique" de Marc Augé', *L'Homme* 185/186, L'Anthropologue et le Contemporain (2008), 357.
39   Samuel N. Eisenstadt, Michel Abitbol and Noami Chazan, 'Les Origines de l'État: Une Nouvelle Approche', *Annales. Histoire, Sciences Sociales* 38/6 (1983), 1232–55.

and philosophy. In so doing, the book disseminated what I would call a partial *colonial* anticolonialism. Despite its contested history and uneven reception, however, *Akan* remains an important book that encapsulates anticolonial aspirations, shaping the political and academic postcolonial worlds alike.

Bibliography

Appiah, Kwame Anthony, *In My Father's House: Africa in the Philosophy of Culture* (Oxford: Oxford University Press, 1992).

Bascom, William R., 'West Africa and the Complexity of Primitive Cultures', *American Anthropologist* 50/1 (1948), 18–23.

Braker, C. J., 'Eschatology and Christian Perfection', *Religion in Education* 12/2 (1945), 46–51.

Burton, Antoinette, and Isabel Hofmeyr, 'Introduction: The Spine of Empire? Books and the Making of an Imperial Commons', in Antoinette Burton and Isabel Hofmeyr, eds, *Ten Books That Shaped the British Empire: Creating an Imperial Commons* (Durham, NC and London: Duke University Press, 2014), 1–28.

Coleman, James S., *Nigeria: Background to Nationalism* (Berkeley: University of California Press, 1971).

Danquah, Joseph B., *The Akan Doctrine of God: A Fragment of Gold Coast Ethics and Religion* (London: Lutterworth Press, 1944).

——, *Gold Coast: Akan Laws and Customs and the Akim Abuakwa Constitution* (London: George Routledge, 1928).

Dickson, Kwesi A., 'Introduction to the Second Edition', in Joseph B. Danquah, *The Akan Doctrine of God: A Fragment of Gold Coast Ethics and Religion* (London: Routledge, 1968 [1944]), xxiii–iv.

Eisenstadt, Samuel N., Michel Abitbol and Noami Chazan, 'Les Origines de l'État: Une Nouvelle Approche', *Annales. Histoire, Sciences Sociales* 38/6 (1983), 1232–55.

Feinberg, Harvey M., 'Review: The Akan Doctrine of God', *African Historical Studies* 2/1 (1969), 149–51.

Fordwor, Kwame D., *The Danquah-Busia Tradition in the Politics of Ghana: The Origins, Mission, and Achievements of the New Patriotic Party* (Accra: Unimax Macmillan, 2010).

Fuller, Harcourt, *Building the Ghanaian Nation-state: Kwame Nkrumah's Symbolic Nationalism* (New York: Palgrave Macmillan, 2014).
Gaba, C. R., 'Review: The Akan Doctrine of God: A Fragment of Gold Coast Ethics and Religion', *Journal of Religion in Africa* 2/1 (1969), 152.
Goody, Jack, 'The Myth of a State', *The Journal of Modern African Studies* 6/4 (1968), 461–73.
Hayford, Joseph Ephraim Casely, *Ethiopia Unbound: Studies in Race Emancipation* (London: C. M. Philip, 1911).
——, *Gold Coast Native Institutions: With Thoughts Upon a Healthy Imperial Policy for the Gold Coast and Ashanti* (London: Sweet and Maxwell, 1903).
Hodgkin, Thomas, *Nationalism in Colonial Africa* (London: Frederick Muller, 1956).
Hountondji, Paulin J., 'Une Pensée Pré-personnelle. Note Sur "Ethnophilosophie et Idéo-logique" de Marc Augé', *L'Homme* 185/186, L'Anthropologue et le Contemporain (2008), 343–63.
Iliffe, John, *Africans: The History of a Continent* (Cambridge: Cambridge University Press, 2007).
Konadu, Kwasi, 'Introduction', in Kwasi Konadu, ed., *Akan Peoples in Africa and the Diaspora: A Historical Reader* (Princeton, NJ: Markus Wiener Publishers, 2015), xi–xix.
McCaskie, Thomas C., *State and Society in Pre-colonial Asante* (Cambridge: Cambridge University Press, 1995).
Markov, Walter, and Fausto Codino, 'Appunti Sulla Storiografia Africana', *Studi Storici* 4/4 (1963), 759–82.
Meyerowitz, Eva L. R., *The Divine Kingship in Ghana and Ancient Egypt* (London: Faber and Faber, 1960).
National Archives, Kew Gardens, London: CO 537/4638, no. 1, 10 March 1949.
Newell, Stephanie, 'Entering the Territory of Elites: Literary Activity in Colonial Ghana', in Karin Barber, ed., *Africa's Hidden Histories: Everyday Literacy and Making the Self* (Bloomington: Indiana University Press, 2006), 211–35.
——, *The Power to Name: A History of Anonymity in Colonial West Africa* (Athens: Ohio University Press, 2013).
Parrinder, Geoffrey, *African Traditional Religion* (London: Hutchinson's University Library, 1954).
——, *Religion in Africa* (London: Pall Mall Press, 1969).
——, *West African Religion: Illustrated from the Beliefs and Practices of the Yoruba, Ewe, Akan, and Kindred Peoples* (London: Epworth Press, 1949).
Smith, Edwin W., 'Religious Beliefs of the Akan', *Journal of the International African Institute* 15/1 (1945), 23–9.

United Nations Statistics Division, 'Composition of Macro Geographical (Continental) Regions, Geographical Sub-regions, and Selected Economic and Other Groupings', *United Nations Statistics Division* (2016) <http://unstats.un.org/unsd/methods/m49/m49regin.htm> accessed 26 November 2016.

Welbourn, Fred B., 'Review: J. B. Danquah, The Akan Doctrine of God', *Journal of Asian and African Studies* 4/4 (1969), 320.

Wilks, Ivor, *Asante in the Nineteenth Century: The Structure and Evolution of a Political Order* (Cambridge: Cambridge University Press, 1989).

——, *One Nation, Many Histories: Ghana Past and Present* (Accra: Ghana University Press, 1996).

JOHANNA RICHTER

9   The Resistant Forces of Myth: Miguel Ángel Asturias's *Men of Maize* (1949)

ABSTRACT

This chapter explores Miguel Ángel Asturias's *Hombres de maíz* [*Men of Maize*], a milestone of narrative resistance to imperialist and colonialist power in Latin America that remains as relevant today as it was when it was published in 1949. The novel addresses issues as wide ranging as conflict over land and resources, capitalist exploitation and the environmental atrocities of the modern agricultural system from the perspective of indigenous people. Its resistance is rooted in its multifaceted engagement with indigenous Mayan literary traditions, mythology and philosophies, which are mobilized to create an alternative vision of the world and to resist the infiltration of an exploitative imperialism.

Introduction

Miguel Ángel Asturias's *Hombres de maíz* [*Men of Maize*] is a milestone of narrative resistance to imperialist and colonialist power in Latin America.[1] Written in Spanish by the Guatemalan poet, journalist and novelist Miguel Ángel Asturias (1899–1974), the novel was first published in 1949 in Buenos Aires by the publishing company Losada. *Men of Maize* addresses the conflicts over land and resources in a postcolonial state, capitalist exploitation,

1   Original Spanish edition: *Hombres de maíz* (Buenos Aires: Losada, 1949). The English translation by Gerald Martin was first published in 1975 (New York: Delacorte Press/S. Lawrence). References in this chapter are to the critical editions in Spanish (1996) and in English (1993), both edited by Gerald Martin.

the environmental atrocities of the modern agricultural system, strategies of resistance and Mayan mythology. Celebrating the enduring resistance of indigenous communities, it is a text about resistant people that is itself resistant at many levels. The novel's rebellious strength lies in its complex engagement with indigenous literary traditions and philosophies. It is one of the most compelling narratives of Latin America, drawing on Mayan poetic and mythological traditions to advance 'a new way of transmitting and understanding our reality', which in turn serves to resist exploitative and colonizing forces.[2]

Asturias had begun writing and publishing pieces that would become part of the novel as early as 1925, but it was only after 1946 that he finished the book while working in Argentina in the new reformist Guatemalan government's diplomatic service.[3] Already recognized for his stories and poems, Asturias's first two novels *El Señor Presidente* [*Mister President*] (first published in 1946) and *Men of Maize* established his career as a successful international novelist, which culminated in his being awarded the Nobel Prize for Literature in 1967. These two books remain Asturias's most influential works. However, while *Mister President* has sold very well and received almost unanimously positive evaluations by scholars, *Men of Maize*, Asturias's personal favourite among his own novels,[4] has elicited conflicting academic reactions and gained a reputation as 'a difficult novel'.[5] Nevertheless, it has been proclaimed by one influential Latin American

2   Ariel Dorfman, '*Men of Maize*: Myth as Time and Language', in Miguel Ángel Asturias, *Men of Maize*, ed. and trans. Gerald Martin (Pittsburgh, PA: University of Pittsburgh Press, 1993), 390.
3   Gerald Martin, 'Introduction', in Miguel Ángel Asturias, *Men of Maize*, xv.
4   See Saúl Hurtado Heras's interview with Rodrigo Asturias Amado, 'Los Hombres de Maíz se volvieron guerrilleros … Miguel Ángel Asturias en la visión de su hijo, el "comandante" Gaspar Ilom', in Saúl Hurtado Heras, *En la tierra del Quetzal* (Toluca: Universidad Autónoma del Estado de México, 2012), 136–7.
5   See Gerald Martin, 'Destinos: La novela y sus críticos', in Miguel Ángel Asturias, *Hombres de maíz*, ed. Gerald Martin, 2nd edn (Madrid et al.: Colección Archivos, 1996), 514 n. 15.

writer, Ariel Dorfman, as 'the source and backbone of all that is being written in our continent today', and many writers and critics consider it to be Asturias's masterpiece.⁶

The Power of Dreams and Myths

The novel begins with Gaspar Ilóm, an indigenous chief and the novel's protagonist, dreaming that the earth of Ilóm is speaking to him. The earth claims that Gaspar must defend her from the maize growers who are burning down the mountain forest: 'Gaspar Ilóm lets them steal the sleep from the eyes of the land of Ilóm. Gaspar Ilóm lets them hack away the eyelids of the land of Ilóm with axes'.⁷ Ilóm means 'place of rest',⁸ and the deforested land or earth cannot sleep without her 'leafy eyelashes'.⁹ Gaspar Ilóm is encouraged to respond to this ecological violence with a violent resistance of his own: to 'hack the eyelids of those who fell the trees,

---

6   Ariel Dorfman, '*Hombres de maíz*: El mito como tiempo y palabra', in Miguel Ángel Asturias, *Hombres de maíz*, 657. The same article published in the English-language critical edition of *Men of Maize* (1993) does not include this original introductory paragraph, but Dorfman makes mention of his famous citation from 1967 in a short introductory text: Ariel Dorfman, 'Men of Maize: Twenty-Five Years Later', in Miguel Ángel Asturias, *Men of Maize*, 385.
7   Asturias, *Men of Maize*, 7.
8   Duncan Talomé, *Ixiles: La pérdida de Ilom* (Guatemala: CEDIM, 2008), 16.
9   Asturias, *Men of Maize*, 7. Land, earth and ground are usually designated by the same word in Spanish: *tierra*. American-Indian cosmovisions see the earth or the ground as the sacred mother of everything: 'To us our Mother Earth is [...] the root and the source of our culture. She guards our memories, she receives our ancestors and she therefore demands that we honor her and that we return to her, with tenderness and respect, the goods she gives us' (Rigoberta Menchú, 'Address by Doña Rigoberta Menchú on the Occasion of the Award of the Nobel Peace Prize 1992', in Miguel Ángel Asturias, *Men of Maize*, 455).

singe the eyelashes of those who burn the forest, and chill the bodies of those who dam the waters of the river that sleeps as it flows'.[10] This dream, which introduces the text's deep engagement with Mayan philosophy and mythology, inspires a rebellion that will turn into a myth in the thirty or forty years the novel covers.

Gaspar heeds the earth's call, taking up arms with his men against the forest clearance and against the capitalist exploitation of the earth that introduced these slash-and-burn methods of corn cultivation. The novel is set around the turn of the twentieth century in Guatemala at a time when, historically, a governmental development plan led to the expansion of modern agriculture into geographically less accessible regions like the Cuchumatanes mountains.[11] The conflict around land-ownership in Guatemala involved (and still involves) not only an ethnically biased and unequal system of distribution, but also a series of clashes between parallel legal systems, ways of living and spiritual traditions. Characters in the novel oppose modern intensive corn agriculture for its deleterious social, cultural, environmental and economic consequences: 'The maize impoverishes the earth and makes no one rich. Neither the boss nor the men. Sown to be eaten it is the sacred sustenance of the men who were made of maize. Sown to make money it means famine for the men who were made of maize'.[12]

Traditional corn cultivation in subsistence agriculture is related to the spiritual meaning of maize in Mayan culture. In Mayan cosmogony, the gods tried to create humans from different materials like clay and wood, but it was only with corn that they succeeded: humankind is literally *made* of maize.[13] As Sariah Acevedo points out, this is 'mitohistoria', a mythical version of actual history – corn is still a primary nutritional source in

---

10   Asturias, *Men of Maize*, 7.
11   Talomé, *Ixiles*, 26. Significantly, the name 'Guatemala' is never mentioned in the novel.
12   Asturias, *Men of Maize*, 11. See also *Men of Maize*, 11, 191, 237, 304.
13   See Dennis Tedlock, trans., *Popol Vuh: The Definitive Edition of the Mayan Book of the Dawn of Life and the Glories of Gods and Kings* (New York: Simon & Schuster, 1985).

Central America, and its domestication thousands of years ago was the basis for the development of civilizations like the Olmec, and later the Mayan.[14] In this view, disrespecting the earth by using corn for profit, as the novel repeatedly affirms, is a profanation tantamount to the selling of one's own children.

Gaspar's violent killing of the maize growers brings the national military to Ilóm. Living in the mountain forests like *guerrilleros*, Gaspar and his men are protected by the earth, that is, by nature itself, and appear invincible. But during a feast in the mountains to celebrate the birth of Gaspar's son, conceived the very night he resolved to take up arms to protect the earth, Gaspar is betrayed by two members of his community who are collaborating with the military. Gaspar survives their attempted poisoning thanks to the cleansing river water, but returns to find his men slaughtered by soldiers. Rather than surrendering to the military, he drowns himself in the river. But his death only increases his power, for his story takes on mythical status, spreading amongst his allies and enemies alike. In the end, he becomes a legendary figure that no one can defeat, the invincible Gaspar Ilóm.

After this spectacular opening the novel narrates the consequences of a powerful curse spoken after Gaspar's death by the firefly wizards (shamans) to punish Ilóm's traitors and their descendants. For by betraying the fight of Gaspar Ilóm, they have also betrayed the land of Ilóm, or the earth herself. The shamans' words come true, reverberating in the minds and hearts of Gaspar's enemies and driving them to destruction. Although the second and third parts of the novel appear initially to be independent stories about two men searching for their wives decades after the dramatic events in Ilóm, these two narratives are closely related to Gaspar's story and to the shamanic curse. In the epilogue, one of the men is reunited with his wife after years of solitary wandering and returns to the land of Ilóm to sow corn with his children and grandchildren according to traditional Mayan subsistence agricultural practices.

---

14 Sariah Acevedo, 'La cosmovisión indígena en la obra de Miguel Ángel Asturias', *Revista Umbrales, Una publicación del Diario Tiempo* 2/1 (2001), 9.

The Book and Its Readers

Many scholars, even those who explicitly admire the book, have suggested that general readers find the novel 'difficult', 'confusing' and 'irritating', but its market performance suggests something rather different.[15] The Spanish publishing history of *Men of Maize* actually shows sustained public interest. There have been thirteen editions by Losada in Buenos Aires. In Julio Cortázar's novel, *Los premios* (1960), the protagonist is so engrossed in reading *Men of Maize* in the cabin of a ship that he is tempted not to go up to dinner.[16] This scene and the thoughts in the protagonist's stream of consciousness suggest that the novel was a much discussed must-read in Buenos Aires literary circles. Moreover, after the first pocket book edition in 1972, there were at least thirteen reprints of it at Alianza in Madrid, and at least thirteen other Spanish editions after 1974 (published in San José, Costa Rica and in Havana, Paris, Barcelona, Madrid and Guatemala City). The first Central American edition, produced by the Editorial Universitaria Centroamericana (EDUCA), was republished seven times in twenty years. The multiple reprints of affordable editions suggest that the novel has found a sizable reading public, and the steady course of new editions and reprints in its original language prove its status as a classic of Latin American literature.

Men of Maize has also been published in many countries outside the Spanish-speaking world, and translated into at least twelve languages.[17] The first translation, into French, took place immediately after its first

---

15   For example: 'Los lectores deben encontrarla aburrida y difícil, conclusión que deduzco de múltiples conversaciones' [Readers seem to find it boring and difficult, a conclusion I draw from many conversations] (Ariel Dorfman, 'Hombres de maíz: el mito como tiempo y palabra', in Miguel Ángel Asturias, *Hombres de maíz*, 657); '*Hombres de maíz* ha confundido e irritado a muchos lectores' [*Men of Maize* has confused and irritated many readers] (Gerald Martin, 'Introducción del coordinador', in Miguel Ángel Asturias, *Hombres de maíz*, xxi).
16   Julio Cortázar, *Los premios* (Madrid: Punto de Lectura, 2007 [1960]).
17   See Gerald Martin, 'Nuestra edición', in Miguel Ángel Asturias, *Hombres de maíz*, xxix n. 1.

publication. German (1956), Swedish (1961), Dutch (1962) and Italian (1967) translations followed. The novel was not published in English until 1975, later than most of Asturias's other work and more than twenty-five years after its first publication. Since then, Russian (1977), Czech (1981), Danish (1985), Slovenian (1989), Greek (1989) and Chinese (1994) translations have appeared. Significantly, *Men of Maize* has also seen several reprints of its translated editions, and a number of retranslations. Given this translation history and the many Spanish editions and reprints, the text is clearly more widely read than the criticism it has received from academics might suggest.

In fact, there is a marked contrast between the positive responses of journalists, writers and the reading public throughout its history and its very mixed scholarly reception – arguably even neglect – in the first decades after its publication.[18] Given the text's structural complexity, avant-garde poetic practices and unique lyrical language, this is perhaps counterintuitive. Yet *Men of Maize* evidently frustrated many scholars of the 1950s and 1960s, who criticized its supposed lack of structure and obscurity, described the text as incoherent and disorientating, and even doubted if the book could be considered a novel at all.[19] I argue, however, that the book's resistant potential is to be found in these very features, which are in turn linked to the Mayan cultural tradition.

Indigenous Form and Fighting Words

The novel presents and exemplifies a worldview that differs markedly from what might be thought of as 'modern' (mostly 'Western') ways of seeing and being in the world, particularly a rationalistic, individualistic and 'realist' position. Its combination of Mayan spiritual and poetic traditions with European avant-garde literary strategies seems to have deeply

---

18 See Martin, 'Destinos: la novela y sus críticos'.
19 See Martin, 'Destinos: la novela y sus críticos'.

unsettled scholars in the mid-twentieth century. Whilst the novel nevertheless remains readable, as the steady enthusiasm of the general reader proves, these traits mean that academics attempting to interpret the text according only to the aesthetic and philosophical models of the European literary tradition find that it resists these frames. *Men of Maize* embodies the power of myths as fighting words and strategies of cultural resistance that have existed for thousands of years, enduring far longer than the logics of capitalism or theories of Marxist revolution, which are inseparable from the project of European modernity and its philosophical and aesthetic traditions.[20] The story of Gaspar Ilóm's fight draws instead on indigenous models of thought, celebrating subsistence agriculture and representing a posthumanist magical worldview in which everything is alive and connected.

Asturias drew many of his references and narrative elements from the ancient literatures of Central America that survived the systematic destruction of pre-Columbian documents in colonial times, such as the *Popol Vuh*, the *Anales de los Xahiles*, *Rabinal Achí* and Aztec myths. In his Nobel Prize address, Asturias articulated a vision of Latin American literature that predated European arrival. Whilst this tradition is generally acknowledged by most Hispanic-American writers today (if only out of political correctness), few writers before or since Asturias have demonstrated a comparable depth of engagement with ancient American intellectual and aesthetic traditions in their work.[21]

---

20 Asturias also operated in this tradition, adopting a more traditional leftist social realist aesthetic and outspoken anti-imperialist politics in his subsequent novels, the 'Banana Trilogy'. These novels were welcomed by the left at the time of their publication; Asturias received an invitation to Cuba in 1959 by Fidel Castro and the 1965 Lenin Prize as a result.

21 In Guatemalan literature, Luis di Lion's *El tiempo principia en Xibalbá* (1985) should be mentioned. Gordon Brotherston argues that grounding an act of resistance in the indigenous cosmology of America rather than the Western perspective – as Asturias does in *Men of Maize* – has no precedents in Latin American literature except for the almost contemporary *Canek* (1940) by Ermilo Abreu Gómez. See Gordon Brotherston, 'Gaspar Ilóm en su tierra', in Miguel Ángel Asturias, *Hombres de maíz*, 594.

In a sense, *Men of Maize* could be read as a retelling of the central story of the *Popol Vuh*, in which the heroic twins Hunahpu and Xbalanque are killed and thrown into the river after they travel to the underworld.[22] At the same time, the character of Gaspar is an echo of a real historical figure, Gaspar Hijom, who once led a local resistance movement in Ilóm. This kind of parallelism, and also the extensive use of syntactic parallelism, is a stylistic device within the Mayan poetic tradition that fascinated Asturias. For Asturias, parallelism creates 'a poetic gradation destined to induce certain states of consciousness which were taken to be magic'.[23] Words are not only rendered philosophically rich through the building up of nuance and meaning, but also become a means of opening up 'magic[al]' experiential states for readers through their aesthetic effects. In *Men of Maize* Asturias also used elements of the popular Mayan epic and the spiritual tradition of nagualism to create secret layers of meaning and sensual experience. The novel, he later reflected, 'explores the hidden dimensions of words: their resonance, their shadings, their fragrance'.[24] It is these 'hidden dimensions of words' and the connecting energy of parallelism that creates and recreates legends, myths and figures such as Gaspar Ilóm.

In this way, *Men of Maize* is one of the first Latin American texts to successfully remould the novel – a European form – so that it adopts an indigenous cosmovision as its 'normal' narrative perspective. On a linguistic level, Asturias's experimental incorporation of elements of the diction, sounds and structures of Mayan languages into the Spanish text alienates the literary prose from the hegemonic colonial language and creates a unique sound linked to local pre-Columbian traditions. Unlike many other novels tackling the problems of land conflict, indigenous rights or the processes of modernization, however, *Men of Maize* eschews ethnic

22 See René Prieto, *Miguel Ángel Asturias's Archaeology of Return*, 85–160.
23 Miguel Ángel Asturias, 'Nobel Lecture: The Latin American Novel: Testimony of an Epoch', trans. The Swedish Trade Council Language Services, Nobelprize. org (2014) <http://www.nobelprize.org/nobel_prizes/literature/laureates/1967/asturias-lecture.html> accessed July 2016.
24 Asturias to Harss, in Luis Harss and Barbara Dohmann, *Into the Mainstream: Conversations with Latin American Writers* (New York: Harper & Row, 1967), 85.

or moral dichotomies, blurring any clear definitions of and opposition between its various groups.

Men of Maize has a history full of contradictions: though written about a highly indigenous and mostly rural region of Guatemala, it was published in Latin America's least indigenous city. Asturias, the author of this celebratory narrative of rebellion against the state authorities, was ironically the diplomatic representative of the (albeit reformist) Guatemalan state in Argentina. Likewise, although the novel demonstrates a profound and in-depth knowledge of Mayan philosophy, literature and mythology, Asturias himself was still a *ladino*, socially and intellectually identified with European culture and language.[25]

Alan Mills proposes the concepts of cyberspace and code as useful analogies for understanding how different cultural systems and languages function; he argues that operating within other systems is only possible through a procedure comparable to hacking.[26] In these terms, Asturias may be thought of as a 'literary hacker': a cultural actor who tries to understand and use unfamiliar codes, and so inhabit other worldviews and cultural systems. Insofar as *Men of Maize* operates within and across both European and indigenous cultural systems, I would suggest that Asturias succeeded in 'hacking' the Mayan literary code, using that system to produce what is, in a European tradition, an avant-garde and deeply subversive literary work. This kind of hacking usually works the other way round: it is far more common for indigenous actors to exploit European cultural codes and framework to exercise their agency, as Diane Nelson has explored using the term 'Maya-hackers'.[27]

---

25 Asturias has been much criticized for the racist thinking he expressed in his youth: as a law student he wrote his thesis on 'El problema social del indio' [The social problem of the Indian], a study full of racist stereotypes that were common in the 1920s. It was only during his doctoral studies in Europe that he engaged with ancient Mayan texts and developed a different, even contrary, view of indigenous Americans that is evident in his first book, *Leyendas de Guatemala* [Legends of Guatemala] (1931).

26 Alan Mills, 'Literatura hacker y el nahual del lector', *Cuadernos Hispanoamericanos* 744 (2012), 13–20.

27 Diane Nelson, 'Maya-Hackers and the Cyberspatialized Nation-State: Modernity, Ethnonostalgia, and a Lizard Queen in Guatemala', in *A Finger in the Wound: Body Politics in Quincentennial Guatemala* (Berkeley: University of California

If the 'hacking' of Mayan literary and philosophical codes is one of *Men of Maize*'s literary and political achievements, it is probably also the reason that the novel has struggled to be accepted by parts of the academy, where it continues to meet with Eurocentric preconceptions. Even studies that have explored the text's engagement with the Mayan written tradition prefer to describe Asturias's procedure as the integration of 'anthropological material' rather than calling it 'intertextuality', which would entail the acceptance of pre-Columbian texts as 'literature' or 'history'. Indeed, I would suggest that it is because of lingering colonial practices and hierarchies that a tendency to confine the texts and intellectual traditions of indigenous Americans to the discipline of anthropology still persists among scholars.[28] Within Mayan communities, however, Asturias's literary works have generally been beloved and acclaimed: the author was officially honoured with the titles of 'Gran Lengua' and 'Hijo unigénito de Tecún Umán'.[29]

Contemporary Resonances

In the 1970s, over two decades after the novel's publication, Asturias's son Rodrigo became a famous leader of a Guatemalan guerrilla organization, which he is rumoured to have financed with his father's Nobel Prize

---

Press, 1999), 245–82. Mills describes contemporary indigenous poets such as Humberto Ak'abal, Jaime Luis Huenún and Roxana Miranda Rupailaf as 'literary hackers'. See Mills, 'Literatura hacker y el nahual del lector', 18–19. Cultural hacking is arguably the basis of all endemic Latin American aesthetic, spiritual and cultural expressions, from the American Baroque (as conceptualized by Bolívar Echeverría) to magical realism and *mestizaje*.

28 For example, Prieto notes: 'Since the 1970s and early '80s, a few critics, […] have begun to read Asturias's fiction from the well-documented perspective of Mayan anthropology.' He adds: 'To grasp the full tenor of [Asturias's] invention, we must venture into the fields of ethnology and anthropology' (Prieto, *Miguel Ángel Asturias's Archaeology of Return*, 7, 261).

29 Acevedo, 'La cosmovisión indígena en la obra de Miguel Ángel Asturias', 10.

money.[30] The note Rodrigo left to his father to inform him that he was going underground said: 'Los hombres de maíz se volvieron guerrilleros' [The men of maize have become *guerrilleros*] – and he signed it 'Gaspar Ilóm'.[31] Gaspar Ilóm had returned, now as a real life *guerrillero*.[32] The armed conflict in Guatemala lasted thirty-six years (1960–96) and revolved primarily around land disputes: the land reform of 1952 was reversed after the coup of 1954, after which several guerrilla movements fought for political change and land reform. As Duncan Talomé has shown, ongoing conflict was often used as a means to expand huge plantations, especially in the so-called 'Ixil Triangle' or 'the land of Ilóm'.[33] Although in *Men of Maize* the name 'Ixiles' is not mentioned, the location and the name 'Ilóm' leave little doubt that both the fictional Gaspar Ilóm and the historical Gaspar Hijom were chiefs of the Ixil people – an indigenous group in Guatemala whose language, 'Ixil', is part of the Mayan language family. Historically, Ixil identity and customs have always been bound to a particular geographic region, and the Ixiles are known as resistance fighters who have fought fierce battles over territory with invading forces since early colonial times.[34] From 1975 onwards, they endured massacres and persecutions, rape, torture and the systematic destruction of their villages.[35] More than two thirds of Ixiles were driven from their native lands and many were forced into model villages in other areas of Guatemala where they were

30   Arturo Arias, 'Miguel Ángel Asturias', in *Latin-American Lives: Selected Biographies from the Five-Volume 'Encyclopedia of Latin American History and Culture'* (New York: Macmillan, 1998), 442.
31   Hurtado Heras and Asturias Amado, 'Los Hombres de Maíz se volvieron guerrilleros', 140.
32   Rodrigo Asturias was so identified with the name of the novel's protagonist that when he died from a heart attack in his swimming pool in 2005, newspaper titles proclaimed 'the death of Gaspar Ilom'.
33   See Talomé, *Ixiles*.
34   Talomé, *Ixiles*, 21–2.
35   Georg Grünberg, *Tierras y territorios* (Guatemala: FLACSO/MINUGUA/CONTIERRA, 2003), 102–3; Barbara Torggler, 'Comunidades de población en Resistencia: Zivile Widerstandsdörfer in Guatemala', Master's thesis, University of Vienna, 1996, 22.

prevented from practising their traditional ways of organizing community life. Some refused to submit to the model village system and founded the CPRs (Comunidad de Población en Resistencia) [communities of people [population/village] in resistance].[36] In these villages, which were regularly subjected to military violence (including bombings as late as the 1990s), indigenous people continue to resist by living their lives and cultivating corn according to their traditional cultural practices. In 2013, the Ixil community took former president José Efraín Ríos Montt to court in Guatemala City. The court process was a momentous event that received attention from – and stimulated debate across – the whole of the Americas: Ixiles in their traditional clothing sat in the courtroom, facing the powerful man whose orders had authorized the torture and murder of many of their relatives and friends twenty years earlier. Ríos Montt was found guilty of genocide and sentenced to eighty years in prison, but the sentence was overturned ten days later.[37]

When Asturias published *Men of Maize* in 1949, while a hopeful reformist and democratic government discussed land reform, he could not have anticipated his novel's continued topicality nearly seven decades later. There has been no land reform in Guatemala since 1952; rather, liberalizing economic reforms like the Free Trade Agreement of 2006 (CAFTA-DR) have increased pressure on the exploitation of natural resources. In recent years, another formerly near-pristine natural forest region, in the department Petén, has been slashed and burned and transformed into huge plantations for palm oil. Indigenous communities continue to fight and resist the encroachments of Canadian and Russian mining companies, whose practices are devastating mountain ecosystems. The communities are also protesting against enormous damn projects that divert 'the flow of the water as it sleeps' and the use of transgenic corn. Mayan resistance to colonial, postcolonial and neocolonial rule has thus been maintained for almost five centuries, and the telling and retelling of their mythical stories of resistance have been crucial to these efforts. It was these stories that Asturias

36 Torggler, 'Comunidades de población en Resistencia', 31–4.
37 The sentence was overturned by the constitutional court, officially due to procedural irregularities.

tapped into and reinterpreted, spreading them across, and shaping, the postcolonial world.[38]

Bibliography

Acevedo, Sariah, 'La cosmovisión indígena en la obra de Miguel Ángel Asturias', *Revista Umbrales, Una publicación del Diario Tiempo* 2/1 (2001), 8–11.
Arias, Arturo, 'Miguel Ángel Asturias', in *Latin-American Lives: Selected Biographies from the Five-Volume 'Encyclopedia of Latin American History and Culture'* (New York: Macmillan, 1998), 440–3.
Asturias, Miguel Ángel, *Hombres de maíz*, ed. Gerald Martin, 2nd edn (Madrid, Paris and México: ALLCA XX; Colección Archivos, 1996).
——, *Men of Maize*, ed. and trans. Gerald Martin (Pittsburgh, PA: University of Pittsburgh Press, 1993).
——, 'Nobel Lecture: The Latin American Novel: Testimony of an Epoch', trans. The Swedish Trade Council Language Services, Nobelprize.org (2014) <http://www.nobelprize.org/nobel_prizes/literature/laureates/1967/asturias-lecture.html> accessed July 2016.
Bastos, Santiago, and Manuela Camus, *El movimiento maya en perspectiva: Texto para reflexión y debate* (Guatemala: FLACSO, 2003).
Brotherston, Gordon, 'Gaspar Ilóm en su tierra', in Miguel Ángel Asturias, *Hombres de maíz*, 593–602.
Callan, Richard J., 'The Quest Myth in Miguel Ángel Asturias' *Hombres de maíz*', *Hispanic Review* 36/3 (1968), 249–61.
Díaz Castellanos, Guillermo, 'Guatemala: una nación, dos países', *Sociedad y Discurso* 27 (2015), 84–100.
Dorfman, Ariel, '*Hombres de maíz*: El mito como tiempo y palabra', in Asturias, *Hombres de maíz*, 657–74.
——, '*Men of Maize*: Myth as Time and Language', in Miguel Ángel Asturias, *Men of Maize*, 389–412.

---

38 Arguably, *Men of Maize* prepared the way for Rigoberta Menchú's Nobel Peace Prize, which was crucial in drawing international attention to the situation of indigenous communities in Guatemala, and which helped to establish the *Agreement on Identity and Rights of Indigenous People* (1996).

——, '*Men of Maize*: Twenty-Five Years Later', in Miguel Ángel Asturias, *Men of Maize*, 385–7.
Grünberg, Georg, *Tierras y territorios indígenas en Guatemala* (Guatemala: FLACSO/MINUGUA/CONTIERRA, 2003).
Harss, Luis, and Barbara Dohmann, *Into the Mainstream: Conversations with Latin American Writers* (New York: Harper & Row, 1967).
Hurtado Heras, Saúl, and Rodrigo Asturias Amado, '*Los Hombres de Maíz* se volvieron guerrilleros … Miguel Ángel Asturias en la visión de su hijo, el "comandante" Gaspar Ilom (entrevista con Rodrigo Asturias Amado [en diciembre de 1997])', in Saúl Hurtado Heras, *En la tierra del Quetzal: ensayos y entrevistas reunidos sobre Miguel Ángel Asturias y su obra* (Toluca: Universidad Autónoma del Estado de México, 2012), 133–44.
Martin, Gerald, 'Destinos: la novela y sus críticos', in Miguel Ángel Asturias, *Hombres de maíz*, 507–38.
——, 'Introducción del coordinador', in Miguel Ángel Asturias, *Hombres de maíz*, xxi–xxviii.
——, 'Introduction', in Miguel Ángel Asturias, *Men of Maize*, xi–xxx.
——, 'Nuestra edición', in Miguel Ángel Asturias, *Hombres de maíz*, xxix–xxx.
Menchú Tum, Rigoberta, 'Address by Doña Rigoberta Menchú on the Occasion of the Award of the Nobel Peace Prize 1992', in Miguel Ángel Asturias, *Hombres de maíz*, 453–8.
Mills, Alan, 'Literatura hacker y el nahual del lector', *Cuadernos Hispanoamericanos* 744 (2012), 13–30.
Nelson, Diane, 'Maya-Hackers and the Cyberspatialized Nation-State: Modernity, Ethnonostalgia, and a Lizard Queen in Guatemala', in *A Finger in the Wound: Body Politics in Quincentennial Guatemala* (Berkeley: University of California Press, 1999), 245–82.
Prieto, René, *Miguel Ángel Asturias's Archaeology of Return* (Cambridge: Cambridge University Press, 1983).
Talomé, Duncan, *Ixiles: La pérdida de Ilom* (Guatemala: CEDIM, 2008).
Tedlock, Dennis, trans., *Popol Vuh: The Definitive Edition of the Mayan Book of the Dawn of Life and the Glories of Gods and Kings* (New York: Simon & Schuster, 1985).
Torggler, Barbara, 'Comunidades de población en Resistencia: Zivile Widerstandsdörfer in Guatemala', Master's thesis, University of Vienna, 1996.

RUTH BUSH

10 The Hip-Hop Legacies of Cheikh Anta Diop's *Nations nègres et culture* (1954)

ABSTRACT

This chapter explores the legacies of a landmark text by Senegalese historian and scientist Cheikh Anta Diop. Best known for its affirmation of the black African origins of pre-dynastic Egyptian culture, *Nations nègres et culture* (1954) paved the way for subsequent research in this area, notably Martin Bernal's *Black Athena* (1987) and the work of Afrocentrists such as Molefi Asante (1994; 2007). This chapter focuses on recent engagement with these polemical ideas on the African continent, and particularly in Senegal. It considers Diop's first book-length publication less in terms of its empirical truth-value, than with an eye to the affective, didactic qualities captured in a range of afterlives, from hip-hop to recent essays by African intellectuals. Through discussion of the contested politics and policing of postcolonial knowledge production, I argue that Diop set the tone for anticolonial thought in the second half of the twentieth century and its fraught relationship with the academic sphere.

'Monsieur le prof! Les Egyptens étaient des négroïdes, où je l'ai su? c'est Cheikh Anta Diop qui me l'a dit ...'[1]

[Hey, Mr Teacher! The Egyptians were negroid. Where did I learn that? Cheikh Anta Diop told me ...]

'Renoi, c'est bien beau d'avoir été Pharaon Mais le passé n'est qu'un caveau si le futur passe par la honte.'[2]

[*Renoi* (*Verlan* slang for Black, inverting syllables of 'Noire'), it's bliss to have been a Pharaoh, but the past is an abyss if the future comes through shame.]

1   Disiz, 'Cours d'histoire', *Jeu de société* (2003). All translations are my own.
2   Youssoupha, 'Noir Désir', *Noir Désir* (2012).

As these epigraphs from Franco-Senegalese hip-hop artists Disiz and Youssoupha confirm, the ideas of historian and scientist, Cheikh Anta Diop (1923–86) remain potent in the twenty-first century. Diop's life-work sought to assert the cultural unity and dignity of the African continent and its peoples through the means of rigorous scientific enquiry. His best-known thesis affirms the black African origins of Ancient Egypt and, by extension, of Greek and European 'civilization'. While this argument was not entirely original – such ideas had been articulated at regular intervals throughout the late eighteenth and nineteenth centuries[3] – Diop's work, developed over a series of articles and books from the 1950s to the 1980s, provided ample new evidence and lodged these ideas firmly within both academic and non-academic spaces. In turn, it catalysed the profound questioning of Eurocentric notions of modernity and progress which characterize the postcolonial world. By the 1980s, Martin Bernal's *Black Athena* trilogy addressed similar questions to those raised by Diop, and Bernal's work has come to dominate debates on the 'Afro-asiatic' roots of European civilization in the anglophone Global North. As two of Bernal's most vocal critics note, his work's success lies in 'the appeal of iconoclasm in an age where everything traditional has been questioned and found wanting'.[4] It is generally acknowledged, however, that Bernal's engagement with Diop's work is limited.[5]

Today, Diop's reputation shifts between three overlapping epistemologies: the rhetoric of what Kwame Anthony Appiah has called 'romantic racialism', often associated with the Afrocentrism of North American scholars such as Molefi Kete Asante;[6] a general awareness of the need to act upon, or with awareness of, a decolonized understanding of the past;

---

[3] See Maghan Keita, 'Believing in Ethiopians', in Daniel Orrells, Gurminder K. Bhambra and Tessa Roynon, eds, *African Athena: New Agendas* (Oxford: Oxford University Press, 2011), 19–39.

[4] Mary R. Lefkowitz and Guy MacLean Rogers, eds, *Black Athena Revisited* (Chapel Hill: University of North Carolina Press, 1996), x.

[5] Stephen Howe, *Afrocentrism: Mythical Pasts and Imagined Homes* (London and New York: Verso, 1998), 158.

[6] Kwame Anthony Appiah, *In My Father's House: Africa in the Philosophy of Culture* (Oxford: Oxford University Press, 1992), 101.

and rigorous, ongoing historical research that traces nuanced patterns of cultural influence on the African continent and in the Mediterranean.[7] In the light of these complex legacies, this chapter focuses on Diop's 'audacious' first book,[8] *Nations nègres et culture* [Negro nations and culture] (1954).[9] I will argue that the book remains a powerful argument against the instrumentalization of historical knowledge and language by colonial ideology, despite widespread critique of many of its arguments.

By contributing to long-running discussions of African history and historiography, and challenging fundamental disciplinary norms, Diop set the tone for anticolonial thought in the second half of the twentieth century and its fraught relationship with the academic sphere. This relationship can be traced most recently in ongoing struggles to decolonize university curricula (including the Rhodes Must Fall movement and perennial debates surrounding postcolonial history and memory), as well as through the popular currency of Diop's ideas in the archive of hip-hop culture. Responses to Diop's broad affirmation of an African contribution to humanity reveal the contested politics and policing of knowledge production. They also signal the need to trace the circulation of those ideas regarding knowledge and truth beyond the covers of this world-changing book. As Diop notes in the preface to the first edition, 'la vérité, c'est ce qui sert et, ici, ce qui sert le colonialisme' [truth is that which serves a purpose, and, in this case, that which serves colonialism].[10] Diop's work continues to wield influence in the United States, and in Senegal, where the country's largest university and a major avenue in Dakar were named (posthumously) after him.[11] While acknowledging that Diop's ideas have found enthusiastic advocates in Europe and America, the

---

7 See also: Orrells, Bhambra and Roynon, *African Athena*, 14.
8 Aimé Césaire, *Discours sur le colonialisme* (Paris: Présence Africaine, 2004 [1955]), 3.
9 Ten chapters of *Nations nègres et culture* were translated into English by Mercer Cook and published with extracts from *Antériorité des civilisations nègres* (1967) as *The African Origins of Civilisation: Myth or Reality* (1974).
10 Cheikh Anta Diop, *Nations nègres et culture*, 4th edn (Paris: Présence Africaine, 1979 [1954]), 14.
11 This is paradoxical given that Diop was ostracized from the higher echelons of academic life in Senegal during his lifetime.

focus in this chapter will be on the recent engagement with these ideas on the African continent, and particularly in Senegal. With this in mind, I consider Diop's first book-length publication less in terms of its empirical truth-value, than with an eye to the affective, didactic qualities captured in a range of afterlives, from hip-hop to recent essays by African intellectuals.

Writing *Nations nègres et culture*

The cultural echoes of Diop's ideas have resounded far beyond the institutionalized contexts of book-publishing and circulation. It is helpful, nonetheless, to start with a summary of the original context and content of *Nations nègres et culture*. Cheikh Anta Diop was born in 1923 into a distinguished Wolof family in Caytu, a town in the Diourbel region of Senegal. He followed Islamic education and then entered the French education system in Dakar and Saint Louis, before moving to Paris in 1946. His interest in language and in particular the linguistic structures of his mother tongue, Wolof, stemmed from his schooldays in Senegal, when he first attempted to create a written alphabet for the language.[12] Once in France, Diop's intellectual ambition was applied to his studies in mathematics and physics, together with further research interests in Egyptology and linguistics. This training in the French higher education system shaped his concern with scientific methods. Encounters with African students during this period also galvanized Diop's political consciousness as a member of the RDA (Rassemblement Démocratique Africain), and his research and writing in the 1950s were closely linked to the political struggle for independence. As early as 1952, Diop advocated the independence of African nation states, the formation of an African federation, and the promotion of national African languages, challenging 'la duperie de l'Union française' [the trickery of the

---

12   Bara Diouf, 'Une interview exclusive de Cheikh Anta Diop', *La Vie Africaine* 6 (1960), 10.

French Union].[13] Unlike the poet and future president, Léopold Sédar Senghor, whose conception of an amicable ongoing relationship between France and Africa would be partly realized by 1960, Diop sought a more radical break with the colonial power. He was briefly imprisoned for this political stance following his return to newly independent Senegal.

The book began as a doctoral thesis produced at the Sorbonne under the supervision of eminent French scientist Gaston Bachelard and archaeologist Marcel Griaule, whose work on the Dogon country (in present-day Mali) shaped a generation of ethnologists in France. This thesis failed to recruit the required number of academics to sit on the viva committee. Despite the absence of consecration by the French academy, the book was published by Présence Africaine in 1954. This was a bold move by the young publishing house, founded in 1949 (following the launch of a journal under the same name in 1947) by Senegalese intellectual Alioune Diop and specializing in texts relating to African and African diasporic experience. Cheikh Anta Diop subsequently renewed his work for the doctoral degree, working under two new titles: 'Etude comparée des systèmes politiques et sociaux de l'Europe et de l'Afrique, de l'Antiquité à la formation des Etats modernes' and 'Domaines du patriarcat et du matriarcat dans l'Antiquité classique'. This thesis passed in 1960, but was awarded a mediocre 'mention honorable', effectively barring Diop from any senior academic post in the French system. Afterwards, he returned to Senegal to set up a scientific laboratory at the University of Dakar, which would play a key role in developing the use of Carbon 14 dating in West African archaeological sites.

Diop's precocious interdisciplinarity was allied with a commitment to spreading new forms of understanding widely and transparently on the African continent. In an interview given shortly before returning to Dakar, he stated:

> Il ne s'agit pas de se créer, de toutes pièces, une histoire plus belle que celle des autres, de manière de doper moralement le peuple pendant la période de lutte pour l'indépendance, mais de partir de cette idée évidente que chaque peuple a une histoire.

---

13   Cheikh M'Backé Diop, *Cheikh Anta Diop: L'homme et l'oeuvre* (Paris: Présence Africaine, 2003), 52–3.

[It is not a matter of creating a history for oneself which is more beautiful than that of others in order to morally dupe the people during the struggle for independence, but to start from the obvious idea that each people has a history.][14]

Even a cursory reading of academic engagement with *Nations nègres et culture* and Diop's subsequent work reveals a smouldering nest of polemical debate and contestation. This was sparked by Diop's fundamental questioning of the temporality, truth and sociocultural role of historical knowledge, combined with his unorthodox interdisciplinary straddling of Egyptology, classics, history and linguistics. *Nations nègres et culture* made a splash when it was first published in the 1950s. As his early articles and accounts of his public doctoral viva show, Diop's ideas provoked animated responses among the generation of African students and writers living in post-war Paris, many of whom would go on to lead significant political careers following the independences of 1960. While by this point Senghor and Aimé Césaire were developing their political projects in Senegal and Martinique, respectively, Diop's vocal and eloquent presence in Paris enabled him to spread and defend his ideas in settings such as the landmark 1956 Congress of Negro Writers and Artists. His style was not universally praised, however, nor did it translate well across some linguistic divides. Following his presentation in 1956, a young James Baldwin wrote in irritation that Diop 'quite refused to remain within the twenty-minute limit and, while his claims of the deliberate dishonesty of all Egyptian scholars may be quite well founded for all I know, I cannot say that he convinced me. He was, however, a great success in the hall'.[15]

14 Diouf, 'Une interview', 10.
15 James Baldwin, *The Price of the Ticket: Collected Non-Fiction 1948–1985* (London: Michael Joseph, 1985), 57.

Reading *Nations nègres et culture*

Nations nègres et culture is structured in two parts. The first outlines Diop's critique of European historiography; the second presents detailed evidence in support of these arguments. Diop's critique of existing accounts of African history targets the creation of a 'mythe du nègre' by nineteenth-century Egyptologists such as Champollion-Figeac and Maspéro, and an ensuing 'falsification' of ancient history.[16] This falsification, Diop claims, tended to focus on the Asian, Phoenician or Arabic origins of Ancient Egypt, overlooking the ethnological and linguistic connections to sub-Saharan Africa, which are explored in the fourth chapter. Diop considers the two-way movement in traditions of circumcision, kingship, social organization and matriarchal social structures, arguing that ancient texts confirm the black African contribution to these 'phénomènes de civilisation'.[17] It is here that a key divergence between Diop and his intellectual and political rival Senghor emerges, which is key to understanding the early reception of the book. Whereas Senghor's claims for négritude as a political as well as cultural system of thought gathered impetus through their praise of cultural *métissage*, Diop's argument sought chronological clarity and scientific precision to posit a more stridently separatist thesis. 'Civilization' for Diop did not emerge from cultural mixing following the encounter of Indo-Europeans and Africans, since civilization had existed on the African continent well before contact with Indo-Europeans.[18] In other words, *métissage* was to be considered a consequence of civilization created within black Africa, rather than the cause of that civilization.

For Diop, Senghor remained an alienated intellectual wedded to a mistaken belief in the inherent, universal reason contained in European thought and the French language:

> Il est fréquent que des Nègres d'une haute intellectualité restent victimes de cette aliénation au point de chercher à codifier ces idées nazies d'une prétendue

---

16   Diop, *Nations*, 49, 59.
17   Diop, *Nations*, 230.
18   Diop, *Nations*, 231.

dualité du Nègre sensible et émotif, créateur d'art, et du Blanc fait surtout de rationalité.

[Highly intellectual negroes often remain victims of this alienation to the extent that they seek to codify these Nazi ideas of a supposed duality between the sensitive and emotional negro artist, and the rational white.][19]

Contrary to Senghor's commitment to the rationality of the French language, Diop advocated the use of indigenous African languages. The book's second section addresses this linguistic material in more detail, stating the need for national languages. Prefiguring later calls to 'decolonize the mind' that have dominated postcolonial critique, it insists that these languages would re-affirm the basis for local knowledge and understanding.[20] For example, Diop demonstrates that Wolof has the capacity to express scientific and abstract concepts by providing Wolof translations of mathematical concepts and a summary of Einstein's theory of relativity, along with examples of contemporary Wolof poetry.[21] Comparative linguistic evidence (much of which was excised from the English translation of the book in the interest of accessibility) is summoned to demonstrate the filial relationship between Egyptian hieroglyphs, Meroitic language and languages spoken in sub-Saharan Africa. These arguments and their evidence have since been revised – indeed, Diop notes explicitly that his hypothesis seeks to lay the groundwork for future research rather than draw definitive conclusions.[22] Nonetheless, his work as a translator and advocate of the transcription of African languages, allied to the project of writing African history rooted in African experience, was path-breaking in providing a scientific basis for affirming the humanity of black Africans.[23]

---

19   Diop, *Nations*, 54–5.
20   Ngũgĩ wa Thiong'o, *Decolonising the Mind: The Politics of Language in African Literature* (Woodbridge and Rochester, NY: James Currey, 1986).
21   Diop, *Nations*, 415–50.
22   Diop, *Nations*, 235.
23   On Diop as translator, see: Paul Bandia, 'Cheikh Anta Diop. Translation at the service of history', in John Milton and Paul Bandia, eds, *Agents of Translation* (Amsterdam and Philadelphia, PA: John Benjamins Publishing Company, 2009).

The book's final chapters deal with issues in African art and, finally, social and political structures. They are amply illustrated with photographs of Egyptian artefacts, Ifé sculptures, masks and bas-reliefs, which provide visual evidence to support Diop's arguments and are complemented by ancient written sources from Herodotus and Homer to Ibn Battuta and Es Sa'di. At points, the argument is presented as a series of assertions without convincing supporting material, though it has been claimed that Diop was reluctant to include more footnotes so that his work would be more accessible and straightforwardly didactic.[24] Diop encourages his African readers to claim historical continuity with the past and to draw from this 'le bénéfice moral nécessaire pour reconquérir sa place dans le monde moderne, sans se verser dans les excès d'un nazisme à rebours' [the moral benefit necessary for reconquering one's place in the modern world, without ending up in the excesses of an inverted Nazism].[25]

He goes on to assert that cultural and political achievement across the arts, architecture, agriculture and social organization is specific to place rather than race:

> La civilisation [...] eût pu être créée par n'importe quelle autre race humaine – pour autant que l'on puisse parler d'une race – qui eût été placée dans un berceau aussi favorable, aussi unique.
>
> [Civilisation [...] could have been created by any other human race – in as far as we can speak of a race – which had been placed in such a favourable and unique context.][26]

Rather than simply affirming black African achievement in Egypt, Diop at times adopts a moderate and reflective tone. This indicates a nuanced line of enquiry, alert to the specificity of geography and climate, and wary of the dangers of racial essentialism. These dangers were especially acute in France, where Diop was living and writing, during the decade that followed the Nazi occupation of France and led to the period of decolonization. This summary gives a sense of the scope and early reception of Diop's book. Its

---

24 François-Xavier Fauvelle, *L'Afrique de Cheikh Anta Diop* (Paris: Karthala, 1996), 36–7.
25 Diop, *Nations*, 401.
26 Diop, *Nations*, 401.

critique of a European origin for the project of modernity is twinned with an acknowledgement of the disciplinary conventions which emerged from that project in the nineteenth and early twentieth centuries. Indeed, debates surrounding black Egyptians cast ample light on the history of academic disciplines and the geographic divisions sustained by them.[27]

Cheikh Anta Diop in the Twenty-First Century

More recent engagement with Diop's ideas has tended to approach them indirectly, via their influence on others: in particular, the work of Afrocentrists such as Molefi Asante and Théophile Obenga, one of Diop's closest interlocutors. In a compelling, if relentless, critique of Afrocentrism, Stephen Howe dissects and dismisses its claims and methods on the basis of ideological distortion. Defending an empirical historical tradition, Howe claims: 'No one is or can ever possibly be "empowered" or "strengthened" by believing in lies and fantasies [...] They [the "poor, oppressed and under-privileged"] need accurate information about their world more than anyone else, if they are ever to change it'.[28] While this may be valid in essence, it takes little account of the mode by which such 'information' may be communicated, elicited, felt, or indeed ignored, by 'them'. What becomes apparent, when juxtaposing such counterarguments with the legacies of Diop's ideas, from hip-hop lyricists to prominent contemporary thinkers, is that Diop's writing set in motion, and subsequently sustained, a powerful engagement with historical consciousness and its mode of expression as a fundamental basis for asserting humanity in the wake of empire.

I will conclude by turning briefly to those legacies in a recent essay by Senegalese writer Boubacar Boris Diop and the work of prominent hip-hop artist, Didier Awadi. In his homage to Cheikh Anta Diop (C. A. Diop),

27 Robert J. C. Young, 'The Afterlives of *Black Athena*', in Daniel Orrells, Gurminder K. Bhambra and Tessa Roynon, *African Athena*, 184.
28 Howe, *Afrocentrism*, 285.

Boubacar Boris Diop (B. B. Diop) outlines the historian's adversarial relationship with Senghor, and emphasizes above all his calls for national languages and African federalism. As B. B. Diop notes, relatively little is known about Diop's own life (unlike that of Senghor) and he is yet to be the subject of a well-documented critical biography. For B. B. Diop, C. A. Diop is not primarily an Afrocentrist, but rather a carefully situated figure in twentieth-century Senegalese intellectual and political history. The opposition between two national father figures reveals some fundamental divides and paradoxes within Senegalese identity: between C. A. Diop the Mouride Muslim and Wolof figurehead, and the Catholic, Serer personality of Senghor. The essay outlines the men's political differences, emphasizing Senghor's (often over-looked) refusal to recognize the political parties founded by C. A. Diop in the 1970s, or hold fully democratic elections. This political 'family secret', and Senghor's devotion to Francophonie, clouds intellectual appreciation of his poetry in Senegal. For C. A. Diop's work in *Nations nègres et culture*, conversely, B. B. Diop insists on the significance of lending scientific weight to what had been expressed until then 'sur un mode purement émotionnel' [in a purely emotional mode] by the négritude poets.[29] He also notes C. A. Diop's mastery of the Wolof language and his adept performance of linguistic code-switching:

> Il connaissait et parlait à la perfection le wolof du pays profond, poussant souvent la malice – en privé ou pendant ses meetings politiques – jusqu'à le prononcer exactement à la manière de ceux qui n'ont jamais mis les pieds dans une école française.
>
> [He knew perfectly the Wolof spoken out in the sticks, and often used this playfully – whether in private or during political meetings – pronouncing it precisely in the way of someone who had never set foot in a French school.][30]

Nonetheless, C. A. Diop's campaign against neocolonialism and his promotion of national languages remain marginal in contemporary political discourse in Senegal. There is an evident line of descent from C. A. Diop's arguments to B. B. Diop's own work to promote Wolof through his writing

---

29   Boubacar Boris Diop, *L'Afrique au-delà du miroir* (Paris: Philippe Rey, 2007), 112.
30   Diop, *L'Afrique*, 115.

(the novel *Doomi Golo*) and literary translation (the Ceytu collection, launched in 2016, publishes francophone literary 'classics' in Wolof translation).

B. B. Diop accepts that the focus on Ancient Egypt might seem distant or indulgent given urgent socio-economic and political challenges in sub-Saharan Africa. Such reactions are not new. In 1967, the Ugandan poet Okot p'Bitek caricatured the cultural alienation of a Western-educated 'modern' man, Ocol, in 'Song of Ocol'. His speaker rejects all types of historical recuperation:

> Why should I care
> Who built the citadel
> Of Zimbabwe?
> Of what relevance is it
> Whether black men
> Architected the Pyramid?
>
> Smash all these mirrors
> That I may not see
> The blackness of the past
> From which I came
> Reflected in them.[31]

Here these historical 'mirrors' only encourage Ocol's frustration with society's present inertia and his quest for newness. He is ensnared between the rhetoric of a glorious material past and a complex modern reality in which that rhetoric co-exists with alternative perspectives. For Ocol, futurity does not appear dependent on uncovering the past. C. A. Diop's pioneering work in *Nations nègres et culture* linked the recuperation of African history to the project of reinforcing indigenous African languages. That his work elicits responses across anglophone and francophone spaces indicates the power of his ideas as they move beyond the printed page, embodying his conviction that Pan-African ideas must have material effects to match their affective energy. B. B. Diop calls for a moderate appraisal of C. A. Diop's

---

[31] Okot p'Bitek, *Song of Lawino and Song of Ocol* (Dar Es Salaam: East African Educational Publishers, 2013 [1967]), 132.

work within Senegalese post-independence history, a reading that necessarily draws *Nations nègres et culture* away from its more radical disciples.

Returning to the epigraphs with which this chapter began, while intellectuals such as Boubacar Boris Diop have shown where C. A. Diop's ideas are open to contestation and further nuance, since the late 1980s the Senegalese hip-hop scene has forged an arena in which ideas of Afrocentricity and the politics of language and shared history are brought up to date. This scene, known as 'Galsen', reveals a 'poetic, sonic, and stylistic dialogue between Africa and the North Atlantic', which both encapsulates and moves some way beyond the routes towards Pan-African cultural unity that Diop mapped out in *Nations nègres et culture*.[32] To cite an example by one of the best-known Senegalese hip-hop artists, Didier Awadi, the track 'Une seule origine' (2010) fuses samples from Diop's recorded lectures with a live musical score and lyrics in French and Wolof, affirming Africa's role as 'le berceau de l'humanité' [the cradle of humankind].[33] Awadi has noted the importance of maintaining Diop's legacy in local popular consciousness: 'Nous devons connaître nos héros. Au Sénégal par exemple, nous ne connaissons pas l'action de Cheikh Anta Diop. Les Américains en savent plus que nous sur celui qui a donné son nom à l'université' [We must know our heroes. In Senegal, for example, we don't know about Cheikh Anta Diop's actions. The Americans know more than us about the person after whom the university is named].[34] If Galsen mirrors the style and production values of North American hip-hop, its lyrics tend towards more local concerns and linguistic traits, fluently mixing the Urban Wolof spoken in Dakar with French and English, and blending elements of reggae, *mbalax* dance music and griot traditions. Transnational trends mix with national politics and the complex role of Sufi Islam in the region. In this light, Diop's calls for national languages and, in particular, the recuperation of African

32 Ali Colleen Neff, 'Senegalese hip-hop', in Justin A. Williams, ed., *The Cambridge Companion to Hip-Hop* (Cambridge: Cambridge University Press, 2015), 271.
33 Didier Awadi, 'Une seule origine', *Présidents d'Afrique*, 2010.
34 Fatou Kandé Senghor, *Wala Bok: Une histoire orale du hip hop au Sénégal* (Dakar: Editions Amalion, 2015), 181.

history, find new audiences and outlets, shaped by the socio-economic and cultural contexts of twenty-first-century Senegal.³⁵

Though much research remains to be done into this medium's critical framing and its mobilization of Diop's agency, these brief examples point to the iconicity of his work, and its translatability into popular forms. Towards the close of the track, Awadi includes the following brief sample from one of Diop's seminars:

> Formez-vous, armez-vous de Sciences jusqu'aux dents [...] et arrachez votre patrimoine culturel. Ou alors traînez-moi dans la boue si, quand vous arriverez à cette connaissance directe vous découvrez que mes arguments sont inconsistants, c'est cela, mais il n'y a pas d'autres voies.
>
> [Train yourselves, arm yourselves to the teeth with science [...] and take back your cultural heritage. Or drag me through the mud if, when you get to that direct knowledge, you discover that my arguments are inconsistent; there is no other way forward.]

Diop's call for rigorous enquiry and ongoing revision, (re)framed here by the beat of an engaged hip-hop aesthetic, are sometimes marginalized characteristics of his work. On closer analysis, this track incites listeners to engage seriously with the process of history-making, rather than accepting or simply repeating a dominant historical paradigm (whether Eurocentric or Afrocentric). That concern with making history is a key element of transatlantic hip-hop culture, emphasizing the form's close links to Diop's intellectual project in *Nations nègres et culture*.³⁶

In conclusion, *Nations nègres et culture* raises the underlying questions that continued to motivate and inform Diop's subsequent writing, setting an important agenda for postcolonial thought. The book catalysed diverse and powerful strands of Afrocentrism, centred particularly around the thesis of black Egypt. It is clear, however, that Diop's work cannot be

---

35 The recent documentary about Cheikh Anta Diop, *Kemtiyu – Séex Anta* (William Ousmane Mbaye, 2016), is a significant step towards giving renewed visibility to his life and work.
36 See, among others, Tricia Rose, *Black Noise: Rap Music and Black Culture in Contemporary America* (Middletown, CT: Wesleyan University Press, 1994).

solely reduced to this. His book drew on linguistics, science and history in ways that continue to inform and provoke critical thinking in Senegal, while advocating greater overlap between academic and popular discourses. *Nations nègres et culture* affirms the need to cultivate alternative points of view within dominant systems of thought, while remaining attentive to the divergent local contexts in which those perspectives emerge.

Bibliography

Appiah, Kwame Anthony, *In My Father's House: Africa in the Philosophy of Culture* (Oxford: Oxford University Press, 1992).
Baldwin, James, *The Price of the Ticket: Collected Non-Fiction 1948–1985* (London: Michael Joseph, 1985).
Bandia, Paul, 'Cheikh Anta Diop. Translation at the service of history', in John Milton and Paul Bandia, eds, *Agents of Translation* (Amsterdam and Philadelphia, PA: John Benjamins Publishing Company, 2009).
Bernal, Martin, *Black Athena: The Afroasiatic Roots of Classical Civilisation*, i. *The Fabrication of Ancient Greece, 1785–1995* (New Brunswick, NJ: Rutgers University Press, 1987).
Césaire, Aimé, *Discours sur le colonialisme* (Paris: Présence Africaine, 2004 [1955]).
Diop, Boubacar Boris, *L'Afrique au-delà du miroir* (Paris: Philippe Rey, 2007).
——, *Doomi Golo* (Dakar: Editions Papyrus Afrique, 2012).
Diop, Cheikh Anta, *The African Origin of Civilization: Myth or Reality*, ed. and trans. Mercer Cook (Chicago: Lawrence Hill Books, 1974).
——, *Nations nègres et culture* (Paris: Présence Africaine, 1979 [1954]).
Diouf, Bara, 'Une interview exclusive de Cheikh Anta Diop', *La Vie Africaine* 6 (1960).
Fauvelle, François-Xavier, *L'Afrique de Cheikh Anta Diop* (Paris: Karthala, 1996).
Howe, Stephen, *Afrocentrism: Mythical Pasts and Imagined Homes* (London and New York: Verso, 1998).
Kandé Senghor, Fatou, *Wala Bok: Une histoire orale du hip hop au Sénégal* (Dakar: Editions Amalion, 2015).
Keita, Maghan, 'Believing in Ethiopians', in Daniel Orrells, Gurminder K. Bhambra and Tessa Roynon, eds, *African Athena*, 19–39.
Lefkowitz, Mary R., and Guy MacLean Rogers, eds, *Black Athena Revisited* (Chapel Hill: University of North Carolina Press, 1996).

M'Backé Diop, Cheikh, *Cheikh Anta Diop: L'homme et l'oeuvre* (Paris: Présence Africaine, 2003).
Neff, Ali Colleen, 'Senegalese hip-hop', in Justin A. Williams, ed., *The Cambridge Companion to Hip-Hop* (Cambridge: Cambridge University Press, 2015). 271–9.
Ngũgĩ wa Thiong'o, *Decolonising the Mind: The Politics of Language in African Literature* (Woodbridge and Rochester, NY: James Currey, 1986).
Orrells, Daniel, Gurminder K. Bhambra, and Tessa Roynon, eds, *African Athena: New Agendas* (Oxford: Oxford University Press, 2011).
p'Bitek, Okot, *Song of Lawino and Song of Ocol* (Dar Es Salaam: East African Educational Publishers, 2013 [1967]).
Rose, Tricia, *Black Noise: Rap Music and Black Culture in Contemporary America* (Middletown, CT: Wesleyan University Press, 1994).
Young, Robert J. C., 'The Afterlives of *Black Athena*', in Daniel Orrells, Gurminder K. Bhambra and Tessa Roynon, eds, *African Athena*, 174–88.

ASHA ROGERS

11 Culture in Transition: Rajat Neogy's *Transition* (1961–1968) and the Decolonization of African Literature

ABSTRACT

Transition, the Ugandan literary magazine edited by Rajat Neogy, sought to create an autonomous East African culture in the aftermath of decolonization. Publishing leading intellectuals and writers from across the continent such as Wole Soyinka, Chinua Achebe, Ali Mazrui and Es'kia Mphahlele, neither the outgoing imperialists nor Milton Obote's overbearing nationalist regime were exempt from its challenge. Neogy's imprisonment for sedition in 1968 consolidated the magazine's resistant position. However, the case of *Transition* also raises larger questions about the relationship between politics and print. By bringing into view the liberal institutions that funded and protected such ventures in the decolonizing world, notably the Congress for Cultural Freedom but also Amnesty International, *Transition* asks important questions about how we conceive of resistance in the long twentieth century.

Launched in Kampala by the self-styled literary beatnik Rajat Neogy (1938–95), *Transition* had one eye on metropolitan modernism and another on establishing an authentic local culture in the vacuum created by the British withdrawal from East Africa in 1962. *Transition*'s project was positively rather than negatively framed, intended not to combat imperialism, but to assert an invigorated cultural life on its own terms and in its place. Committed to publishing creative writing of merit, Neogy's journal was a blueprint for literary and intellectual production in 1960s anglophone Africa.[1] It furthered the early careers of leading postcolonial writers: at least

---

1   *Transition* has been remarkably durable, and I use the term 'Neogy's *Transition*' to refer specifically to the Kampala years when the magazine was under his editorship.

two of the continent's foremost novels of postcolonial resistance (Chinua Achebe's *Arrow of God* (1964) and *A Grain of Wheat* (1967) by Ngũgĩ wa Thiong'o) started out in the magazine. Equipped with a quietly confident black Atlanticism, *Transition* maintained a transnational cosmopolitan perspective in the face of postcolonial nationalism and Cold War antagonism.

Transition deliberately did not divorce its aesthetic commitment to culture on its own terms from the pressing social and political realities that surrounded it, which included growing anxieties about its Africanness (and that of its Bengali editor) in an ethnically divided region. As antinational as it was anti-imperial, neither the outgoing British colonial authorities nor Uganda's overbearing political elite were exempt from its censure. Within a few short years the magazine would publicly intervene in the narrowing down of Ugandan political life. Neogy's arrest for sedition in 1968, and his subsequent adoption as a prisoner of conscience by Amnesty International, consolidated the magazine's resistant position and assured it a global status.

The case of *Transition* raises both material and structural questions about how we understand the relationship between print and resistance in the long twentieth century. As a periodical, its inbuilt polyvocalism worked against the monumentality of 'the book' and of authorship conventionally interpreted, and instead rivalled the 'extensive network of periodicals that carpeted Empire'.[2] At the same time, *Transition* brings into view the structures that propped up resistance, as decolonization intersected with the Cold War in the non-aligned Third World. Part-financed by the Congress for Cultural Freedom, an organization with funds traceable to the CIA, *Transition* exemplifies the funding complexities undergirding the print outlets dismantling empire, particularly those committed to artistic or political freedom.[3]

---

2   Antoinette Burton and Isabel Hofmeyr, 'Introduction: The Spine of Empire? Books and the Making of an Imperial Commons', in Antoinette Burton and Isabel Hofmeyr, eds, *Ten Books That Shaped the British Empire: Creating an Imperial Commons* (Durham, NC and London: Duke University Press, 2014), 4.

3   Giles Scott Smith has termed this 'the politics of apolitical culture'. See Scott Smith, *The Politics of Apolitical Culture: The Congress for Cultural Freedom, The CIA, and Post-War American Hegemony* (London: Routledge, 2002).

Neither glossy magazine nor serious scholarly volume, *Transition* falls outside of conventional definitions we normally ascribe to 'the book'. Nonetheless, the ephemeral qualities of a periodical (often published irregularly) can aid how we understand the relationship between print and political resistance in the African sphere. As Caroline Davis and David Johnson have reiterated recently, to talk of 'the book' *and* or *in* 'Africa' is to register a long and chequered history partly bound up in the forces of colonization.[4] By contrast, *Transition* and its counterparts in the 1960s like *Black Orpheus* operated in the tradition of the cyclostyled 'little magazines' emerging out of the universities: in West Africa, the student poetry magazine *The Horn*, in the East, the University of Makerere's *Penpoint*. In South Africa, the cosmopolitan *Drum* magazine contrasted with lo-fi anti-apartheid newssheets such as *The Voice*, produced in the Orlando township just outside of Johannesburg.[5] As this chapter argues, then, it is precisely the vulnerability and versatility of a publication like *Transition* that can transform our understanding of 'the book', alerting us to a multitude of small-scale literary and political acts and encounters. *Transition*, like the Heinemann African Writers Series, created a space for literary and critical intervention in the decolonizing world, yet with none of the heavy lumber of the AWS's institutional framework, however adaptable the latter sought to be. Although seemingly unbookish – particularly when compared to the thick paper and hard spine of *Black Orpheus* – it was ultimately *Transition*'s status as a print object that mobilized its supporters in the US foundations, and struck fear into its detractors in the Ugandan state.

---

4   Caroline Davis and David Johnson, eds, *The Book in Africa: Critical Debates* (Basingstoke: Palgrave Macmillan, 2015).
5   Mphahlele brought experience of both *The Voice* and *Drum*, where he was fiction editor, to the CCF's African programme. See Corinne Sandwith, *A World of Letters: Reading Communities and Cultural Debates in Early Apartheid South Africa* (Durban: University of Kwazulu-Natal Press, 2014), 216–43.

Culture in Transition

Transition was founded in 1961 by Neogy, a Ugandan of Bengali descent recently returned to Kampala from study at the University of London. For Neogy, *Transition* was first and foremost a literary-cultural review designed to spark new creative and intellectual interventions in the wake of colonial retreat. This 'Journal of the Arts, Culture and Society', as the subtitle of its early issues indicated, had a specifically literary objective, as well as one that was more broadly cultural. Modelled on the Nigerian little magazine *Black Orpheus*, founded by the German émigré Ulli Beier in 1960, Neogy sought to stimulate a modern literary and cultural movement in East Africa. Given economies of space and the alternative publishing opportunities available for novels (Heinemann had launched its African Writers Series in 1962), *Transition* typically published poetry and short stories, though plays, fictional extracts, translations and transcribed forms of orature were also featured. Controversially for some, literary and critical contributors included European and American expatriates such as Paul Theroux and Gerald Moore, and (less controversially) African American and Caribbean writers such as Langston Hughes and Denis Williams. Regular African contributors included Achebe, Wole Soyinka and Christopher Okigbo from Nigeria; South African writers such as Bessie Head, Richard Rive, Dennis Brutus and Nadine Gordimer; John Nagenda from Uganda; and Rebecca Njau and Ngũgĩ from Kenya. The lively and tendentious letters pages documented *Transition*'s international reach, not least in the US where it was heralded by *The New York Times* as 'Africa's slickest, sprightliest and occasionally sexiest magazine'.[6]

Transition provided the material and conceptual conditions for a resistant African critical discourse, publishing Obiajunwa Wali's provocative essay 'The Dead End of African Literature?' in Issue 10, Achebe's proclamations on 'English and the African Writer' in Issue 18, and Soyinka's

---

[6] Alfred Friendly Jr, 'Slick African Magazine Gains a Wide Following', *The New York Times* (11 August 1968), 3.

'The Writer in an African State' in Issue 31. These pieces on the worldly context of African literature reflected Neogy's own self-conscious efforts to use the magazine to 'culture' – that is, to grow or to stimulate – debate. He famously declared his editorial responsibilities by announcing that 'a well-edited magazine should, like sour milk, be capable of perpetuating itself. One issue should have enough germs to be capable of generating another'.[7] In this respect, *Transition* was successful. As the critic Bernth Lindfors commented at the time, the magazine was the 'least antiseptic' of all African publications and the most capable of 'spreading germs in all directions'.[8]

The magazine was underpinned by a conscious desire to capture the cutting edge of an autonomous East African culture. As Neogy observed in his opening editorial, titled 'Culture in Transition' and written the year before Ugandan Independence:

> Africa is undergoing various and exciting changes. It is a time when idealism and action merge with various degrees of success. It is also a time for testing intellectual and other preconceptions and for thoughtful and creative contributions in all spheres. One of the questions this journal will address itself to is: What is an East African culture?[9]

Surprisingly, given the atmosphere of cultural as well as political independence from the British metropole, Neogy drew on T. S. Eliot's conjectures about Englishness to develop his vision for what a decolonized East African culture should look like. Quoting from *Notes Towards the Definition of Culture* (1948), Neogy listed Eliot's fancy for 'Wensleydale cheese, boiled cabbage cut into sections, beetroot in vinegar, 19th century Gothic churches and the music of Elgar' as metonyms for an Englishness that was troubled neither by its Eurocentrism nor Eliot's own status as a self-made Englishman and an outsider. Neogy appropriated Eliot's essentialist and whimsical logic

---

7   Rajat Neogy, 'Do Magazines Culture?', *Transition* 24 (1966), 32.
8   Bernth Lindfors, Letter, *Transition* 26 (1966), 5.
9   Rajat Neogy, 'Culture in Transition', *Transition* 1 (1961), 2.

as a model for his own ends.[10] 'These are some aspects of English culture', he mused, before asking, 'What is East African?'

Despite its high literary beginnings, by the mid-1960s concerns had grown about the under-privileging of literature in *Transition*. The critic John Nagenda, a former editor of the Makerere College's little magazine *Penpoint*, warned that the magazine's success as a journal of current affairs put its 'original intention' at risk.[11] However, the flexible relationship that *Transition* maintained between the literary and the political, and between cultural versus social critique, was more complex than prevailing accounts allow. The magazine expressed its aesthetic commitments less in terms of literary purity or the exclusion of 'non-literary' content than in the cultivation of an intellectual openness to difference. Neogy conceived of *Transition*'s broad focus as providing a distinctly fertile context for literature, rather than one that deprived it of attention. Indeed, he would gladly provoke readers of *Transition* who complained of 'too much poetry'. In his introduction to one issue, he delightedly suggested that it was 'bound to be an offender'.[12]

Transition's literary commitments also had a bearing on anxieties about its Africanness. When questioned in interviews about the racial profile of the magazine's writers and readers, Neogy tended to elide narrow questions of race in favour of a more universal set of commitments, preferring to talk of his 'ideal conception' of the magazine, and the 'standards [...] implicit in the material', rather than in the racial or ethnic affiliation of its writers.[13]

---

10 This argument is taken further by Peter Kalliney in 'Modernism, African Literature, and the Cold War', *Modern Language Quarterly* 76/3 (2015), 333–68.

11 John Nagenda, 'Review of Transition no. 9', *African Writers Club*, Transcription Centre recording (n. d.).

12 'We receive complaints whenever some of our readers feel an issue contains too much poetry. This issue is bound to be an offender. There is quite a lot of poetry. But we do not feel we have to apologise for this'. Rajat Neogy, *Transition* 3 (1962), 6.

13 In one interview for the Transcription Centre, contributor Es'kia Mphahlele waded in to waylay the interviewer's dogged efforts to make Neogy name individual readers. Mphahlele offered an anecdote about a Nairobi shopkeeper who was an avid reader of *Transition*, though given the racial essentialism that lurked beneath the question, he did not mention the reader's name. See 'Interview with Rajat Neogy and Es'kia Mphahlele', *African Writers Club*, Transcription Centre recording (n. d. [c. 1963]).

Transition's resistance might therefore be understood in at least two ways: first, through its opposition to 'facile standards and answers',[14] a goal it expressed by publishing everything from James Baldwin's stark social realism to Christopher Okigbo's notoriously difficult 'Ibadan modernism'; and second, by cultivating an African print modernity positioned outside of commercialized mass culture.[15] *Transition* thus expressed its commitment to literature not only by the quality of what it published, but also by its location outside the parameters of the sensationalist news media. In a paper insert announcing a special introductory offer for subscription, Neogy conceded that 'revolutionary changes' had taken place in the East African print and news media, all of which indicated a 'healthy' democratic trajectory.[16] Yet, he declared, 'TRANSITION is not a journal which is involved in this competition'. Describing it as a monthly 'reflection' of East African affairs (whose 'constant aim' was to 'search and encourage writers and poets from East Africa'), Neogy distinguished *Transition* from its media competitors, marking it out as a publication requiring longer temporal cycles of writerly contemplation and editorial deliberation, and slower modes of reading, than a daily newspaper or weekly magazine. Starting with an initial print run of 2,000 copies in 1961, production of the journal ran up to 12,000 copies at its peak in 1968 – though, as Neogy astutely pointed out, 'in Africa you should multiply that by about 10 for the number of readers'.[17]

However, Neogy's high cultural positioning of the magazine and assurances to readers of its intellectual sophistication when compared to the popular press were undermined by its reliance on commercial advertising.

14   Louis James, 'The Protest Tradition', in Cosmo Pieterse, ed., *Protest & Conflict in African Literature* (London: Heinemann Educational, 1969), 120.
15   The term is taken from Nathan Suhr-Sytsma, 'Ibadan modernism: Poetry and the literary present in mid-century Nigeria', *Journal of Commonwealth Literature* 48/1 (2013), 41–59.
16   'An Introductory Offer', *Transition* 1 (1961).
17   Friendly Jr, 'Slick African Magazine Gains a Wide Following', 3; Pendennis, 'Voice of Africa', *The Observer* (14 July 1968), 34.

Advertisements from the Uganda Tourist Association regularly greeted *Transition*'s international readers; more worrying were those for products such as Coca-Cola (see Figure 11.1). Dependent on reader subscriptions and local advertising, the economic vulnerability of the magazine left it dangerously susceptible to foreign interference. Indeed, the advertisement for Coca-Cola that accompanied Neogy's inaugural editorial arguably undermined the magazine's self-proclaimed intellectual sophistication. As a product synonymous with Brand America, free and available to all – especially the non-aligned Third World – Coke targeted *Transition*'s younger readers, promoting American cultural ideals of affluence ('after you pour there's still lots more'), dominance (the king-size bottle), and a consumer-based community ('there's Coke to spare when you want to share'). Positioned dangerously close to Neogy's Eliotic ruminations on autonomous culture, the advertisement was emblematic of the transfer of power taking place in the 1960s from Pax Britannica to Pax Americana and the lurking threat of cultural imperialism.[18] Twinned on the page, the advertisement and editorial were emblematic of Neogy's anxieties about the diluting effects of mass culture. They demonstrated the competing visions of modernity and modernization running through *Transition*, rendering all too starkly the tensions in Neogy's vision.

Global Sponsors, Government Readers

Clearly, Neogy's cultural ambitions required support from outside of the market if they were to survive. Sponsorship by the international Congress for Cultural Freedom (CCF) ensured that *Transition* would be dependent on neither commercial advertising nor the Ugandan state. Neogy approached

---

18   See Reinhold Wagnleitner on 'Cocacolonialization' as a historical concept in post-war Europe. Wagnleitner, *Coca-colonization and the Cold War: The Cultural Mission of the United States in Austria after the Second World War*, trans. Diana M. Wolf (Chapel Hill and London: University of North Carolina Press, 1994).

TRANSITION

Culture in Transition

This journal appears when East Africa is undergoing various and exciting changes. It is a time when idealism and action merge with various degrees of success. It is also a time for testing intellectual and other preconceptions and for thoughtful and creative contributions in all spheres. One of the questions this journal will address itself to is: «What is an East African culture?» Much is included in this word «culture». T.S. Eliot has written it includes all the characteristic activities and interests of a people: Derby Day, Henley, Regatta, Cowes, the twelfth of August, a cup final, the dog races, the pin table, the dart board, Wensleydale cheese, boiled cabbage cut into sections, beetroot in vinegar, 19th century Gothic churches and the music of Elgar. These are some aspects of English culture. What is East African?

In future issues we hope to devote space to articles of scientific interest, science being one of the two cultures, and also to news of developments in the medical world where several new advances have recently taken place.
The next issue (December) is a special Tanganika number with several contributions by Tanganikans and others, and is published to mark her birth as an independent nation.
Also in this issue will be printed TRANSITION's choice of the best play performed at the Uganda Drama Festival. There is also an original, and hitherto unpublished short story for children by Edward Fry, a Fulbright lecturer at Makerere. John Butler writes on the Individual and the Establishment, the first of a series which will inquire into individuality within the special context of Africa. Abu Mayanja will follow with the second article.
David Cook, Lecturer in English at the University of Southhampton writes about his short visit to Uganda, where he hopes to return. Semei Nyanzi, lecturer in Economics at Makerere will write on the prospects of an East African Common Market. There will also be book reviews including «Kwame Nkrumak and the Future of Africa» by John Phillips, reviewed by Geoffrey Engholm; and prose, poetry and other criticism.
Erisa Kironde has been investigating changing notions of beauty, and we shalls print his findings - « In Search of Black Venus» in the near future.

Figure 11.1: The inaugural editorial by Rajat Neogy, *Transition*, Issue 1 (1961), 2. Reprinted with permission of Indiana University Press.

the CCF's funding representative Ezekiel (later Es'kia) Mphahlele in 1962 after three self-funded issues, and what began as an agreement to clear Neogy's debts was formalized into an arrangement to fund bi-monthly issues of the magazine. The CCF thus came to support postcolonial Africa's most dynamic cultural outlet of the 1960s. *Transition* became the Eastern vertex of the republic of African letters over which Mphahlele presided, a triangulated network of CCF-financed little magazines sharing poetry, short stories, and criticism from each of the regions of sub-Saharan Africa.[19]

The CCF was founded in Berlin in 1950 as a response to the ground gained by the USSR among left-leaning intellectuals, writers and artists. Motivated by what it perceived as the 'positive obligation' to offer 'new and constructive answers to the problems of [its] time', the CCF took steps to globalize its liberal principles by undertaking a comprehensive programme of worldwide cultural sponsorship.[20] In particular, the CCF was committed to the social, cultural and political significance of literary magazines. Under the influence of the Chicago sociologist Edward Shils, it was convinced that a publication like *Transition* could create a liberal elite in postcolonial East Africa. The notoriously high mortality rate for little magazines – especially in economically underdeveloped regions – made them all the more deserving of outside subsidy. Meanwhile, from the perspective of journals like *Transition*, the CCF was an ideal patron: its strong anti-interventionism (lest it be accused of neocolonial interference) and supposedly apolitical stance equated to full editorial freedom. Thus, when questioned about *Transition*'s financial sustainability, Neogy confessed to having been 'rather glad that [the CCF] have been able to help us, because one of our primary concerns was to remain as independent as possible'; he continued, 'the way the Congress has given us help [...] has been really

---

19 *Transition* was flanked by the journals *Black Orpheus* in West Africa and *The Classic* in South Africa.
20 See Peter Coleman, *The Liberal Conspiracy: The Congress for Cultural Freedom and the Struggle for the Mind of Postwar Europe* (London and New York: Free Press, 1989), 249–51.

without any kind of influence'.²¹ This would be a crucial qualification: by late 1967, revelations about covert funding links between the private trusts behind the CCF and the CIA would be splashed across the pages of *The New York Times*, threatening to discredit the organization and its projects.

Transition's roots in a version of European cosmopolitanism ensured a sufficient, albeit superficial, endorsement of the CCF's Euro-American liberalism.²² In practice, however, it was not a straightforward fit: occasional Marxist commentary and debates on African socialism accompanied characteristically provocative pieces. One piece by a Russian translator of Richard Rive, Achebe and Lewis Nkosi calculated that over 7 million books by African writers had been published in the USSR, and advised publishers in search of authors, as well as writers looking for translators, to connect 'through the editorial board of the magazine *Transition*'.²³ Such articles highlight the complexity of the magazine's position amid international development agendas inexorably bound up with Cold War imperatives.

These tensions accelerated unexpectedly in the late 1960s as the magazine found itself at the centre of a direct struggle with the Ugandan state. True to his 'sour milk' ethos, Neogy printed a number of pieces critiquing changes to the Ugandan constitution that would consolidate the power of the ruling regime.²⁴ Two particularly provocative pieces in *Transition* 32 and 34 – by opposition MP Abu Mayanja and a university student writing under the pseudonym Steve Lino – triggered the 1968 arrest of the contributors, the editor and even the printer for sedition. Though the journal had been brought to its knees, President Obote was somewhat paradoxically still eager for *Transition* to continue in order to model Uganda's liberal image.²⁵ Indeed, the source of the Obote government's displeasure was not

21   Rajat Neogy, 'African Intellectualism. Interview with Lewis Nkosi', *African Writers Club*, Transcription Centre recording (n. d. [c. 1965]).
22   The former was signalled by the allusion to Eugene Jolas's interwar avant-garde magazine *transition*.
23   Victor Ramzes, 'African Literature in Russia', *Transition* 25 (1966), 42.
24   Proposals included the political affiliation of the judiciary to the ruling government, and increases to presidential power.
25   These declarations prompted the CCF to explore patenting the name of the magazine, lest a dummy version be set up by state officials.

just *Transition*'s seemingly 'un-Ugandan' content, but also its prestigious status internationally. Questioned on the *Transition* arrests at the 1969 Commonwealth Conference in London, Obote downplayed state repression of the press by identifying himself as a 'very, very religious' reader of *Transition*.[26] Suggesting instead that the case was really about Neogy's involvement with 'certain international organisations' – the revelations of the CIA's links to the CCF had broken the previous year – Obote framed the revised Ugandan constitution as actually protecting press freedom by shielding it from hijacking by 'foreign ideas'.[27]

Acquitted after a lengthy period in solitary confinement, and briefly re-imprisoned under emergency laws, Neogy soon became the subject of widespread international protest. His case rallied not only the CCF but also NGOs like Amnesty in Britain. Indeed, Neogy's strife bolstered these projects considerably by drawing attention to threatened principles such as the liberty of views and freedom of the press.[28] In an article titled 'How It Feels to be a Political Prisoner' published in *The New York Times* shortly after his release in 1969, Neogy described the profound effects of the episode. Despite the widespread promotion of 'Western' concepts of democracy and freedom during decolonization, the plight of Africa's 'real martyrs' persisted; those 'who remain silently behind bars, waiting for justice'.[29]

Yet his article revealed something else: though the CCF was delighted by his release, Neogy's failure to acknowledge the organization as among those lobbying for his freedom (he singled out Amnesty International as representative of the international bodies that had come to his aid) caused

26 Barbara Lapček-Neogy, 'A Matter of Transition', *Transition* 75–76 (1997), 247. For a detailed description of the events see Rajat Neogy, 'Notes in Transition', *Transition* 38 (1971), 43–9. The case against Neogy and Mayanja was heard on 9–11 January 1969 in Kampala. British MP and former solicitor General Dingle Foot acted as Mayanja's legal representation and an observer for Amnesty International.
27 Lapček-Neogy, 'A Matter of Transition', 244.
28 Amnesty's 'Postcards for Prisoners' newsletter featured the case of both Neogy and Mayanja over several months in 1968 and 1969.
29 Rajat Neogy, 'How It Feels to be a Political Prisoner', *The New York Times* (25 October 1969), 32.

considerable trouble for the Congress. Rapidly trying to disentangle itself from the CIA scandal, the CCF faced decreased influence and diminished credibility, and the *Transition* case appeared to be one way in which it might salvage its reputation.[30] Conscious of the two-way flow of symbolic, as well as economic, capital between a journal and its sponsor, the CCF perceived Neogy as having betrayed his side of the deal. 'A line in an article like yours in a paper like [*The New York Times*]', wrote one dejected official to the editor, would have 'secured [the CCF's] reputation' and could 'carry weight with Foundations' in order 'to get outlets like Transition going' again.[31]

Neogy's failure to identify the CCF publicly signalled how rapidly the sponsor had fallen out of favour. Against perceptions of the CCF's brand of Cold War liberalism as outmoded and undeniably tainted, the international human rights organization Amnesty International was clearly a more agreeable choice. Amnesty had been founded in the same year as *Transition*, 1961, by the British lawyer Peter Benenson to mobilize the public in defence of afflicted individuals. The organization grew in profile and stature as the CCF declined, and won the Nobel Peace Prize in 1977 – the year after the last vestiges of the CCF finally disappeared. Whereas the CCF's traditional liberal roots meant it vociferously denied its entanglements with the US government, Amnesty made direct representation to governments, even as it refused state funding, thereby remaining 'resolutely, almost neurotically, non-political'.[32]

The *Transition* case documents the struggle of one incisive if little-known magazine against the might of the nationalist state and of transnational organizations. However, the vastly different fates of the CCF and Amnesty as liberal institutions in the postcolonial world reveals much

---

30   The CCF reformed as the International Association of Cultural Freedom under Ford Foundation Executive Shepherd Stone. Stone was heavily involved in the relocation of *Transition* to Ghana, where the next edition appeared in 1971. In 1973 the editorship was handed over to Soyinka.
31   David Goldstein, Letter to Rajat Neogy, 29 October 1969, International Association for Cultural Freedom archives, Special Collections Research Center, University of Chicago Library, series 2, box 73, folder 2.
32   John de St Jorre, 'Prisoners of Conscience', *The Observer* (17 November 1968), 9.

about the pitfalls and opportunities presented by the Third World for mid-century liberalism. Both defenders of literature's capacity to 'fight' in the world, these contemporaneous bodies shared a belief in the power of words as a means of political action. Whereas Amnesty allocated Neogy's plight to a Dutch group of letter-writers, the Congress rallied devotees of its other journals as well as readers of *Transition* (contributors had already donated their fees to cover legal costs). Obote's response criticized the moralizing of the West. A believer in the written word as well as a 'religious' reader, he pointedly addressed an open letter defending Ugandan justice to 'All Foreign Governments, all Foreign press and journalists, the Syracuse University, U. S. A., Amnesty International, London Headquarters and Branches Overseas'.[33]

Conclusion

Neogy's aim with *Transition* was less to dismantle empire than to cultivate something definitive in its place. As antinational as it was anti-imperial, the magazine sought to establish an East African culture on its own terms. Yet, as this chapter has shown, this most dynamic of literary and cultural outlets of African decolonization was thoroughly contingent on the world outside its East African location, whether through Anglo-European modernism or US mass culture, even before it became entangled in the geopolitics of sponsorship during the Cold War.

Nonetheless, the case of *Transition* has much to suggest about the relationship between print and resistance in the long twentieth century. For one thing, the magazine's small-scale format – constituting a portmanteau assemblage of different elements, intricately connected to contributors, readers, and sister publications – contrasts with the monumentality of both colonial and anticolonial works, indicating something defter and

---

33   Quoted in Rajat Neogy, 'Notes in Transition', *Transition* 38 (1971), 45

harder to trace. Whether through remastering European modernist ideals of aesthetic autonomy to fashion political neutrality during the Cold War, or in making and materializing the otherwise forgotten history of erstwhile literary movements, *Transition* played a central and deeply significant role in galvanizing an African cultural modernism and postcolonial modernity.[34]

However, *Transition* also reminds us of the importance of asking who supported these ventures at this time and why, and of incorporating such questions into frameworks for thinking about the relationship between print and politics. In *Transition*'s case, its literariness, understood as the dogged pursuit of literary freedom, made it more, not less, appealing to the CCF, a sponsor committed to developing cultural enclaves that were critically resistant to the spread of global communism. To explore *Transition*'s example in this way necessarily takes us away from interpreting resistance on 'pure' versus 'impure' terms (as good versus bad money) and toward something more complex and entangled, but ultimately more interesting and affective. The legacy of *Transition* lies partly in the collective agency of the magazine to negotiate these contingencies and, both because and in spite of them, still to cultivate an important and resistant cultural practice.

Bibliography

Bulson, Eric, 'Little Magazine, World Form', in Mark A. Wollaeger and Matt Eatough, eds, *The Oxford Handbook of Global Modernisms* (Oxford: Oxford University Press, 2013), 267–85.

Burton, Antoinette, and Isabel Hofmeyr, 'Introduction: The Spine of Empire? Books and the Making of an Imperial Commons', in Antoinette Burton and Isabel

---

[34] Recent re-evaluations of African little magazines include Simon Gikandi, 'Preface: Modernism in the World', *Modernism/modernity* 13 (2006), 419–24; and Eric Bulson, 'Little Magazine, World Form', in Mark A. Wollaeger and Matt Eatough, eds, *The Oxford Handbook of Global Modernisms* (Oxford: Oxford University Press, 2013), 267–85.

Hofmeyr, eds, *Ten Books That Shaped the British Empire: Creating an Imperial Commons* (Durham, NC and London: Duke University Press, 2014), 1–28.

Coleman, Peter, *The Liberal Conspiracy: The Congress for Cultural Freedom and the Struggle for the Mind of Postwar Europe* (London and New York: Free Press, 1989).

Davis, Caroline, and David Johnson, eds, *The Book in Africa: Critical Debates* (Basingstoke: Palgrave Macmillan, 2015).

De St Jorre, John, 'Prisoners of Conscience', *The Observer* (17 November 1968), 9.

Eliot, T. S., *Notes Towards the Definition of Culture* (London: Faber, 1948).

Friendly, Alfred, Jr, 'Slick African Magazine Gains a Wide Following', *New York Times* (11 August 1968), 3.

Gikandi, Simon, 'Preface: Modernism in the World', *Modernism/modernity* 13 (2006), 419–24.

Goldstein, David, Letter to Rajat Neogy, 29 October 1969, International Association for Cultural Freedom archives, Special Collections Research Center, University of Chicago Library, series 2, box 73, folder 2.

'Interview with Rajat Neogy and Es'kia Mphahlele', *African Writers Club*, Transcription Centre recording (n.d. [c. 1963]).

James, Louis, 'The Protest Tradition', in Cosmo Pieterse, ed., *Protest & Conflict in African Literature* (London: Heinemann Educational, 1969), 109–24.

Kalliney, Peter, 'Modernism, African Literature, and the Cold War', *Modern Language Quarterly* 76/3 (2015), 333–68.

Lapček-Neogy, Barbara, 'A Matter of Transition', *Transition* 75–76 (1997), 244–8.

Lindfors, Bernth, Letter, *Transition* 26 (1966), 5.

Nagenda, John, 'Review of Transition no. 9', *African Writers Club*, Transcription Centre recording (n.d.).

Neogy, Rajat, 'African Intellectualism. Interview with Lewis Nkosi', *African Writers Club*, Transcription Centre recording (n.d. [c. 1965]).

——, 'Culture in Transition', *Transition* 1 (1961), 2.

——, 'Do Magazines Culture?', *Transition* 24 (1966), 30–2.

——, 'How It Feels to be a Political Prisoner', *The New York Times* (25 October 1969), 32.

——, 'An Introductory Offer', *Transition* 1 (1961).

——, 'Notes in Transition', *Transition* 38 (1971), 43–9.

——, *Transition* 3 (1962), 6.

Pendennis, 'Voice of Africa', *The Observer* (14 July 1968), 34.

Ramzes, Victor, 'African Literature in Russia', *Transition* 25 (1966), 40–2.

Sandwith, Corinne, *A World of Letters: Reading Communities and Cultural Debates in Early Apartheid South Africa* (Durban: University of Kwazulu-Natal Press, 2014).

Scott Smith, Giles, *The Politics of Apolitical Culture: The Congress for Cultural Freedom, the CIA, and Post-War American Hegemony* (London: Routledge, 2002).

Suhr-Sytsma, Nathan, 'Ibadan modernism: Poetry and the Literary Present in Mid-Century Nigeria', *Journal of Commonwealth Literature* 48/1 (2013), 41–59.

Wagnleitner, Reinhold, *Coca-colonization and the Cold War: The Cultural Mission of the United States in Austria after the Second World War*, trans. Diana M. Wolf (Chapel Hill and London: University of North Carolina Press, 1994).

JOHN NARAYAN

12 Frantz Fanon's *The Wretched of the Earth* (1961): The Spectre of the Third World Project

ABSTRACT
Since its publication, *The Wretched of the Earth* has become a text to which generations of scholars and activists have returned in order discover their own mission of liberation. Frantz Fanon's take on decolonization and liberation is as relevant today as it was fifty years ago. Whilst commentators often focus on *The Wretched of the Earth* as a manifesto for the emergent Third World Project, what is too frequently forgotten is the neo-imperial future that Fanon believed humanity was hurtling towards. This chapter argues that *The Wretched of the Earth* remains a text for our time because its premonitions about the pitfalls of the Third World Project, national independence and neo-imperialism have come to pass in the formation and hegemony of neoliberal globalization. The book, and its evocation of an alternative 'project' of human liberation, continues to haunt our geopolitical order because Fanon foresaw the conditions of our neo-imperial present.

> I get Huey's book, *The Wretched of the Earth* by Frantz Fanon. I lie down, unconscious of my family's presence, my mind totally absorbed with the Party and politics, eager to absorb the lessons of what Huey called 'the black bible'.[1]

Ex-Black Panther Chief of Staff David Hilliard's description of his first encounter with Frantz Fanon's (1925–61) *The Wretched of the Earth* is telling. 'The black bible' was recommended to him by Black Panther leader, Huey P. Newton, and Hilliard initially struggled with Jean-Paul Sartre's preface. He reached for the 'dictionary' after finding himself 'lost' in the 'foreign language' of Fanon's most famous work. That night, Hilliard drove

---

1   David Hilliard and Lawrence Cole, *This Side of Glory: The Autobiography of David Hilliard and the Story of the Black Panther Party* (Boston, MA: Little, Brown, 1993), 121.

to Newton's house, 'furious' with him for recommending such a 'bedeviling book', and angry with himself 'for not understanding it'. However, Newton convinced Hilliard to persevere, and after redoubling his efforts with the text, Hilliard came to the startling conclusion that in *The Wretched of the Earth*, Fanon was talking not only about the peasants, but 'about us, myself, J. J. Ernest, Chico'.[2]

Since its publication in 1961, *The Wretched of the Earth* has been a touchstone text for numerous struggles and resistances. In Hilliard's case, Fanon's text travelled some 6,000 miles from the Algerian War of Independence to the Black Power movement in Oakland, California.[3] The book's ability to travel is rooted in its evocation of a sense of immediacy in its reader. As Hilliard's story makes clear, *The Wretched of the Earth* seemed to speak directly to him, convincing him that Fanon was talking about the experiences of not only rural peasants in Algeria, but also Afro-Americans living in poverty-stricken inner cities across America. From the revolutionary activities of national independence movements across the Third World to the revolutionary suicide of the Black Panthers, and the postcolonial scholarship of Edward Said, Gayatri Spivak and Homi Bhabha (among many others), *The Wretched of the Earth* has functioned as an essential companion for multiple struggles.

This chapter explores the immediacy of *The Wretched of the Earth*. Whilst commentators generally agree that the book outlines the dreams of the emergent Third World, they frequently forget that Fanon believed humanity was heading towards a neo-imperial future at great speed.[4]

---

2   Hilliard and Cole, *This Side of Glory*, 121–2.
3   What the English-speaking world has come to know as *The Wretched of the Earth* was originally published in French in 1961 as *Les Damnés de la Terre*. Fanon's text, along with Sartre's preface, was first translated into English in 1963 by Constance Farrington under the title *The Damned*. This translation was reprinted by Grove Press as *The Wretched of the Earth* in 1965 and became the standard English translation of the text for over forty years. In 2004 Richard Philcox updated the translation, correcting many of the typographical errors and awkward translations in Farrington's text.
4   This chapter deliberately adopts the contentious term 'Third World' in the light of its extensive use by anticolonial writers during the period of formal decolonization, as outlined by Vijay Prashad.

This chapter will argue that *Wretched* remains a text of our time because Fanon's premonitions of the limits of the Third World Project, national independence and neo-imperialism have come to pass in the formation of a hegemonic neoliberal globalization. The discussion is divided into three parts. The first outlines how the book presents a Third World 'manifesto', which centres on the hope that decolonization will deliver an expanded humanism encompassing all of humanity. The second section outlines how Fanon believed such a vision was unlikely in the short term because of neo-imperialism and the pitfalls of national liberation. The final section addresses how Fanon's vision of the postcolonial world is still relevant today because of its foresight about what was likely to follow colonialism. *The Wretched of the Earth*, and its evocation of an alternative 'project' of human liberation, continues to haunt our geopolitical order because in it Fanon anticipated our neo-imperial present long before it fully materialized.

Third World Dreams

> The Third World today is facing Europe as one colossal mass whose project must be to try and solve the problems this Europe was incapable of finding the answers to.[5]

The Wretched of the Earth is a revolutionary text.[6] For Fanon, the onset of decolonization in the middle of the twentieth century signalled the greatest insurrection in human history. European empires that had dominated vast swathes of the globe for over 400 years disintegrated in a few decades. This shattering of the European-centred world was driven by the rise and unity

---

5   Frantz Fanon, *The Wretched of the Earth* (Grove Press, 2004 [1963]), 238.
6   My argument here and in the next section are drawn from John Narayan, 'Fanon's Decolonized Europe: The Double Promise of Coloured Cosmopolitanism in the Age of Austerity', in John Narayan and Gurminder K. Bhambra, eds, *European Cosmopolitanism: Colonial Histories and Postcolonial Societies* (London: Routledge, 2016), 153–71.

of what Vijay Prashad has called the Third World's 'darker nations'.[7] Third World unity initially pivoted on what W. E. B. Du Bois had famously called the preeminent problem of the twentieth century: the 'color-line', which Reiland Rabaka explores in his chapter in this volume.[8] This was the dark meridian along which Western imperialism had divided the world into blocs of light and dark races. Anticolonial protagonists turned the color-line to their own advantage, forging unity between 'dark' or 'coloured' peoples and nations across the world. This unity centred on a common history of colonial exploitation and a political present of pursuing national independence under a climate of Western neo-imperialism.

Prashad, echoing Fanon, argues that the Third World 'was not a place' but a 'project'.[9] Under the rubric of the 'Third World', the coloured world would come together to liberate those who had been denied access to the economic and democratic fruits of European modernity, and to avoid the *fait accompli* that was the Cold War's mutually assured nuclear destruction. The political embodiment of this project took place in 1955 at the first Afro-Asian Conference in Bandung, Indonesia, where national leaders such as Jawaharlal Nehru, Gamal Abdel Nasser and Kwame Nkrumah pledged transcontinental unity in support of anti-imperialism and the development of the darker nations. Through organizations such as the Non-Aligned Movement (NAM), and later the UN Group of 77 (G77) and the United Nations Conference on Trade and Development (UNCTAD), the Third World would critique neo-imperialism and pursue planetary democracy and justice.[10]

---

7   Vijay Prashad, *The Darker Nations: A People's History of the Third World* (New York: The New Press, 2007), xv.
8   W. E. B. Du Bois, *The Souls of Black Folk: Essays and Sketches* (Oxford: Oxford University Press, 2007 [1903]).
9   Prashad, *The Darker Nations*, xv.
10 Vijay Prashad, *The Poorer Nations: A Possible History of the Global South* (London: Verso, 2013), 1–13. See also Giuliano Garavini, *After Empires: European Integration, Decolonization, and the Challenge from the Global South* (Oxford: Oxford University Press, 2012); Christopher Lee, *Making a World after Empire: The Bandung Moment and Its Political Afterlives* (Athens: Ohio University Press, 2010); Pankaj Mishra, *From the Ruins of Empire: The Revolt against the West and the Remaking of Asia* (London:

The Wretched of the Earth remains enthralling today because the text provides a snapshot of the zenith of the Third World as a political actor. It marks a point in time when the Third World had begun to move with increased political confidence and vigour in global affairs. Nkrumah's ideas about Pan-Africanism had emerged; Nasser had dismissed European powers at Suez; and the Cuban revolution had helped nurture the idea of guerrilla warfare. *Wretched* therefore speaks with confidence about the 'Third World' as an emergent political project, one not reducible to the conduct of the Cold War.

For most first-time readers and many commentators, *Wretched*'s Third World swagger is exemplified in its first chapter's theorization of decolonization as a violent process.[11] Fanon believed decolonial violence was a necessity engendered by the very conditions of colonialism. Colonialism, he wrote, was a 'machine' of 'naked violence', which was not 'capable of thinking' or 'endowed with reason'. Decolonization could only occur when such a machine was confronted with 'greater violence'.[12] However, as *Wretched*'s subsequent chapters made clear, decolonization would have to transcend the Manichean subject positions of 'colonizer' and 'colonized' if it were ever to be more than a repeat of colonial violence.[13] *Wretched*'s idea of liberation is not to be found in its evocation of decolonial violence but in its belief that a new and expanded humanism was possible after the violence of colonization.

    Penguin, 2012); and Mark Mazower, *Governing the World: The History of an Idea* (London: Allen Lane, 2012). For a more critical take on the Third World Project see David Scott, *Conscripts of Modernity: The Tragedy of Colonial Enlightenment* (London: Duke University Press, 2004).

11   The classic take on Fanon as a prophet of unrestrained decolonial violence and ultimate corruptor of the New Left can be found in Hannah Arendt, *On Violence* (New York: Harvest, 2007 [1970]). For a more modern focus see Elizabeth Frazer and Kimberley Hutchings, 'On Politics and Violence: Arendt Contra Fanon', *Contemporary Political Theory* 7/1 (2008), 90–108.

12   Fanon, *Wretched*, 23.

13   This is what Fanon famously called the 'double narcissism' of European colonialism. See Fanon, *Black Skin, White Masks* (New York: Grove Press, 2008 [1961]).

This expanded humanism is outlined in the book's concluding pages. Decolonization had revealed the hypocrisy of European humanism by showing the disjunction between its promises of equality and liberation for all, and its practices of colonialism that enslaved, exploited and often exterminated non-Europeans for economic profit. For Fanon, this disjunction between theory and practice was no mistake, as the West's narcissistic 'spiritual adventure' with humanism had actually justified its capitalist crimes against 'four fifths of humanity'.[14]

Fanon's indictment of Europe was not confined to its economic elites and cultural order, but also included the European masses. He focused on Europe's workers and socialist ideas to argue that humanism, refracted through colonial racism, had corrupted not only Europe's bourgeois but also its proletariat, which had failed to heed Marx and Engels's call for workers of the world to unite. This led to a situation where Europe's workers, and their brand of socialism, had often benefitted and gained from the death and destruction of the colonized outside Europe. Both bourgeois European humanism and European socialism were therefore two sides of the same coin, and their hypocrisy was indicative of a Europe which 'never stops talking of man yet massacres him at every one of its street corners, at every corner of the world'.[15]

This hypocrisy on both the left and the right fuelled Fanon's belief that Europe was now heading at 'dizzying speed towards the brink', soon to be torn apart by its economic and political contradictions as it teetered between atomic destruction and spiritual disintegration.[16] Fanon cautioned that newly independent Third World countries and those seeking independence needed to avoid European models of economic and political development. These paradigms of capitalist modernity were premised, Fanon argued, on the denial of humanism and reliant on the exploitation of humanity and nature. The Third World would have to combine its

---

14 Fanon, *Wretched*, 237.
15 Fanon, *Wretched*, 235.
16 Fanon, *Wretched*, 235–7.

'muscles and brains' to head in a 'new direction', one that moved beyond the limitations of the European project. Fanon believed that this new direction could be pursued through a new, expansive humanism that could support the dual emergence of both democratic national sovereignty and international solidarity that would transcend, and eventually erase, the color-line.

Fanon argued for a redefinition and innovation of humanism within the confines of the Third World nation-state, and what he called 'national consciousness'. He advocated a range of changes at the national and local levels: the creation of anti-capitalist economies and decentralized governments; a reappraisal of the relationship between the rural (peasant) and urban (worker); female equality in reality and not just legislation; the need to limit the power of capital cities; and even the use of sports stadiums for popular rather than commercial interests.[17] In addition, Fanon warned that to avoid Europe's compartmentalization of humanism within ethnocentric boundaries, the Third World would have to realize that it is 'at the heart of national consciousness that international consciousness establishes itself and thrives'.[18] Third World nations would use educative practices to 'develop a human landscape' for the sake of their 'enlightened and sovereign inhabitants', and pursue policies of economic and political cooperation with other Third World nations on regional and global levels. Europe's hypocrisies had shown that the pursuit of humanism at home had to be interrelated with the pursuit of humanism abroad.[19]

---

17   Fanon, *Wretched*, 97–144.
18   Fanon, *Wretched*, 180. See also John Narayan, *John Dewey: The Global Public and its Problems* (Manchester: Manchester University Press, 2016).
19   Fanon, *Wretched*, 238. It should be noted that Fanon's vision of a new and expanded humanism in the Third World did not exclude its former colonizers. Fanon's hopes, albeit faint, were that Europe's masses would realize the implication of their so-called 'socialism' within colonialism and forge a new decolonized Europe that could stand with the Third World and participate in the liberation of all of humanity.

Neo-imperial Nightmares

The Wretched of the Earth's call for a new humanism is intoxicating, designed to convince readers that a better world is possible. In this sense, and as suggested earlier, *Wretched* is best seen as a manifesto and map for the decolonization process, centred around Fanon's plea for the Third World not to follow in the footsteps of the West's capitalist modernity: 'we must look elsewhere besides Europe'.[20] Whilst decolonization had evicted European powers from non-European lands, this had not ended the regime of European imperialism. As *The Wretched of the Earth* states, the 'apotheosis of independence' often became the 'curse of independence'. European powers withdrew their armies from newly independent countries but then surrounded new nations with an 'apparatus of economic pressure', making them once again subservient to European interests. This created a neo-imperial order in which independent Third World countries remained on the periphery of the global economy, providing raw materials and natural resources to industrialized countries in the West, and unable to develop their own industries and infrastructure free of Western interference.[21]

Neo-imperialism was accompanied by what Fanon called a betrayal by the native bourgeoisie. National liberation movements often led to an uneasy alliance between the urban and educated middle classes, who led political movements for independence, and the rural and uneducated masses, whose hopes of 'land and bread' provided the physical energy needed to propel the independence movement towards victory. Fanon predicted the fragmentation of these fragile relationships post-independence. In *Wretched*, he argued that Third World nations were unlikely to develop an adequate national consciousness because of the 'apathy of the national bourgeoisie, its mediocrity, and its deeply cosmopolitan mentality'. Isolated through the West's neo-imperialism, and unable to match the level of education of their metropolitan counterparts, the native bourgeois

---

20   Fanon, *Wretched*, 239.
21   Fanon, *Wretched*, 53–5.

would, Fanon believed, secure their own position and prosperity by acting as 'agents' of Western neo-imperialism. Independence, he lamented, would fail to bring a change of direction. Rather, it would turn the Third World into the 'bordello' of the West.[22]

For Fanon, the postcolonial moment marked the point where the certainty of the colonial-era color-line would be superseded by a less certain, less stable, neo-imperial color-line.[23] With this blurring of the color-line in mind, it becomes clear that Fanon's manifesto for the Third World's expanded humanism was more specifically designed to shape the postcolonial (rather than colonial) world. *Wretched* was aimed not only at Europe's white colonizers but the native bourgeois class and the masses in the Third World. Its enemies were not only European empires and their racial subdivision of wealth, land and humanity, but also the neo-imperialism of the West and the treachery of one-party states, regressive nationalisms and military dictatorships that would come to dominate much of the Third World. In this sense, *Wretched* was a repository for not only the dreams of the Third World Project, but also the nightmares of neo-imperialism that would follow independence.

Spectres of Liberation

How then is *The Wretched of the Earth* relevant today? In a recent polemic attack on Slavoj Žižek, Iranian scholar Hamid Dabashi declared the end of the era of colonialism that Fanon and *Wretched* seemingly represent. Dabashi argues that neoliberal globalization, along with its globalized forms of production, trade and finance, has all but erased the color-line that defined earlier forms of globalization through imperial regimes. In a world of truly global capital, which apparently recognizes neither borders nor colour, the suggestion is that the natives have gone native. There is no

---

22   Fanon, *Wretched*, 97–9, 105–7.
23   Fanon, *Wretched*, 93–4.

longer a white colonizer and coloured colonized but rather a total spectrum of the dominance of capital. Fanon's book can be confined, Dabashi therefore concludes, to the historical dustbin:

> The condition of coloniality that had given intellectual birth to us – from Césaire through Fanon to Said – has run its course. That episteme is no longer producing any meaningful knowledge. We are free, but not aimless; liberated, but not futile. The 'we' is no longer we folks in the global South, for some of us have migrated to the global North chasing after their capital in search of jobs, as their capital had gone positively transnational and chases after our cheap labour in the global South. So this 'we' is no longer colour coded or continental and includes all those disenfranchised by the global cooperation of capital whether in the north or the south.[24]

However, Dabashi misses Fanon's prophetic vision of the nightmare that would engulf the Third World Project. The 'breaking' of the 'colour-coded we' in the name of 'capital' rather than humanism accords exactly with Fanon's fears. Whilst he would have been surprised by neoliberal globalization's disarticulated Fordism, which has seen large transfers of wealth and income from labour to capital in the Global North (Europe and other advanced economies) through a new geography of production and the exploitation of cheap labour across the Third World (or what we today call the Global South), the broad contours of neoliberal globalization align with the world foreseen in *The Wretched of the Earth*. Fanon's anxieties that the Third World would be coerced, through both external and internal forces, to abandon its project of human liberation and take up the norms of capitalist development were well founded. Although *Wretched* did not predict the miraculous economic growth, pockets of extreme wealth, and the emergence of real political power in select countries in the Global South (such as the BRICS bloc), Fanon would not have been surprised that the rise of the South would see its elites and middle classes benefit from the exploitation and impoverishment of their fellow citizens.[25] As a

---

24 Hamid Dabashi, 'Fuck You Žižek!', *Zed Books* (26 July 2016) <https://www.zedbooks.net/blog/posts/fuck-you-zizek> accessed 26 July 2016.

25 This neo-imperial situation is complicated by the BRICS (Brazil, Russia, India, China and South Africa) and their rise as economic powers. The group is best seen

narration of the 'de-Europeanization' of global capital, *Wretched* is all too tragically prescient.

Fanon envisaged that the color-line of imperialism would be blurred, though not erased, in the postcolonial era. Whilst the rise of neoliberal globalization in the 1970s has seen the collapse of Fordism in the Global North, the global economy is still based on the exploitation of non-white labour, and is largely controlled by, and for, Western nations and their multinational corporations.[26] The link between this regime of neo-imperialism and everyday life in the West is all-pervading: it extends from the minerals, resources and labour found in the production of mobile phones, to the cheap shirts that are stitched in the South and worn in the North, and the illicit flows of money from the Global South into the West's banking systems.[27] Today, a blurred color-line divides humanity, cutting across lines of nation and citizenship in a way that still resembles imperial cartography.[28]

However, Fanon's prescience lay not only in his understanding of global capital after decolonization but also in his belief in humanity's redemption. *The Wretched of the Earth* remains committed to liberation through the development of a new humanism inclusive of all humanity. Fanon's hope lay with the masses who, he wrote, 'two or three years' after independence would realize that 'their hopes have been dashed' and that independence, whilst bringing about formal political freedom, has brought about no real

---

as a geopolitical bloc, which is developing its own challenge to the dominance of the Global North. This, however, resembles more a form of inter-imperialist rivalry between neoliberal blocs than the resistance of the Third World Project. See Prashad, *The Poorer Nations*.

26   See Utsa Patnaik and Prabhat Patnaik, 'Imperialism in the Era of Globalization', *Monthly Review* 67/3 (2015) <http://monthlyreview.org/2015/07/01/imperialism-in-the-era-of-globalization> accessed 26 July 2016; John Bellamy Foster, 'The New Imperialism of Globalized Monopoly-Finance Capital', *Monthly Review* 67/3 (2015) <http://monthlyreview.org/2015/07/01/the-new-imperialism-of-globalized-monopoly-finance-capital> accessed 20 December 2015.

27   See John Bellamy Foster, Robert W. McChesney and R. Jamil Jonna, 'The Global Reserve Army of Labour and the New Imperialism', *Monthly Review* 63 (2015), 1–15.

28   On the persistence of racialized capitalism and how Fanon's work on decolonization illuminates its workings, see Narayan, 'Fanon's Decolonized Europe'.

'immediate change' in their life. Fanon believed the ensuing resentment would harbour the potential for either the completion of the decolonization process, or utter destruction: 'Any observer with a keen eye is aware of a kind of latent discontent which like glowing embers constantly threatens to flare up again.'[29] One of the book's overriding messages is that the masses are, and always have been, the agents of liberation.

From The Black Power Revolution in Trinidad to Thomas Sankara's Burkina Faso, the First Palestinian Intifada and the Arab Spring, such mass uprisings have normally been deprived of political oxygen and extinguished through military authoritarianism or neo-imperial meddling. As a result, in the aftermath of the treachery and subterfuge of both the West and elites in the Third World, the energy of the masses has increasingly been targeted by regressive forces of criminality, regressive nationalism or religious fundamentalism, who resent capitalist modernity but offer no worthy form of expanded humanism. But Fanon's text continues to believe in the power of popular uprisings and mass rebellions, drawing on these to hope for a better, more humane and just world – a world still within the grasp of the masses who inhabit the confines of neoliberal globalization.

In South Africa today, students under the banner of Rhodes Must Fall and Fees Must Fall are fighting, often literally, with the state, for the right to a free education. Their fight is against not only privatized higher education but also the ingrained, neoliberal-induced inequality of post-apartheid South Africa, and an African National Congress that has forgotten the tenets of its own people's charter. Concurrently, African Americans are imploring white America to recognize that Black Lives Matter, as they protest against police brutality and extrajudicial murder. Their struggle is not only with the police but also the regime of racialized capitalism that structures American society. Uniting these movements is an increased resentment at the failures of perceived moments of independence (in these cases the end of apartheid and the establishment of civil rights in the US) to secure the political and economic freedoms that would bring about liberation. These movements, and others like them across the world – whether they be the Dalit struggle

---

29   Fanon, *Wretched*, 34–5.

in India, the struggles of indigenous peoples in Latin and North America, or anti-austerity activism in Europe – embody to varying degrees an idea articulated by Fanon: that national consciousness can unite the globally interconnected masses in the struggle for liberation. In this sense, these movements are repositories of the possibilities of the Third World Project, defined by their refusal to be dimmed by the darkness of neo-imperialism.

Wretched's relevance today centres on that fact that it is a text that was written about, and for, these pockets of revolutionary energy in an age in which the color-line has been blurred. Contemporary movements are proof that Fanon's evocation of an alternative project of human liberation still haunts our neoliberal, geopolitical present; that the desire for liberation, as Fanon knew all too well, cannot be eradicated amongst the wretched of the earth, no matter their colour or location. Just as David Hilliard found fifty years ago, *Wretched*'s fighting words continue to provide inspiration, instruction and a sense of solidarity across the globe. Whether in Cape Town, Ferguson, Baltimore, Rio, Mexico City, Addis Ababa, Dakar and Harare or Athens, Madrid and Lisbon, the book waits for those masses to realize that they too are the wretched of the earth, and that the flames of revolution can be reignited. This is *The Wretched of the Earth's* promise: that the fire next time will bring to fruition the hopes and dreams of the project that was the Third World.

Bibliography

Alessandrini, Antony C., *Frantz Fanon and the Future of Cultural Politics* (London: Lexington Books, 2014).
Arendt, Hannah, *On Violence* (New York: Harvest, 2007 [1970]).
Dabashi, Hamid, 'Fuck You Žižek!', *Zed Books* (26 July 2016) <https://www.zedbooks.net/blog/posts/fuck-you-zizek> accessed 26 July 2016.
Du Bois, W. E. B., *The Souls of Black Folk: Essays and Sketches* (Oxford: Oxford University Press, 2007 [1903]).
Fanon, Frantz, *Black Skin, White Masks* (New York: Grove Press, 2008 [1961]).
——, *The Wretched of the Earth* (New York: Grove Press, 2004 [1963]).

Foster, John Bellamey, 'The New Imperialism of Globalized Monopoly-Finance Capital', *Monthly Review* 67/3 (2015) <http://monthlyreview.org/2015/07/01/the-new-imperialism-of-globalized-monopoly-finance-capital> accessed 20 December 2015.

——, Robert W. McChesney and R. Jamil Jonna, 'The Global Reserve Army of Labour and the New Imperialism', *Monthly Review* 63 (2011), 1–15.

Frazer, Elizabeth, and Kimberley Hutchings, 'On Politics and Violence: Arendt Contra Fanon', *Contemporary Political Theory* 7/1 (2008), 90–108.

Garavini, Giuliano, *After Empires: European Integration, Decolonization, and the Challenge from the Global South* (Oxford: Oxford University Press, 2012).

Hilliard, David, and Lawrence Cole, *This Side of Glory: The Autobiography of David Hilliard and the Story of the Black Panther Party* (Boston, MA: Little, Brown, 1993).

Lee, Christopher, *Making a World after Empire: The Bandung Moment and Its Political Afterlives* (Athens: Ohio University Press, 2010).

Mazower, Mark, *Governing the World: The History of an Idea* (London: Allen Lane, 2012).

Mishra, Pankaj, *From the Ruins of Empire: The Revolt against the West and the Remaking of Asia* (London: Penguin, 2012).

Narayan, John, 'Fanon's Decolonized Europe: The Double Promise of Coloured Cosmopolitanism in the Age of Austerity', in John Narayan and Gurminder K. Bhambra, eds, *European Cosmopolitanism: Colonial Histories and Postcolonial Societies* (London: Routledge, 2016), 153–71.

——, *John Dewey: The Global Public and its Problems* (Manchester: Manchester University Press, 2016).

Patnaik, Utsa, and Prabhat Patnaik, 'Imperialism in the Era of Globalization', *Monthly Review* 67/3 (2015) <http://monthlyreview.org/2015/07/01/imperialism-in-the-era-of-globalization> accessed 26 July 2016.

Prashad, Vijay, *The Darker Nations: A People's History of the Third World* (New York: The New Press, 2007).

——, *The Poorer Nations: A Possible History of the Global South* (London: Verso, 2013).

Scott, David, *Conscripts of Modernity: The Tragedy of Colonial Enlightenment* (London: Duke University Press, 2004).

BENJAMIN MOUNTFORD

13   'The Match is in the Spinifex': Frank Hardy's *The Unlucky Australians* (1968)

ABSTRACT

During the 1960s author Frank Hardy played an important role in the Wave Hill Walk Off – when a group of Aboriginal stockmen and their families embarked on one of the longest strikes in Australian history. Hardy's account of the Walk Off, *The Unlucky Australians* (1968), carried the story of the Gurindji people and their demand for improved pay and conditions – and ultimately the return of their traditional lands – to readers across Australia. While scholars have devoted considerable attention to the domestic impact, literary merits and historical accuracy of Hardy's book, however, we know relatively little about its international resonance. This chapter sets out to revisit *The Unlucky Australians* and to locate Hardy's work in relation to a broader transnational discourse on race and resistance during the 1960s and 1970s.*

In a television interview in 1966, the radical Australian author Frank Hardy (1917–94) explained his next venture: 'I'm going on a journey shortly across and around Australia to try to rediscover Australia, to think about what I'm going to write about next, to have a look inside myself'. Fleeing Sydney's cynicism, mounting debts and a range of personal and professional anxieties, Hardy would seek fresh inspiration in the land. 'Of course, I'll be there when I arrive at my destination', he informed his interviewer, 'I know I can't escape from myself'.[1] Travelling overland into the interior, Hardy channelled the spirit of the pre-eminent colonial poets, Lawson

---

*   I wish to acknowledge the Gurindji people of Kalkarindji and Daguragu in Australia's Northern Territory, and to pay my respects to their Elders past, present and future. In the course of editing this book and writing this chapter, I was honoured to be invited to the Fiftieth Anniversary Freedom Day Festival in the Northern Territory, to learn more about the Gurindji story and Frank Hardy's involvement in the Wave Hill Walk Off.

1   Frank Hardy, *The Unlucky Australians* (London: Pan, 1978 [1968]), 16.

and Paterson; looked askance at the country and its people through the eyes of his alter ego, the larrikin yarn-spinner Billy Borker; and wondered at the expanse of 'primitive ugly Australian bush, brown and grey, as aloof as an Aborigine'.[2] As he whiled away the hours, his thoughts concentrated on the situation of Aboriginal Australians. In dusty country towns he recoiled at the prevalence of overt white chauvinism. Questions of race and history began to preoccupy his mind and invade his dreams. 'You have travelled into the heart of the land and all you have learnt is what you have known for more than twenty years: the Aboriginal people are treated worse than any minority on earth and Australians don't care or, caring, turn their backs'.[3]

A writer lost for words, Hardy reached Darwin in June 1966. On arriving he stumbled into the middle of one of the great political struggles of post-war Australia, one deeply embedded in the nation's unresolved colonial past. On the cattle stations, frustration was mounting amongst Aboriginal workers over poor conditions and wage discrimination, whereby pastoralists were able to pay their Indigenous staff considerably less than their white counterparts. In May Aboriginal stockmen had gone on strike at Newcastle Waters Station before eventually returning to work. In Darwin Hardy met one of the architects of the protest: Dexter Daniels, a Nunggubuyu man raised at the Roper River mission, who was the Aboriginal organizer for the North Australian Worker's Union.[4] Daniels educated Hardy about the anger of Indigenous people in the Territory, their frustration at the sluggish pace of reform and the Gurindji's particular struggle against the inequities of white Australia: 'He conjured up a vision of an ancient people ready to awake from a long sleep'.[5]

---

2   Hardy, *Unlucky Australians*, 18.
3   Hardy, *Unlucky Australians*, 28.
4   Charlie Ward, '"That's Not Right!" Dexter Daniels in 1968', *The Webworld of Charlie Ward* <https://1charlieward.files.wordpress.com/2011/10/thats-not-right-dexter-daniels-in-1968.pdf> accessed 31 March 2016; Charlie Ward, *A Handful of Sand: The Gurindji Struggle, After the Walk Off* (Melbourne: Monash University Publishing, 2016), 23–7.
5   Hardy, *Unlucky Australians*, 48.

For tens of thousands of years, the Gurindji had lived in the Victoria River District of the Northern Territory. From the 1880s, when the enormous Wave Hill Cattle Station was established, their traditional way of life came under increasing pressure from the advance of European settlement. In 1914 Wave Hill Station was acquired by the international food company Vestey Brothers. Vesteys employed local Aboriginal people on their station as stockmen and domestic servants. At Wave Hill's native settlement, Aboriginal workers and their families lived in decrepit housing and survived on a meagre diet of salt beef, bread, tea and tobacco. By 1966, however, the Gurindji had had enough. In August elder Vincent Lingiari led his people off Wave Hill Station and out on strike. Although many of their white supporters assumed the struggle was primarily about wages and conditions, nine months later Lingiari and his people marched on to Daguragu (Wattie Creek) and began to set up their own village and cattle station. The Gurindji's actions showed that they were interested not only in improving their material conditions, but also in reclaiming their traditional lands.[6]

During the late 1960s and early 1970s Frank Hardy became a central figure in the Wave Hill Walk Off and in the Gurindji's campaign for land rights.[7] Shaking off his writer's block and his acute personal anxieties, Hardy set out to support the Gurindji through his writing – to translate the wishes, aspirations, and grievances of the (illiterate) community into a set of powerful fighting words.

His vivid account of the Walk Off, *The Unlucky Australians* (1968) transmitted the story of Gurindji struggle throughout the country and to interested observers beyond the sea. Since its initial release in 1968, *The Unlucky Australians* has inspired considerable discussion amongst scholars. Of particular interest have been two issues: the accuracy of the book's account of the Wave Hill Walk Off, and Hardy's depiction of his own role in those events. While drawing on this scholarship, this chapter sets out

---

6   The pre-eminent study is Ward, *Handful of Sand*.
7   Jenny Hocking, *Frank Hardy: Politics, Literature, Life* (Melbourne: Lothian, 2005), 157–79; Pauline Armstrong, *Frank Hardy and the Making of Power Without Glory* (Melbourne: Melbourne University Press, 2000), 163–6.

Figure 13.1: Frank Hardy, with his tape recorder by his side, during a discussion about the Gurindji plan to move to Daguragu. With kind permission of Robin Jeffrey.

instead to explore the international resonance of *The Unlucky Australians* and its connection to wider transnational debates about race and resistance circulating across the postcolonial world during the 1960s and 1970s.

'For the first time in years a book is demanding to be written'[8]

Written in the Northern Territory and Sydney, *The Unlucky Australians* relates the story of Hardy's own journey to the north and the unfolding course of events as the Gurindji marched off Wave Hill Station to the banks

---

8   Hardy, *Unlucky Australians*, 272.

of the Victoria River, and then on to Daguragu. At times the action shifts to the south, following Hardy and his efforts to garner support for the Gurindji amongst the wider Australian community. The subject and the structure of the book enabled Hardy to overcome a series of literary and political frustrations. At odds with the leadership of the Communist Party of Australia (which he had joined in 1940) and interested in a more fluid approach to social realism, Hardy found inspiration, clarity and catharsis in the opportunity to write about race as a threat to social justice and the unresolved legacy of European colonization:

> I lay awake with the ancient fire that I thought was dead in me, that was burned into my soul in the hungry thirties [...]. I had seen whites debased and robbed of their self-respect. But no white man, even in the depths of the depression, had suffered as much as the black man suffers now in the heart of the nation's boom. I knew I had reached the last line of the retreat of the rebel without a cause: where he makes his final stand with the dispossessed black minority.[9]

As the ancient fire burned, it warmed Hardy's typewriter and his pen. He contemplated a number of potential literary projects, yet prioritized the work that would become *The Unlucky Australians* as it 'would directly assist the Aborigines'.[10] To achieve this end he was eager to publish quickly, regardless of 'all the defects of a story written as it happened'.[11] Back in Sydney, he worked tirelessly on the manuscript, fending off all external pressures:

> The urge to gamble; it can bring no exultation or despair, no hope of salvation. The anxiety over finance can be switched off; it's only money. Lock yourself in with a machine gun nest at the top of the stairs to keep the bailiffs out, and 'write it down for them'. Only one commitment to white Australia, to convince it that 'while black men are in chains, no white man can be free'; and that it will need all its luck until it sets the black man free. No other literary work is thinkable.[12]

---

9   Hardy, *Unlucky Australians*, 49.
10 Hardy, *Unlucky Australians*, 272.
11 Hardy, *Unlucky Australians*, 273.
12 Hardy, *Unlucky Australians*, 271–2.

While writing the book Hardy was particularly conscious of his whiteness. Determined to understand the Gurindji and their experience 'well enough to write meaningfully about it', he wrestled with his own place in the story and with the issue of narrative hierarchy.[13] 'Perhaps, I see now, I would have been better to dive straight into the story of the Aborigines', he wrote to his friend Cecil Homes as the text developed. But as the story was told in the first person, it was 'necessary for the "I" to register on the reader sincerely and frankly in order that the reader can identify with what the first person sees, says and does, and identify sympathetically with the Aborigines'.[14] Hardy resolved this tension by adopting a 'polyphonic' structure and by alternating between documentary style and fictionalized representation. As the story unfolds, multiple contrasting voices – Hardy himself, members of the Gurindji community (via taped interviews reproduced verbatim) and others involved in the struggle – assume the role of narrator.[15]

In Hardy, the Gurindji leaders recognized a *Kartiya* [non-Indigenous] ally with the communication skills they required.[16] During their long campaign, he remained a passionate advocate, on the street and on the stump, on the radio and on television, but particularly in print. 'I'll tell a lotta people in the South', he enthused, 'write in newspaper, write in book'.[17] Through a process of narrative accrual and coalescence, he helped to transmit the Gurindji story from the outback into the homes of white Australians.[18] Aboriginal people in the north needed such a writer, argued Dexter Daniels; 'this story has to be told'.[19] After a series of delays, following the threat of legal action

13 Hardy, *Unlucky Australians*, 207.
14 Hardy to Holmes, 14 October 1967, Hardy Papers, National Library of Australia (NLA), MS4887/13/2.
15 Hocking, *Frank Hardy*, 168–9; Paul Adams, *The Stranger from Melbourne: Frank Hardy, A Literary Biography 1944–1975* (Perth: University of Western Australia Press, 1999), 85–105.
16 Ward, *Handful of Sand*, 35.
17 Hardy, *Unlucky Australians*, 263.
18 Bain Attwood, 'The Articulation of "Land Rights" in Australia', *Social Analysis* 44/1 (2000), 4–5; and his *Rights for Aborigines* (Sydney: Allen & Unwin, 2003), 257–82.
19 Hardy, *Unlucky Australians*, 128.

by Vesteys and others, the book was eventually released by Melbourne publisher Thomas Nelson.[20] Reviews were largely sympathetic, though criticism over the way Hardy had depicted his own role in events evidently proved frustrating even before publication. 'I have suffered the agonies of creative hell over this book', he wrote in October 1967, 'and no longer have any patience with those who condemn it for the wrong reasons and motives – without having read a line'.[21]

How Do *You* Plead?

When Frank Hardy first signed a memorandum of agreement with Thomas Nelson in January 1967, it was simply for the 'Aboriginal book'.[22] The title Hardy eventually settled on responded to Donald Horne's influential characterization of 1960s Australia as *The Lucky Country*. In Horne's estimation Australia's remarkable prosperity owed little to its rather unremarkable population. Their good fortune was simply the result of an abundance of natural resources and inherited British institutions.[23] Like Horne's book, Hardy's was intended as a wake-up call that would shatter the complacency of most Australians and force them to confront the continuing legacies of colonization and dispossession.

In Australia, as in the other former British dominions, the process of decolonization was marked by a sense of uncertainty as to what should replace 'Britishness' as a cultural ideal. During the 1960s increasing numbers of Australians turned to the country's Aboriginal heritage for an alternative grand narrative to the expansion of England. At the same time, Australian governments came under increasing domestic and international pressure

---

20 Armstrong, *Frank Hardy*, 164.
21 Hardy to Holmes, 14 October 1967, Hardy Papers, NLA, MS-4887/13/2.
22 Memorandum of Agreement, 9 January 1967, Hardy Papers, NLA, MS-4887/2/21.
23 Donald Horne, *The Lucky Country: Australia in the Sixties* (Harmondsworth: Penguin 1964). Horne provided the foreword for *The Unlucky Australians*.

to improve the country's record on racial issues.[24] In 1967 a constitutional referendum empowered the Federal government to make laws on behalf of Aboriginal people. To many Australians the success of the 'Yes' vote (90.77 per cent) signalled a new recognition of 'Aboriginal rights', but the reality was rather more modest.[25] In his account of the Gurindji struggle Hardy mocked white Australia's half-hearted engagement with Aborigines and sought to expose the racial chauvinism that he suspected lay at the heart of Australian history and culture. Forget Vesteys, he reflected while visiting the abandoned native settlement at Wave Hill Station, forget the government; 'White Australia is to blame [...]. If Australia is the Lucky Country, the Aborigines must be the unluckiest people in the world'.[26]

Hardy was deeply conscious of Australia's place within a grander postcolonial narrative. 'White Australia', he contended, had begun 'as the furthest outpost of Old England's power and that power was based on the white man's inhumanity to the coloured man'. Indigenous dispossession and imperial violence were the foundation of European settlement. Turning to the decimation of Aboriginal communities in nineteenth-century Tasmania, *The Unlucky Australians* compares white Australia with Nazi Germany. For all the horrors perpetuated by the British and French in Africa, by Stalin in the USSR, and by Americans in the slave-owning South and along the Western frontier, only white Australia and Hitler's Germany stood guilty of the 'ultimate crime of genocide'. Railing against the sunny, suburban satisfaction of 1960s Australia, Hardy demanded that the country stand up and recognize the racial antagonism upon which its modern identity rested. The crimes of the colonial era had imparted

---

24　James Curran and Stuart Ward, *The Unknown Nation: Australia After Empire* (Melbourne: Melbourne University Press, 2010), 77–9.
25　Russell McGregor, *Indifferent Inclusion: Aboriginal People and the Australian Nation* (Canberra: Aboriginal Studies Press, 2011), 162–3. Bain Attwood and Andrew Markus, 'Representation Matters: The 1967 Referendum and Citizenship', in Nicholas Peterson and Will Sanders, eds, *Citizenship and Indigenous Australians* (Cambridge: Cambridge University Press, 1998), 118–40.
26　Hardy, *Unlucky Australians*, 136.

racism 'into the Australian character like a Pavlovian reflex, conditioning our policies towards Aborigines, Asia and immigration'.[27]

Beyond these legacies of empire, in *The Unlucky Australians* Hardy also sought to emphasize the links between the Gurindji struggle and the history of the Civil Rights and Black Power movements in America.[28] Citing Stokely Carmichael's famous assertion that the 'United States is going to fall', Hardy predicted the emergence of Indigenous leaders who would declare: 'White Australia will fall'. His awareness of the postcolonial and trans-Pacific resonance of the Gurindji struggle reflects the extent to which global and transnational discourses on race and resistance took hold in Australia in the late 1960s. If the Gurindji story was being played out on an Australian stage, Hardy recognized, it was part of a far grander international, post-imperial drama. 'It is in the Supreme Court of the world of race relations that the final verdict will be given', the author declares to his readers: 'how do *you* plead?'[29]

The Long Crossing

By the 1960s Frank Hardy was one of Australia's most well-known authors. His first book, the political novel *Power Without Glory* (1950), had caused a sensation in Australia and was eventually translated into more than twenty languages. Infused with a distinctly Australian, iconoclastic approach to socialist realism, the book resonated with audiences overseas and particularly in Britain and Eastern Europe. Its success (along with Hardy's communist affiliations) enabled the young author to head abroad and to forge literary and personal relationships around the world. In time his social

---

27 Hardy, *Unlucky Australians*, 313–14.
28 John Maynard, *Fight for Liberty and Freedom: The Origins of Australian Aboriginal Activism* (Canberra: Aboriginal Studies Press, 2007). Reviewers also made the link: see *Canberra Times* (20 July 1968), 13.
29 Hardy, *Unlucky Australians*, 315–16.

circle came to include Arthur Miller and the dissident Soviet poet Yevgeny Yevtushenko. He maintained several literary and personal connections with the Eastern Bloc, where many of his royalties remained, inaccessible from Australia.[30]

If Hardy was already well known overseas, the focus of *The Unlucky Australians* – the plight of Australia's Aboriginal people – was also attracting increasing attention on foreign shores. Indigenous activists played a vital role in stimulating this interest and connecting the Australian situation to postcolonial struggles elsewhere. In December 1964, for instance, Davis Daniels (Dexter's brother) and fellow Aboriginal campaigner Philip Roberts, travelled to Kenya to witness decolonization first-hand at the invitation of Kenya's Minister for Justice and Constitutional Affairs, who had visited Australia earlier that year. In 1968, with the Gurindji holding out at Daguragu, Dexter Daniels himself travelled overseas. Invited to Sofia to attend the World Youth Festival, Daniels promised 'to raise my people's claims and let the injustices of my people be known'.[31] By the 1970s Indigenous campaigners, artists and writers were heading abroad, sharing insights on the Australian situation and canvassing support from international audiences and institutions. In the other direction came a stream of activists, artists, religious leaders and academics, both black and white, seeking fresh insights into Australian attitudes to race and to the welfare of Aboriginal people. Many responded with horror and disdain over what they saw. The black British sociologist Chris Mullard declared Australia 'second only to South Africa in racism'. Janet McLeod, a Native American member of a research team investigating racism in Queensland, struck an equally sombre note. 'In America', she lamented, 'the Indians have at least hope whereas here there is racism and apathy in every policy'.[32] In Sydney, the Hardy family was directly involved in the visit of at least one prominent American observer – the great African American singer Paul

---

30 Hocking, *Frank Hardy*, 137, 160–3.
31 Ward, 'That's Not Right'.
32 Australian Commission for Community Relations, 'World Perceptions of Racism in Australia', Community Relations Paper No. 12, Australian Commission for Community Relations Report (1981).

Robeson. Part of the Communist Party delegation to welcome Robeson to Australia, Hardy hosted the singer at his flat at Manly. Alan Hardy (Frank's son) recalls Robeson becoming inconsolable after watching a documentary on Aboriginal people in Western Australia: 'I remember this great tall man, standing in silence, tears streaming down his face'.[33]

The international resonance of *The Unlucky Australians* needs to be read against this backdrop of increasing interest in Indigenous affairs overseas. As early as August 1968, Hardy was writing to Thomas Nelson, asking them to expedite the publication of overseas editions for the UK, USA and Canadian markets and offering to meet their agents in France and Italy to discuss translations.[34] Further east, he began negotiations with publishers in the Eastern Bloc and was soon sending articles on the Gurindji to *Ogonyok* (Moscow), *Lumea* (Bucharest) and the Czechoslovak Theatrical and Literary Agency in order to stimulate interest in the book.[35] Although Hardy's correspondence suggests these articles were warmly received, they evidently failed to generate sufficient interest to secure contracts. In March 1969 he wrote with regret about Thomas Nelson's failure to promote the book overseas, even through its London office. By that stage he had offered international rights to another British publisher, Bodley Head, assuring them that *The Unlucky Australians* 'might well make its way in, for example, UK, Italy, France and Romania'.[36]

If Hardy, like many Aboriginal activists, saw the Australian situation as part of a wider postcolonial narrative, his efforts to have the book published overseas nonetheless revealed the peripheral status of Australia in the minds of foreign publishers. Given the connection between the American Civil Rights movement and the campaign for Aboriginal rights, one might have expected Hardy's book to find a respectable market in the US. Yet, despite the interest of a number of prominent Americans in Aboriginal

---

33 Benjamin Mountford, interview with Alan Hardy, Daguragu, August 2016.
34 Hardy to Rosenberg, 12 August 1968, Hardy Papers, NLA, MS-4887/3/19.
35 Hardy to Sofronov, 2 November 1966, Hardy Papers, NLA, MS-4887/13/5; Cǎrje to Hardy, 24 February 1967, Hardy Papers, NLA, MS-4887/13/2; Bernau to Hardy, 21 January 1970, Hardy Papers, NLA, MS-4887/74/1.
36 Blackley to Hardy, 16 October 1969, Hardy Papers, NLA, MS-4887/3/20.

affairs, Hardy's attempts to have his book published in America foundered. In early 1968 the Manhattan literary agent John Hawkins wrote that the manuscript was well-written and interesting, but would struggle to find an audience. Selling the book in America would be as difficult as trying to sell a book about Native Americans in Australia. When he received a similar response from William Morrow & Co. of New York, Hardy professed to have 'lost faith in America'.[37]

He was spurred on over the next few years, however, by two champions working in the US academy: Dr Alan Weinstein and Professor Mervyn Meggitt. Hardy had met Weinstein, a historian at Smith College, when he had been briefly based in Adelaide, guest lecturing on the US Civil Rights movement. Queensland-born Meggitt, meanwhile, whose ground-breaking work on the Warlpiri people of the Northern Territory had provided Hardy with some inspiration, was Professor of Anthropology at City University in New York. Believing *The Unlucky Australians* to be deserving of an American edition, Weinstein and Meggitt pitched the book to several publishers including Knopf, Random House, Oxford, Yale and Prentice-Hall. Despite their endorsement it failed to secure a release. American readers, Weinstein finally conceded, were becoming 'weary and exhausted' of exposés on racial problems. Hardy had written a fascinating book, certainly, but locating an American audience would be difficult.[38] Mentioned in passing in the American press, the book mostly failed to register – a potent reminder of the dominance of American attitudes in determining the nature of cultural exchange across the Pacific.[39] 'One always hopes for the best', Hardy lamented, 'but learns to be aware of the shortcomings of the work and the irrelevance of Australia':

> It must be extremely difficult to sell Australian books in America, for example, where the vast majority of people seem to be quite unaware of our existence. In fact, I have come to the conclusion that the more relevant that a book is to Australia the more

---

37 Hawkins to Hardy, 17 January 1968, Hardy Papers, NLA, MS-4887/13/4; Hardy to Hawkins, 29 February 1968.
38 Weinstein to Hardy, 20 December 1970, Hardy Papers, NLA, MS-4887/3/21.
39 For a rare glimpse, *The New York Times* (26 October 1969), 34.

irrelevant it becomes elsewhere. Processes at work in Australian society are out of date and irrelevant to processes elsewhere.[40]

It was ironic, perhaps, that *The Unlucky Australians* found its strongest international audience in Britain and in the other former dominions of Canada and New Zealand. In Britain, interest in Aboriginal Australia in the late 1960s and 1970s was closely bound up with escalating debates on race, decolonization and the struggle against apartheid in South Africa. By the early 1970s several sympathetic organizations had taken up the cause, including the Minority Rights Group, Colonialism and Minorities Research and Action (CIMRA), and the World Council for Indigenous Peoples. As the World Council of Churches lobbied Lord Vestey on behalf of the Gurindji, a group calling itself the Movement to Combat Australian Racism launched its own campaign in the British press.[41] Hardy himself played an active role in promoting the Gurindji's struggle, writing articles for *The Sunday Times*, making appearances on the BBC, and leading demonstrations in London. In November 1968, *The Times* reported:

> The battle for the rights of Australia's Aborigines reaches London this week. Tomorrow Vesteys' office at Smithfield in London will be picketed in an attempt to draw Britain's attention to the plight of the aborigine [...]. The picket, composed of London Australians, will be led by the Australian author Frank Hardy, a sort of 1930s communist, who became involved with the aborigines when writing his book *The Unlucky Australians*.[42]

'I was over in England', Hardy later reported to Vincent Lingiari, 'We had a big meeting outside where the big bosses of VESTEYS live in London.'[43]

In October 1968, J. B. Blackley of Bodley Head in London wrote to Hardy about the prospects for a British edition.[44] Nothing appears to have come of these discussions, although British readers evidently already had access to Australian editions of the book – the title of which was absorbed

---

40 Hardy to Cameron, 25 March 1969, Hardy Papers, NLA, MS-4887/74/1.
41 'World Perceptions of Racism'.
42 *The Times* (14 November 1968), 10.
43 Hardy to Lingiari, undated, Hardy Papers, NLA, MS-4887/13/1.
44 Blackley to Hardy, 8 October 1968, Hardy Papers, NLA, MS-4887/74/1.

into British discourse on Aboriginal affairs. 'Aborigines are still the Unlucky Australians', *The National Times* reflected in 1973. 'Many of them live under dictatorial control on reserves which were once their tribal land. They face similar hardships to black South Africans.'[45] In June 1974 Hardy's agent Curtis Brown reported that of an Australian print run of 19,000, 200 copies had been used for publicity, 13,287 had been sold locally and 2,595 had been exported – the majority presumably to Britain.[46] By that stage, awareness of Hardy's work in the UK had been further enhanced by his involvement with a documentary on the Wave Hill Walk Off commissioned by Associated Television UK. Directed by John Goldschmidt and narrated by Hardy, the film 'The Unlucky Australians' screened on British television in 1973.[47] Although Hardy felt the success of the film justified a new hardcover release, it was not until 1978 that a British (paperback) edition appeared through Pan Books. Of the 22,000 copies printed, surviving records suggest that 1,803 were sold in Britain, while another 11,600 were exported to Australia, New Zealand and Canada.[48]

Pan's 1978 second edition included a long epilogue by Hardy, who was by then living in France. It offered an uncompromising assessment of the slow progress of Aboriginal affairs since 1968, reiterated the international context and included some of the narration from Goldschmidt's documentary. This second edition also featured a powerful new introduction from former Australian Prime Minister Gough Whitlam, who in 1975 had finally travelled to Daguragu to bestow land rights on the Gurindji. '*The Unlucky Australians*', Whitlam began, 'is justly regarded as a landmark in the struggle for aboriginal advancement. It was not the first book to draw attention to the plight of Australian Aborigines, but it was the first by a noted and popular author to bring their living conditions and just demands to the notice of a wide audience.'[49]

---

45 *National Times* (7–13 September 1980), cited in 'World Perceptions of Racism'.
46 Curtis Brown to Hardy, 6 June 1974, Hardy Papers, NLA, MS-4887/2/12.
47 Benjamin Mountford and Keir Reeves, 'The Fiftieth Anniversary Freedom Day Festival and John Goldschmidt's "The Unlucky Australians" (1973)', forthcoming.
48 Hardy to Blakely, 6 June 1974, Hardy Papers, NLA, MS-4887/3/26; Benjamin Mountford, correspondence Macmillan Archive, 17 February 2016.
49 Hardy, *Unlucky Australians*, preface by E. Gough Whitlam.

Reissued for a third edition in 2008, but now again out of print, Frank Hardy's *The Unlucky Australians* remains a vital text for anyone wishing to understand Australia's place in a wider postcolonial narrative of race and resistance during the second half of the twentieth century. That the book's publication was limited to Australian and British editions, and its distribution apparently concentrated within Australia, Britain, Canada and New Zealand, reflects the continuing importance of old Commonwealth cultural connections. But in helping the Gurindji to shape and transmit their fighting words Hardy remained convinced of the wider significance of their struggle. Deep in the Australian outback, in the land of their ancestors, the Gurindji had taken a stand against the legacies of empire – a stand that Hardy believed would echo from the heart of the island continent, and across the postcolonial world.

Bibliography

Adams, Paul, *The Stranger from Melbourne: Frank Hardy, A Literary Biography 1944–1975* (Perth: University of Western Australia Press, 1999).
Armstrong, Pauline, *Frank Hardy and the Making of Power Without Glory* (Melbourne: Melbourne University Press, 2000).
Attwood, Bain, 'The Articulation of "Land Rights" in Australia', *Social Analysis* 44/1 (2000), 4–5.
——, *Rights for Aborigines* (Sydney: Allen & Unwin, 2003).
——, and Andrew Markus, 'Representation Matters: The 1967 Referendum and Citizenship', in Nicholas Peterson and Will Sanders, eds, *Citizenship and Indigenous Australians* (Cambridge: Cambridge University Press, 1998), 118–40.
Australian Commission for Community Relations, 'World Perceptions of Racism in Australia', Community Relations Paper No. 12, Australian Commission for Community Relations Report (1981).
Broome, Richard, *Aboriginal Australians: A History Since 1788* (Sydney: Allen & Unwin: 2010 [1982]).
Curran, James, and Stuart Ward, *The Unknown Nation: Australia After Empire* (Melbourne: Melbourne University Press, 2010).
Frank Hardy Papers, National Library of Australia, MS-4887.
Hardy, Frank, *The Unlucky Australians* (London: Pan Books, 1978 [1968]).

Hocking, Jenny, *Frank Hardy: Politics, Literature, Life* (Melbourne: Lothian, 2005).
Hokari, Minoru, 'From Wattie Creek to Wattie Creek: An Oral Historical Approach to the Gurindji Walk Off', *Aboriginal History* 24 (2000), 98–116.
Horne, Donald, *The Lucky Country: Australia in the Sixties* (Harmondsworth: Penguin, 1964).
McGregor, Russell, *Indifferent Inclusion: Aboriginal People and the Australian Nation* (Canberra: Aboriginal Studies Press, 2011).
Maynard, John, *Fight for Liberty and Freedom: The Origins of Australian Aboriginal Activism* (Canberra: Aboriginal Studies Press, 2007).
Mountford, Benjamin, correspondence with Macmillan Archive, 17 February 2016.
——, interview with Alan Hardy, Daguragu, August 2016.
——, and Keir Reeves, 'The Fiftieth Anniversary Freedom Day Festival and John Goldschmidt's "The Unlucky Australians" (1973)', forthcoming.
Ward, Charlie, *A Handful of Sand: The Gurindji Struggle, After the Walk Off* (Melbourne: Monash University Publishing, 2016).
——, '"That's Not Right!" Dexter Daniels in 1968', *The Webworld of Charlie Ward* <https://1charlieward.files.wordpress.com/2011/10/thats-not-right-dexter-daniels-in-1968.pdf> accessed 31 March 2016.
Wilson, Deborah, *Different White People: Radical Activism for Aboriginal Rights, 1946–1972* (Perth: University of Western Australia Press, 2015).

MICHAEL R. GRIFFITHS

14   Provenance, Identification and Confession in Sally Morgan's *My Place* (1987)

ABSTRACT
This chapter surveys the impact and success of Sally Morgan's 1987 memoir *My Place*. It is one of the most successful, widely read and widely disseminated (and translated) books ever to come out of Australia. Therefore, this chapter also aims to account for the cultural meaning of the book in Australian identity politics and its transnational dissemination. It examines the range of academic responses to Morgan's book in order to position its use of genre, its invocation of Aboriginal history and the basis of its appeal. Drawing on this criticism, the chapter identifies attempts to implicate Morgan's book in the dominant white settler discourse around Aboriginality and authenticity, as well as efforts to defend it from such accusations. Ultimately, the book's importance lies not only in its wide and global readership, but in the way its success has stimulated renewed debate about Aboriginality.*

Since Sally Morgan (1951–) first published her memoir *My Place* in 1987, critics have been trying to make sense of the book's phenomenal success. Indeed, *My Place* is one of the most popular, widely disseminated and translated books ever to come out of Australia. The book has had nine printings, several of which have been new editions. By 1992, the Australian edition had sold over 330,000 copies – an enormous achievement in the often lean domestic book market – prompting historian Bain Attwood to claim that '[n]o other Aboriginal writing has achieved anything like its readership'.[1] That the book was immediately abridged into a 'youth'

---

*   Acknowledgement: My colleague at the University of Wollongong, painter and scholar Garry Jones (Gamilaroi) advised on key aspects of legislative history in this piece. His advice is warmly appreciated and was incorporated.

[1]   Bain Attwood, 'Portrait of an Aboriginal as an Artist: Sally Morgan and the Construction of Aboriginality', *Australian Historical Studies* 25/99 (1992), 317.

edition is indicative of two of the book's aims: to describe a particular kind of Aboriginal experience to the Australian public and to educate its young constituents about that experience.[2] Furthermore, its impact is not limited only to Australia. In the English language alone, the book was published immediately in the United Kingdom and the United States (in the latter across two print runs between 1989 and 1990). It later appeared in India, where Indigenous Australian writing is increasingly popular, and has since been translated into fourteen languages: initially German and Dutch, and later Indonesian, Malay and Chinese.[3]

Does this global circulation of confessional resistance make *My Place* a book of fighting words? And, if so, how might it be conceived as such? Several early critical accounts of the book identified it as political, resistant, even revolutionary writing.[4] Morgan herself has spoken of her suspicion of the legacy of the British Empire and its cultural dominance in Australia: 'I've always had problems knuckling under to authority [...] whenever I met people who were very much into King and Country and Commonwealth I would just find it very irritating'.[5] The text's confessional mode of resistance emerges in the tension between the undisclosed and under-represented nature of histories of Aboriginal dispossession. Within the text itself, it is on this basis that Daisy – Sally's grandmother, or 'Nan' – agrees to tell her story:

---

[2] See Sally Morgan, *My Place for Young Readers*, ed. Barbara Ker Wilson (Fremantle: Fremantle Press, 1990).

[3] On the translation and reception of Sally Morgan and of Aboriginal writing more generally in German, see Oliver Haag, 'Representations of Aboriginality in German Translations of Aboriginal Literature: A Study of Peritexts', *Antipodes: A Global Journal of Australian and New Zealand Literature* 26/1 (2012), 203–8. For an example of South Asian criticism that deals seriously with Morgan, see Anjali Gera Roy, 'Voice of Australia: Who Speaks for the Aborigine', in Santosh K. Sareen, Sheel C. Nuna and Malathi Mathur, eds, *Cultural Interfaces* (New Delhi: Indialog, 2004), 18–29.

[4] Jody Broun, 'Unmaking White Myths: Your Laws, My Place', in Delys Bird and Dennis Haskell, eds, *Whose Place? A Study of Sally Morgan's* My Place (Pymble: Angus and Robertson, 1992), 23–9.

[5] Delys Bird and Dennis Haskell, 'Interview with Sally Morgan', in Bird and Haskell, eds, *Whose Place?*, 13.

Sally Morgan's My Place *(1987)* 233

'Why shouldn't she write a book?' Mum said firmly. 'There's been nothing written about people like us, all the history's about the white man. There's nothing about Aboriginal people and what they've been through.'⁶

My Place was not the only story of Aboriginality to emerge at this time, but the book successfully tapped into one particular history of Aboriginal people that was beginning to resonate in public discourse: the revelation of the Australian government's attempt at genocide through the removal of Aboriginal children from their parents.⁷ Indeed, *My Place*'s publication in 1987 places it between this revelation by historian Peter Read – which he would name 'the Stolen Generations' – and the eventual government response of a Royal Commission in 1995 (which eventually led to the 1997 *Bringing Them Home* report).⁸

6   Sally Morgan, *My Place* (Fremantle: Fremantle Arts Centre Press, 1987), 161. Throughout this chapter, while invoking Lejeune's notion of 'the autobiographical pact' that states that readers are solicited by texts to see a correspondence between author, narrator and protagonist, I nonetheless employ 'Morgan' to refer to the author and 'Sally' to refer to the protagonist of the text. See Philippe Lejeune, *On Autobiography* (Minneapolis: University of Minnesota Press, 1987).
7   Assimilation was the culturally oriented form of a policy stretching back to the early twentieth century, which was aimed at incorporating Aboriginal people into the wider polity, often by force. Initially a eugenic policy named 'absorption', this biologically oriented form of the policy culminated in a 1937 conference on 'Native Welfare' held in Canberra, which recommended the forced removal of Aboriginal children from their parents. Following the Second World War, the policy was replaced by a culturally (and ostensibly non-racially) targeted policy of 'Assimilation', though this latter form continued to operate through child removal. See Anna Haebich, *Spinning the Dream: Assimilation in Australia* (Fremantle: Fremantle Press, 2008); Russell McGregor, 'Governance Not Genocide', in Dirk Moses, ed., *Genocide and Settler Society* (New York: Bergahn Books, 2004), 290–311. I contest McGregor's strict periodization of absorption and assimilation in 'Interventions: Race, Culture, and Population via the Thought of A. P. Elkin', in Bruno Cornellier and Michael R. Griffiths, eds, 'Globalizing Unsettlement', a Special Issue of *Settler Colonial Studies* 6/4 (2016), 385–402.
8   Peter Read, *The Stolen Generations: The Removal of Aboriginal Children in NSW 1883–1969* (Sydney: Government Printer, 1982); *Bringing Them Home: A Report into the Forced Separation of Aboriginal and Torres Strait Islander Children from the Families* (Canberra: Government Printer, 1997).

My Place's impact was not only literary, but also activist in the awareness it raised around an issue of profound political importance for many Aboriginal people. The *Bringing Them Home* report estimated that 'between one in three and one in ten Indigenous children were forcibly removed from their families and communities in the period from approximately 1910 until 1970' and that '[m]ost families have been affected, in one or more generations, by the forcible removal of one or more children'.[9] Not only was *My Place* published close to the bicentenary of Australia's settlement by Europeans; Sally's own date of birth in 1951 positions her lifetime as near coterminous with the introduction of the assimilation policy by the Australian government. In this way, Sally's life story parallels the historical shift from race toward culture in justifications of policies like child removal, even as it also documents a period during which removals continued to take place.[10]

Provenance

Although *My Place* was not the first piece of life-writing by an Aboriginal author (from the early 1970s, books were published by men from traditional backgrounds such as Dick Roughsey and Jack Mirritji), it was one of the first Stolen Generations narratives, and transformed life-writing into the primary genre employed by Aboriginal writers.[11] At the time of writing, almost 800 books of life-writing, memoir and autobiography have been published by Aboriginal authors.[12]

---

9   *Bringing Them Home*, 31.
10 See Anna Haebich, *Broken Circles: Fragmenting Indigenous Families 1800–2000* (Fremantle: Fremantle Arts Centre Press, 2000); Haebich, *Spinning the Dream*.
11 Dick Roughsey, *Moon and Rainbow: The Autobiography of an Aboriginal* (Artarmon: Reed, 1971); Jack Mirritji, *My People's Life: An Aboriginal's Own Story* (Milingimbi: Milingimbi Language Resource Centre, 1976).
12 Estimate taken from *Blackwords* section of *Austlit* database as at 22 August 2015.

Yet the paradox identified by many critics is that this most successful of Aboriginal texts is, at least initially, not recognizably Aboriginal. This is not only because it does not aim to conform to the expectations of what 'traditional' Aboriginal society 'should' look like (as texts like Roughsey's and Mirritji's arguably do), but also because, for almost the first third of the book, there is no sense that the narrative of growing up in the southern suburbs of Perth has anything to do with Aboriginal people's lives or cultures. As another renowned and highly successful Aboriginal writer of life-writing, Jackie Huggins, recalls of her first reading of the book: 'I read the first three chapters and thought I was reading the life of a middle class Anglo woman'.[13] This is in spite of the fact that in an early interview (prior to Huggins's essay) Morgan identified her upbringing as '[v]ery much working class [...] "poor working class" would be more appropriate'.[14] Indeed, the structure of *My Place* – which perhaps explains something of its appeal – hinges on its withholding of its protagonist's recognition of her and her family's Aboriginality. The slow revelation of this identity is a driving force of the memoir's plot, a feature that led many critics to follow Attwood in describing the book as, in part, a detective story.[15] The plot is propelled by first the suspicion, and then the revelation, that Sally's family are in fact Aboriginal. For this reason, Sue Thomas usefully contrasts the book with black women's autobiography: '[b]lack women's autobiographies usually contain a recognition scene, an incident that makes the authors conscious of their blackness and its significance'.[16] For Morgan's protagonist, Sally, this comes through questions that arise from her surrounding community, as it subtly foregrounds the prevalence of whiteness and the interrogation of difference in Australia.

Early in the text, Sally finds her cultural identity queried by schoolmates, curious about her slightly different complexion. 'Tell them you're

---

13   Jackie Huggins, 'Always Was Always Will Be', *Australian Historical Studies* 25/100 (1993), 461.
14   Haskell and Byrd, 'Interview with Sally Morgan', 7.
15   Attwood, 'Portrait of an Aboriginal as an Artist', 305.
16   Sue Thomas, 'Aboriginal Subjection and Affirmation', *Meanjin* 47/4 (1988), 755.

Indian', Sally's Nan instructs.[17] As the text progresses, it is revealed to Sally that Nan is not in fact 'Indian' but Aboriginal, after she responds with frustration to the idea that Sally and her siblings might be ashamed of their ethnicity. While Sally is confused, she is not, it seems, ashamed:

> Inside, I felt all churned up, but I didn't know why. I had accepted by now that Nan was dark, and that our heritage was not that shared by most Australians, but I hadn't accepted that we were Aboriginal. I was too ignorant to make such a decision, and too confused. I found myself coming back to the same old question: if Nan was Aboriginal, why didn't she just say so?[18]

Here we see the beginnings of the revelation described by Thomas, the 'little pieces of a huge jigsaw [that] were finally fitting together'.[19]

This detective quest for identity eventually leads Sally to track down and meet *Palyku* relatives in the north of Western Australia. Her uncle Arthur Corunna's story, as well as those of her mother (Gladys) and Nan (Daisy), then form the backdrop to the final sections of the text. Sally's story becomes contingent upon the re-narration of the Aboriginality of a community – a family – that had been unable to name itself as such. In this way, telling the story of extended family becomes not only a personal revelation but also a healing of communal bonds. Revelation of identity and the reconnection of this identity to a wider community becomes an act of both resistance and healing.[20] As Sally puts it:

> We were different people, now. What had begun as a tentative search for knowledge had grown into a spiritual and emotional pilgrimage. We had an Aboriginal consciousness now, and were proud of it. How deprived we would have been if we had been willing to let things stay as they were. We would have survived, but not as a whole people. We would never have known our place.[21]

---

17 Morgan, *My Place*, 38.
18 Morgan, *My Place*, 105.
19 Morgan, *My Place*, 232.
20 Fran De Groen, 'Healing, Wholeness and Holiness in *My Place*', in Bird and Haskell, eds, *Whose Place?*, 32–47.
21 Morgan, *My Place*, 233.

The motif of survival 'as a whole people' positions the story as a means of resisting the cultural genocide to which Aboriginal people were subjected. Indeed, this moment, with its sense of community survival, becomes the leitmotif of the text and is transposed to the front matter to become the book's epigraph. Sally's search for her place becomes a search for 'our place', one that is completed primarily through the relation between the individual identity of the protagonist and the collective identity of the extended *Palyku* family. Put another way, this collective identity is made possible by the individual's quest, even as it in turn makes possible the affirmation of identity that is this individual quest's goal. In this way, the trope of revelation connects Sally's story to black women's autobiography as Thomas conceives it, as the meaning of gender and race identity becomes the basis for a quest which is fulfilled throughout the course of the text.

Identification

Sally's gradual discovery of her Aboriginality in part explains the book's popularity. As Eric Michaels suggests, Morgan's text positions its protagonist as the simultaneous object of Aboriginality and the subject who uncovers it.[22] Furthermore, because Sally is both subject and object of the book's quest, the reader participates in the initial conundrum of identity which is eventually solved by Aboriginality. However, this identification of implied reader with protagonist is also, for some critics, the text's largest political limitation. Indeed, these critics are more reluctant than Thomas to grant Morgan's book the status of 'black women's autobiography'. In particular, Attwood's 1992 article reverberated through the Australian literary, historical and Indigenous studies scenes by critiquing Morgan's framing of Aboriginality. Where Thomas saw the use of genre as opening *My Place*

---

22   Eric Michaels, 'Para-Ethnography: A Review Article of Bruce Chatwin, *The Songlines*, and Sally Morgan, *My Place*', *Art and Text* 30 (1988), 49–50.

to a broader transnational discourse on the identity of black women, this typicality irks Attwood:

> The success of *My Place* might be said largely to reside in the ease with which Morgan's Aboriginality can be understood by all non-Aborigines – that, unlike most other Aboriginal life histories, it requires little if any translation. What is the significance of this comparative lack of difference or otherness for Morgan's identity? Rather than strengthening her new sense of self, it could be argued that it weakens her identity – at least on the terms in which she has defined her Aboriginality.[23]

Aboriginal author and academic Jackie Huggins built on Attwood's charges and quite vehemently condemned the book from her own Aboriginal perspective: 'To me that is *My Place*'s greatest weakness – requiring little translation (to a white audience), therefore it reeks of whitewashing in the ultimate sense'.[24] Paradoxically then, for these critics it is precisely the success of *My Place*, its accessibility to a wide non-Indigenous audience, that might be said to limit its resistant potential.

For Attwood, if the book is widely legible as an Aboriginal text, it is *not* sufficiently Aboriginal. Accounting for its success in this way is convincing but also, perhaps, somewhat self-defeating. I would like to suggest that the ambivalence of Aboriginality in the text – which is revealed through a cautious but ultimately rewarding investigation rather than being overtly on display from the outset – is a reflection of a particularly Australian condition of imperial legacy. As Tim Rowse suggests in a rejoinder to Attwood, '[t]he phenomenon *My Place* – that is, the pleasure it gives to so many Australians – is a challenge to an historical understanding of the changing apprehensions of "Aboriginality" within Australia's settler colonial culture'.[25] In this way, *My Place* can be read not so much as a typical or totalizing account of the experience of being Aboriginal in Australia, but rather as challenging a particularly settler colonial attitude to Aboriginality rooted in authenticity. Scholars such as Marcia Langton, Jeffrey Sissons and Elizabeth Povinelli have each argued that Aboriginality should not

---

23 Attwood, 'Portrait of an Aboriginal as an Artist', 318.
24 Huggins, 'Always Was Always Will Be', 460.
25 Tim Rowse, 'Sally Morgan's Kaftan', *Australian Historical Studies* 25/100 (1993), 468.

only, or even principally, be evaluated against an authenticity or tradition when the emergent mode of authenticity, ironically, serves the appropriative demands of non-Indigenous people for an idealized vision of the other.[26] Langton argues that:

> Aboriginality is not just a label to do with skin colour or the particular ideas a person carries around in his/her head which might be labeled Aboriginal, such as an Aboriginal language or kinship system. [...] Aboriginality arises from the subjective experience of both Aboriginal people and non-Aboriginal people who engage in intercultural dialogue, whether in actual lived experience or through a mediated experience such as a white person watching a program about Aboriginal people or reading a book.[27]

In this way, for Langton, Aboriginality is discursively produced and inter-subjectively negotiated between Aboriginal and non-Aboriginal people. *My Place* highlights a particular mode of settler colonial dispossession, specifically as it was perpetrated under the legacy of the Stolen Generations. As *My Place* represents it, there is a direct connection for subjects of the Stolen Generations between being Aboriginal and the process of making sense of the experience of the revelation of this fact. That this is a process made vicariously available to the reader implies Eric Michaels's sense of doubleness.

Daisy's fear about Sally discovering her Aboriginal ancestry perhaps reflects the way that Aboriginal people who had survived the forced removal of children might be wary of revealing their children's identity to the wider non-Indigenous community, and particularly to figures in government. For example, in a significant chapter entitled 'The Black Grandmother', Sally narrates the shift in Australian currency from pounds to dollars. When her Mum and Nan frantically begin stashing away the

---

26 See for instance Jeffrey Sissons, *First Peoples: Indigenous Cultures and Their Futures* (London: Reaktion, 2005), 37–60; Elizabeth Povinelli, *The Cunning of Recognition: Indigenous Alterities and the Making of Australian Multiculturalism* (Durham, NC: Duke University Press, 2002), 6.

27 Marcia Langton, 'Aboriginal Art and Film: The Politics of Representation', in Michele Grossman, ed., *Blacklines: Contemporary Critical Writing by Indigenous Australians* (Carlton: Melbourne University Press, 2003), 116.

old form of money, Sally is told not to reveal this act to any strangers, with a special warning that 'you never trust anybody who works for the government'.[28] Sally is perplexed, as the reader may well be, and wonders, 'why on earth would anyone be frightened of the government?'[29] Later in the same chapter, Nan reveals that she (and therefore by inference, Sally) is Aboriginal. This is the hinge moment on which the text pivots, as it transforms from an autobiography of a working-class woman in suburban Perth into a revelatory narrative of Aboriginality. The fulcrum for this pivot, however, is the simultaneous revelation to the reader that there may well be very good reasons for Aboriginal people to have been, or indeed to be, afraid of government intervention. When Nan reveals the family's Aboriginality, it is immediately understood by Sally in terms of the assimilationist repression of Aboriginal life. As she observes, '[t]here was a great deal of social stigma attached to being Aboriginal at our school'.[30] Sally's slow discovery of her and her family's Aboriginality leads to the unveiling of the government policies that motivated such secrecy on the part of the colonized.

Yet if Aboriginality forms a kind of cypher in the text, this cypher is redoubled in its paradoxical relation to whiteness. Sally's discovery of her family's Aboriginality is also connected to their discovery of the history of miscegenation and sexual subjugation by white men that defined the lives of many Aboriginal women, as it has Daisy's. When Nan begins reluctantly to tell her story for Sally's book, she reveals her suspicion that she is the child of the white station owner Howden Drake-Brockman. Sally treats the revelation as a successful instance of confession for Nan and for the family: 'It was a small victory but an important one. Not so much for the knowledge, but for the fact that Nan had finally found it possible to trust her family with a piece of information that was important to her'.[31] As

---

28   Morgan, *My Place*, 96.
29   Morgan, *My Place*, 96.
30   Morgan, *My Place*, 98.
31   Morgan, *My Place*, 162.

Hodge and Mishra point out, there is a paradox here: 'Morgan's search for her Aboriginal identity is accomplished primarily by disclosing her White ancestors'.[32] Yet this paradox does not necessarily result in a displacement of authenticity, but a further revelation that for many Aboriginal people such identity and its concealment is a response to assimilationist government policies – indeed, a way of surviving them. As Hodge and Mishra continue, by revealing Aboriginality in relation to whiteness, 'she discloses to nonAborigines [sic] a pattern of White complicity in the destruction of Aboriginal society that is their own buried secret'.[33] If the success of the novel relies on white readers' identification with the protagonist, this reader is nonetheless alienated from full identification by the revelation of their complicity in colonial subjugation.

Simultaneously, however, Aboriginality becomes a space of white vicariousness in problematic ways in the text. If Aboriginality is withheld from Sally, and if the legacy of the Stolen Generations means this withholding is the basis of at least one valid experience of Aboriginality, then the position of the implied reader as proxy detective means that they too might feel potentially Aboriginal. For this reason, Langton foregrounds the possibility that *My Place* might succeed for the implied (likely non-Aboriginal) reader in crafting a possible identification as Aboriginal through the very complexity of Sally's own journey of self-discovery and the reader's identification with it:

> *My Place* raises the possibility that the reader might also find, with a little sleuthing in the family tree, an Aboriginal ancestor? This indeed would be a startling perception. Yes, Morgan raises the possibility for the reader that he or she would thus acquire the genealogical, even biological ticket ('my great-great grandmother was Aboriginal') to enter the world of 'primitivism'.[34]

---

32   Bob Hodge and Vijay Mishra, *Dark Side of the Dream: Australian Literature and the Postcolonial Mind* (North Sydney: Allen and Unwin, 1990), 100.
33   Hodge and Mishra, *Dark Side of the Dream*, 100.
34   Langton, 'Aboriginal Art and Film: The Politics of Representation', 117.

Confession

I have suggested so far that the book's popularity relies on the double reading that first enables readers to empathize with Sally in her struggle to unravel a concealed identity, whilst this disclosure then forms the basis of the challenge to what Hodge and Mishra term 'white complicity'. Yet, as Langton suggests, the text's reliance on identification to mobilize this challenge might also be the source of an over-identification that risks the appropriation of Aboriginal experience by the text's white readers. Early in the text, when Sally first goes to school, this experience (also implicitly universal) is used simultaneously to recall the threat of removal associated with the Stolen Generations, and to frame this as a threat to which all Australian children are vulnerable. As Sally's teacher escorts her away from her mother, she is left crying, 'rooted to the bitumen playground, screaming and clutching for security my spotted, plastic toilet-bag and a Vegemite sandwich'.[35] If Vegemite – the archetypically Australian sandwich spread – is a symbol *par excellence* of Australian childhood, then the fear of removal becomes something all Australians – not only Aboriginal people – can, as readers, experience vicariously. The fact that this fear is manifest in the text before Sally is even aware of the legacy of policies of child removal emphasizes the experience's pervasive universality. Yet, in narrating a route towards this identification Morgan's text perhaps also risks occluding the specifically Aboriginal experience of cultural genocide associated with forced removal.

There is, then, both a potential critique of whiteness in the confessional mode of the story and also the danger that such confession might be assimilated by the colonizing culture. Stephen Muecke draws on Foucault to critique the confessional logic of sentiment and expression in the text, which seems to assert that all that is needed to challenge repressive power is self-expression. Instead, he suggests that power is exercised through the demand for confession. Langton's suggestion of appropriation might be

35 Morgan, *My Place*, 18.

one problematic consequence of the over-identification of confession and disclosure as a resistant writing practice. Muecke argues that what is needed is 'scrutiny of these social fields where power relations are exercised'. Making the colonized responsible for revealing the crimes of colonialism might lead to 'the endorsement of romances of liberation which often conceive of the social/political sphere as the negative side of a free self-expression'.[36] Muecke provocatively suggests that Daisy Corunna's resistance to Sally sharing 'our business' is, in fact, the most resistant act in a book that relies on resistance constituted as 'self-expression': 'if we take into account the fact that the shift from Sally to her grandmother represents a shift to more traditional Aboriginality, then could it be the case that the grandmother is resisting the very form of the confessional [?]'[37] Here we find that the logic of resistance that is fostered through confession in *My Place* has also been read, conversely, as the application of a further layer of power. *My Place* should thus be read not only as a text invested with the potentiality to mobilize a resistant practice, but also as a critical site to think through the limits of certain rhetorical modes of constituting that resistance as such.

With these arguments in mind, then, *My Place* should be seen as a node around which numerous 'fighting words' have been mobilized. *My Place* is the *topos* of a critical debate over the place of Aboriginal writing in the act of decolonizing settler colonial space. That it reflects some of the dialectical aspects of the dispossession of Aboriginal people through child removal accounts for its strength and widespread legibility, even if this legibility also has its limits. As we have seen, the text's confessional mode of critique can be made available to a kind of textually based mode of assimilation through identification. The most productive legacy of Sally Morgan's memoir is, in this sense, the discussion it generated about the limits of narrating Aboriginal dispossession in writing. *My Place* is important not only because it has been influentially read and celebrated, but also because of the further revelations that have been made through the debates arising from its significance and success.

36 Stephen Muecke, 'Aboriginal Literature and the Repressive Hypothesis', *Southerly* 48 (1988), 405–18.
37 Muecke, 'Aboriginal Literature and the Repressive Hypothesis', 410.

Bibliography

Attwood, Bain, 'Portrait of an Aboriginal as an Artist: Sally Morgan and the Construction of Aboriginality', *Australian Historical Studies* 25/99 (1992), 302–18.

Bird, Delys, and Dennis Haskell, eds, *Whose Place? A Study of Sally Morgan's* My Place (Pymble: Angus and Robertson, 1992).

Griffiths, Michael R., 'Interventions: Race, Culture, and Population via the Thought of A. P. Elkin', in Bruno Cornellier and Michael R. Griffiths, eds, 'Globalizing Unsettlement', A Special Issue of *Settler Colonial Studies* 6/4 (2016), 385–402.

Haag, Oliver, 'Representations of Aboriginality in German Translations of Aboriginal Literature: A Study of Peritexts', *Antipodes: A Global Journal of Australian and New Zealand Literature* 26/1 (2012), 203–8.

Haebich, Anna, *Broken Circles: Fragmenting Indigenous Families 1800–2000* (Fremantle: Fremantle Arts Centre Press, 2000).

——, *Spinning the Dream: Assimilation in Australia 1950–1970* (Fremantle: Fremantle Press, 2008).

Hodge, Bob, and Vijay Mishra, *Dark Side of the Dream: Australian Literature and the Postcolonial Mind* (North Sydney: Allen and Unwin, 1990).

Huggins, Jackie, 'Always Was Always Will Be', *Australian Historical Studies* 25/100 (1993), 459–64.

Langton, Marcia, 'Aboriginal Art and Film: The Politics of Representation', in Michele Grossman, ed., *Blacklines: Contemporary Critical Writing by Indigenous Australians* (Carlton: Melbourne University Press, 2003).

Lejeune, Philippe, *On Autobiography* (Minneapolis: University of Minnesota Press, 1987).

McGregor, Russell, 'Governance Not Genocide', in Dirk Moses, ed., *Genocide and Settler Society* (New York: Bergahn Books, 2004), 290–311.

Michaels, Eric, 'Para-Ethnography: A Review Article of Bruce Chatwin, *The Songlines*, and Sally Morgan, *My Place*', *Art and Text* 30 (1988), 49–50.

Mirritji, Jack, *My People's Life: An Aboriginal's Own Story* (Milingimbi: Milingimbi Language Resource Centre, 1976).

Morgan, Sally, *My Place* (Fremantle: Fremantle Arts Centre Press, 1987).

——, *My Place* (New York: Seaver, 1988).

——, *My Place for Young Readers*, ed. Barbara Ker Wilson (Fremantle: Fremantle Press, 1990).

Muecke, Stephen, 'Aboriginal Literature and the Repressive Hypothesis', *Southerly* 48 (1988), 405–18.

Povinelli, Elizabeth, *The Cunning of Recognition: Indigenous Alterities and the Making of Australian Multiculturalism* (Durham, NC: Duke University Press, 2002).

Roughsey, Dick, *Moon and Rainbow: The Autobiography of an Aboriginal* (Artarmon: Reed, 1971).

Rowse, Tim, 'Sally Morgan's Kaftan', *Australian Historical Studies* 25/100 (1993), 465–8.

Roy, Anjali Gera, 'Voice of Australia: Who Speaks for the Aborigine', in Santosh K. Sareen, Sheel C. Nuna and Malathi Mathur, eds, *Cultural Interfaces* (New Delhi: Indialog, 2004), 18–29.

Sissons, Jeffrey, *First Peoples: Indigenous Cultures and Their Futures* (London: Reaktion, 2005).

Thomas, Sue, 'Aboriginal Subjection and Affirmation', *Meanjin* 47/4 (1988), 755–61.

ERICA LOMBARD

15 Freedom Fighter/Postcolonial Saint: The Symbolic Legacy of Nelson Mandela's *Long Walk to Freedom* (1994)

ABSTRACT

This chapter explores the influence of Nelson Mandela's *Long Walk to Freedom* (1994), placing the autobiography within the context of the global Mandela phenomenon. Focusing on the symbolic function of Mandela's life story, which was concretized by the autobiography but taken up in multiple media and disseminated widely both in South Africa and globally, the chapter examines the shaping of Mandela as an embodiment of racial reconciliation. Mandela was a figure of hope embraced by the global media and rendered a postcolonial saint at the end of a cataclysmic century in which the history of decolonization represented but one disappointing utopian project among many. The chapter suggests that, while the African-centred humanism outlined in *Long Walk to Freedom* held radical resistant potential, Mandela's value as a symbol proved equally available to conservative uses. This ambivalent legacy is being increasingly contested in South Africa.

Long Walk to Freedom (1994) tells one of the defining stories of the twentieth century, whose influence has been felt not only in South Africa, but also across the world. With more than 15 million copies sold globally since its publication (more than Chinua Achebe's *Things Fall Apart* and Kahlil Gibran's *The Prophet*), its reach has been extraordinarily wide.[1] More significantly, the book gave substance and definition to the story of Nelson Mandela (1918–2013), whose contemporary international influence as 'a

1 'Long Walk Sales Spike', *City Press* (8 December 2013) <http://www.news24.com/Archives/City-Press/Long-Walk-sales-spike-20150429> accessed 24 January 2016.

universal symbol of social justice' and 'moral giant',[2] 'an absolutely upright man'[3] and 'moral hero',[4] is unparalleled. Few names and few faces are as internationally recognizable, and few political figures attract the unbridled praise that followed Mandela's passing on 5 December 2013. But while no one can dispute Mandela's impact on the contemporary global political and cultural landscape, the precise nature of this impact continues to inspire debate within the academy and beyond.

Although Mandela played an important material role in the struggle against South Africa's racist system of apartheid and the country's eventual transition to multiracial democracy, this chapter argues that his global influence is primarily symbolic in nature. It is what Mandela *stands for* that is most important, though this too continues to be a matter of debate. Known at various times as a terrorist, a militant freedom fighter, the world's most famous political prisoner, a Nobel Peace Prize laureate, elder statesman and 'President of the World', Mandela has meant very different things to different groups in different contexts.[5] In Wole Soyinka's words, he is 'a symbol that is already stretched to an almost inhuman dimension'.[6] What is clear is that he is associated less with a particular political ideology than a set of human ideals, chief among them freedom and reconciliation. In this chapter, I view Mandela's autobiography in the context of this wider symbolic terrain in South Africa and beyond, in order to trace the multifaceted and sometimes ambivalent implications for *Long Walk to Freedom* as a book of anticolonial resistance.

---

2   Elleke Boehmer, *Nelson Mandela: A Very Short Introduction* (Oxford: Oxford University Press, 2008), 1.
3   Fidel Castro quoted in Boehmer, *Nelson Mandela*, 2.
4   Susan Sontag, 'For Nelson Mandela', *The Threepenny Review* 28 (1987), 27.
5   He was dubbed 'President of the World' when his statue in Westminster Square was unveiled in 2007. See Boehmer, *Nelson Mandela*, 2.
6   Wole Soyinka, 'Views from a Palette of the Cultural Rainbow', in Xolela Mangcu, ed., *The Meaning of Mandela: A Literary and Intellectual Celebration* (Cape Town: HSRC Press, 2006), 25.

The Book

In its discussion of fifteen books that have shaped the postcolonial world, this collection encompasses various forms of the material text, from printed and bound books to pamphlets, magazines and written speeches. *Long Walk to Freedom* complicates our discussion of the book further still. Mandela's story reached its climax in the late 1980s and early 1990s at a moment of intensifying globalization, as a new global form of cultural and political consciousness was developing due to advances in communications technology (including the rise of international media outlets, such as CNN).[7] The impact of *Long Walk to Freedom* cannot be isolated from the larger Mandela phenomenon, a hybrid creation of multiple media, including visual art, film and video, songs and performance, as well as news stories and printed books. The autobiography alone has circulated in various forms: as an illustrated coffee table edition, a comic book, a children's picture book and a film, *Mandela: Long Walk to Freedom*, directed by Justin Chadwick and starring British actor Idris Elba, which was released in December 2013.[8] Yet I would argue that, for all its diverse manifestations, the kernel of the Mandela phenomenon resides in its narrative. At the heart of what Richard Pithouse calls 'the bright strength of the idea of Nelson Mandela' is Mandela's life story.[9] It is this story that *Long Walk to Freedom* played an essential role in concretizing. Although at least two biographies of Mandela had been published before it, *Long Walk to Freedom* was the first comprehensive account of Mandela's life told in his own words, though

---

7   See Manfred B. Steger, *The Rise of the Global Imaginary: Political Ideologies from the French Revolution to the Global War on Terror* (Oxford: Oxford University Press, 2008).
8   On the comic series, see Lize van Robbroeck, 'The Visual Mandela: A Pedagogy of Citizenship', in Rita Barnard, ed., *The Cambridge Companion to Nelson Mandela* (Cambridge: Cambridge University Press, 2013), 244–66.
9   Richard Pithouse, 'Nelson Mandela's Crossing', The South African Civil Society Information Service (6 December 2013) <http://www.sacsis.org.za/site/article/1865> accessed 15 April 2016.

produced with the help of a team that included American collaborator/ ghost-writer, Richard Stengel, and comrades such as Ahmed Kathrada.[10]

Long Walk to Freedom was published by Little, Brown in December 1994, just over half a year after the African National Congress's (ANC) landslide victory in South Africa's first democratic elections, and at the height of international interest in Mandela and South Africa. The book itself is in many ways a typical postcolonial leader's autobiography, following examples set by Jawaharlal Nehru (explored by Elleke Boehmer in Chapter 7), Kwame Nkrumah and others. Like these forebears, it is an anticolonial *Bildung* narrative, charting the political education and development of its subject, who must undergo significant trials and sacrifices before emerging as a leader capable of ushering a new, liberated nation into being.[11] Its 115 short chapters, which proceed chronologically through Mandela's life, were compiled from various sources. These include an early manuscript produced while Mandela was in prison on Robben Island and smuggled out covertly, a collection of speeches and clippings, and a series of interviews with Stengel. The facts it recounts have been well documented: a Xhosa boy, Rolihlahla, begins his journey in rural colonial Transkei; has a series of political awakenings as a young man in Fort Hare and Johannesburg; becomes involved in the ANC and helps to found the ANC Youth League, rising through the movement's ranks to become a central figure in the struggle against apartheid and the ANC's considered decision to embark on a programme of armed resistance.[12] The book documents the relentlessness and violence of the apartheid state's repression of opposition, as well as Mandela's multiple banning orders, trials and nearly three decades of

---

10   The two biographies are Mary Benson, *Nelson Mandela* (Harmondsworth: Penguin, 1986); and Fatima Meer, *Higher than Hope: The Authorized Biography of Nelson Mandela* (London: Hamish Hamilton, 1990).

11   On *Long Walk to Freedom* as *Bildungsroman*, see Daniel Roux, 'Mandela Writing/ Writing Mandela', in Rita Barnard, ed., *Cambridge Companion*, 205–23.

12   See Anthony Sampson, *Mandela: The Authorised Biography* (London: HarperCollins, 1999); Tom Lodge, *Mandela: A Critical Life* (Oxford: Oxford University Press, 2006); Boehmer, *Nelson Mandela*.

incarceration, most of which took place on Robben Island. It details the dehumanizing prison system – a microcosm of the world beyond prison bars, and conversely an extension of the everyday indignities suffered by black South Africans – but also the resistance and resourcefulness of the prisoners. Throughout, the autobiography emphasizes Mandela's consistent and stubborn assertion of his own selfhood, how he maintained his dignity in a system that deliberately denied it to black South Africans. In covering the run-up to Mandela's long-awaited release, the book also recounts the tense drama of negotiation between the ANC and the National Party, the threat of civil war and finally the country's purportedly miraculous peaceful transition to democracy. Mandela's inauguration as the first president of the 'new' South Africa ends the book, with the country poised hopefully on the brink of a reconstructed future.

Long Walk to Freedom therefore tells an essentially postcolonial story, dramatizing a metaphorical journey from tradition to modernity, from oppression to liberation and from a colonial to a postcolonial world. The narrative binds Mandela's biography to that of the South African nation, so that Mandela's 'long walk to freedom' becomes the embodiment of South Africa's own protracted struggle for liberation – this, too, is in common with other nation-founding autobiographies.

Freedom Fighter/Postcolonial Saint

Just what this freedom would mean, and exactly whom it was fought and won for, is crucial to the impact of *Long Walk to Freedom* and to Mandela's symbolic legacy more broadly. The narrative heart of the autobiography is the development of Mandela's commitment to an ethical principle inextricable from, but more fundamental than, political ideology, which is most clearly stated in the book's final passages. There, Mandela describes how he came to understand his individual freedom as inseparable from that of his fellow black South Africans, that 'the chains on any one of my people were the chains on all of them, the chains on all of my people were the chains on me'.[13] This understanding of freedom is aligned with the traditional African philosophy of *ubuntu*, which holds that selfhood is constituted interpersonally, that one is a person through other people, and so one's humanity, wellbeing and freedom are inextricable from those of others. Apartheid, which systematically prevented mutuality and commonality between people, represented a fundamental violation of this principle. It is this humanist ideal that undergirded Mandela's dedication to, and extraordinary sacrifice for, 'the ideal of a democratic and free society in which all persons live together in harmony and with equal opportunities'.[14]

Crucially, Mandela then describes how he came to extend this relational ethic to his *oppressors*, the white South Africans who perpetrated or benefitted from the systemic and systematic injustice of apartheid. During the 'long and lonely years' of incarceration he realized that 'the oppressor must be liberated just as surely as the oppressed', for both 'are robbed of their humanity' by a relationship of domination. 'A man who takes away another man's freedom is a prisoner of hatred', he notes, 'locked behind the bars of prejudice and narrow-mindedness'. On his release, he took up the project 'to liberate the oppressed and the oppressor both'.[15] *Long Walk to Freedom* is therefore also a story of inclusivity replacing sectarian politics, narrating Mandela's shift from exclusive African nationalism to a steadfast commitment to non-racialism. Consequently, Mandela considers immature those who advocate exclusionary politics, such as the Pan Africanist Congress and Black Consciousness activists he encounters, who argue for the exclusion of white South Africans from participating in the making of the new South African nation. In this way, as Pithouse notes, Mandela's 'ethical choices transcended rather than mirrored those of his oppressors'.[16]

As Boehmer emphasizes, whereas the 'African' has been a concept against which notions of freedom, humanity and civilization have tended to be defined in Western discourse, Mandela's humanism was anchored in an African concept of selfhood. Subtly, but also radically, Mandela undermined

---

13   Nelson Mandela, *Long Walk to Freedom: The Autobiography of Nelson Mandela* (London: Abacus, 1995 [1994]), 751.
14   Mandela, *Long Walk*, 438.
15   Mandela, *Long Walk*, 751.
16   Pithouse, 'Nelson Mandela's Crossing'.

the spurious oppositions on which the colonial and apartheid projects rested – between Africanness, on the one hand, and humanity, rationality and modernity, on the other.[17] The expansive, inclusive ethos he set out in *Long Walk to Freedom* did more than simply resist oppression based on racism and white supremacy: it rejected their fundamental logic, seeking out a redemptive space beyond binary oppositions.[18]

From this empathetic premise, Mandela assumed the task of founding a new, united South African nation from a deeply fragmented population. Centuries of legislation, discrimination and violence would be replaced with an aspirational constitution based on the protection of universal human rights and equality. For white South Africans fearful of their future in a black-majority democracy, Mandela fulfilled what Deborah Posel has called their 'longing to be spared the dreaded brunt of black rage'.[19] This was certainly a pragmatic move too, for the South African economy was (and remains) largely controlled by whites; the country, already crippled by anti-apartheid economic sanctions, could ill afford their desertion.

Although Mandela forswore his being singled out as the hero of South Africa's narrative (even as he also utilized this status in strategic ways), he became both author and perfecter of the new South Africa in popular discourse. Madiba (to use the clan name by which he is popularly and affectionately known) is frequently referred to as 'Tata' [father] by South Africans. In the years following his retirement from public life, Mandela iconography became pervasive in South Africa. Since 2013, his face has appeared on every South African banknote, and Mandela memorials and monuments have proliferated across the country, from his capture site in KwaZulu-Natal and the giant benedictory statue that stands before the Union Buildings in Pretoria, to the smaller shrines of street art and faded posters on the walls of corner stores around the country.

17 Boehmer, *Nelson Mandela*, 180.
18 It is worth recalling Jacques Derrida's messianic description of Mandela as the fulfilment of 'the law above laws'. See Jacques Derrida, 'Admiration of Nelson Mandela, or The Laws of Reflection', trans. Charles Gelman, *Law & Literature* 26/1 (2014), 11.
19 Deborah Posel, '"Madiba Magic": Politics as Enchantment', in Rita Barnard, ed., *Cambridge Companion*, 77.

Figure 15.1: Tributes to Mandela in a fishmonger in Woodstock, Cape Town, and on the side of the Cape Town Civic Centre building.

Nelson Mandela's Long Walk to Freedom *(1994)*

His influence, however, went far beyond South Africa's borders. Mandela's story reached its climax at a crucial moment of intersection between the decline of the nation-state and the rise of the global mass media. *Long Walk to Freedom*'s shaping of the world has much to do with this particular historical juncture. Since the 1980s, Mandela had become, and was in fact deliberately promoted as, a messianic figure at the centre of the international movement to end apartheid.[20] Through the highly effective Free Mandela campaign, an initiative of the British Anti-Apartheid Movement and the ANC, he came to be 'the world's most famous political prisoner' and the personification of the struggle against apartheid. The sanctions campaign, as Tom Lodge observes, was 'the most widely supported single-issue protest in the world' between 1959 and 1994, helping to pressure the apartheid government into negotiating with the ANC.[21] Mandela's walk through the gates of Victor Verster prison on 11 February 1990 was watched by a global television audience of millions. The 1993 Nobel Peace Prize, shared with the last apartheid president, F. W. de Klerk, followed soon after.

Although Mandela's struggle was against a very specific system of racial oppression in South Africa, through the international media he came to embody resistance to oppression, the defence of human rights and racial reconciliation in a much broader (and vaguer) sense. South African race relations in turn became a proxy for similar issues elsewhere. With its message of extraordinary forbearance and forgiveness, *Long Walk to Freedom* confirmed and extended the mythical status of Mandela that had been fashioned in the years of his imprisonment. By the early 1990s, in an age of ambiguity, this story of moral victory was one that everyone, more or less, could agree on. The end of the racist system of apartheid, too, seemed unequivocally a thing to be celebrated. Above all, the Mandela narrative, with its essentially upward trajectory, is a story of hope. Coming at the end of a calamitous century, in which the disappointing history of decolonization elsewhere in Africa represented merely one failed utopian project among many, Mandela's story seemed to affirm that the world could be changed

---

20 See Rob Nixon, 'Mandela, Messianism, and the Media', *Transition* 52 (1994), 42–55.
21 Lodge, *Mandela*, 155.

for the better: racism could give way to reconciliation, and freedom and equality could triumph over oppression. Thus, Sarah Nuttall and Achille Mbembe observe that Mandela represents 'the twentieth century in some of its deepest dreamscapes'.[22] Put another way, the world found in Mandela the postcolonial saint it needed, an individual whose story might redeem the aspirations of a cynical and violent age.

If Mandela symbolized a new, enlightened humanism, and perhaps a new ethical direction for the twenty-first century, the book, *Long Walk to Freedom*, had a particular talismanic power. To purchase Mandela's autobiography was in some way to grasp hold of his symbolic potency in object form, to affirm and share in his goodness, and to gain entry into the enlightened humanity he embodied. For many white South Africans, the book functioned more specifically as a symbolic ticket into the new South Africa, which could be displayed with pride on the living-room bookshelf. That *Long Walk to Freedom* has featured on lists of the least-read bestselling books suggests that it was not necessary even to read the autobiography – the act of acquisition was sufficient.[23]

Mandela himself became a kind of talisman in his later years. Indeed, the phrase 'long walk to freedom' (adapted, incidentally, from Nehru's writing) now has the status of cliché. For the ANC, Mandela became a trump card to be played during election seasons to drum up support among wearying voters. For international celebrities of the late 1990s and early 2000s, a photograph with Madiba proved an essential status symbol, for 'Mandela's fame confirmed the fame of others'.[24] His facility for accommodating, connecting with and appealing to a variety of views and characters across a spectrum of political, cultural and economic divides led in the years following his release to at times curious, even absurd, juxtapositions:

---

22 Sarah Nuttall and Achille Mbembe, 'Mandela's Mortality', in Rita Barnard, ed., *Cambridge Companion*, 287.
23 John Rentoul, 'The Top Ten: Books People Buy but Don't Read', *The Independent* (2 June 2013) <http://www.independent.co.uk/arts-entertainment/books/features/the-top-ten-books-people-buy-but-dont-read-8636866.html> accessed 20 April 2016.
24 Rita Barnard, 'Afterword', in Rita Barnard, ed., *Cambridge Companion*, 292.

photographs show him equally at home with Fidel Castro and Muammar Gaddafi as Queen Elizabeth II, Michael Jackson and the Spice Girls.

But the transformation of Mandela from anticolonial firebrand into secular saint has also frequently dampened the incendiary potential of his African-centred humanism and his anticolonial resistance. Like all symbols, Mandela is open to reinterpretation. For instance, when *Long Walk to Freedom* is quoted in popular discourse, emphasis tends to fall on the text's very general contemplations on the nature of freedom, forgiveness and human virtue. Floating free of their specific twentieth-century South African context, these humanist concepts transform into internet memes that pair beatific images of Mandela with quotations from *Long Walk to Freedom*. In Twitter and Facebook feeds these become nebulous self-help-style mantras to be posted and reposted: for example, 'I learned that courage was not the absence of fear, but the triumph over it. [...] The brave man is not he who does not feel afraid, but he who conquers that fear'.[25]

At its worst, this co-opting of Mandela has transformed him into an analgesic, used by the powerful to preserve an unequal status quo. Clint Eastwood's 2009 Oscar-nominated film *Invictus* provides a pertinent example of this trend. As a number of critics have suggested, Eastwood's hagiographic depiction of Mandela, played by Morgan Freeman, and the film's simplification of the history it relates, results in what is ultimately a wish-fulfilling tale of interracial reconciliation told through the appealing stereotype of the victorious underdog sports team.[26] In response to contemporary (American) anxieties about race, anger and deepening inequality, *Invictus* offers a sentimental and consoling account of the 1995 Rugby World Cup that broaches little of the economic, political or social complexity of race relations in South Africa, or indeed elsewhere.[27] Litheko Modisane observes that Eastwood's Mandela in fact *silences* voices of opposition in the film that insist on the legitimacy of black pain in the past and present, and so becomes 'a vehicle to contain and delegitimize black social and

25 Mandela, *Long Walk*, 748.
26 See Albert Grundlingh et al., 'Roundtable on *Invictus*', *Safundi* 13/1–2 (2012), 115–50.
27 See Lily Saint, in Albert Grundlingh et al., 'Roundtable on *Invictus*', 133.

political aspirations'.²⁸ Promoting an amnesic commitment to national unity, Mandela functions as an elder sage character (another well-worn stereotype in sports films) through which 'the redemption of young white men' may be secured.²⁹ In other words, whites are re-centred in the narrative of race and reconciliation – a point to which I will return below.

Justin Chadwick's 2013 film of *Long Walk to Freedom* performs similar flattening work, reproducing and confirming the heroic Mandela narrative even as it attempts to depict less saintly aspects of Mandela's life, such as his adulterous relationships. With Mandela's comrades and confidantes reduced to sidekicks, Mandela is the force that all but single-handedly revolutionizes the ANC and leads the struggle against apartheid. As with the dissenting voices in *Invictus*, Winnie Madikizela-Mandela is styled conversely as an unregenerate antagonist, and her anger and pain as obstinate impediments to Mandela's far more heroic project of national reconciliation and renewal.

These adoptions and interpretations of Mandela's story in the global cultural landscape – the focus on his forgiveness or redemption of white South Africans and on Mandela as saviour – are central to the contestation of his legacy in South Africa in recent years.

Post-Mandela

In her 2008 biography of Mandela, Boehmer noted: 'It remains clear that we must seek the lasting legacy of Mandela's long struggle for freedom in the domain of the ethical and not the economic, the figural and not the material'.³⁰ In recent years, however, as the racial and economic fault lines of South African (and global) society have become increasingly conspicuous,

---

28   Litheko Modisane, 'Mandela in Film and Television', in Rita Barnard, ed., *Cambridge Companion*, 225.
29   Modisane, 'Mandela in Film and Television', 234.
30   Boehmer, *Nelson Mandela*, 174.

the validity of these distinctions is being questioned. Along with it, the adulation of Mandela as national liberator and the triumphalist 'rainbow nation' rhetoric of the early post-apartheid years have come under intensifying scrutiny, especially since the emergence of the Rhodes Must Fall and Fees Must Fall student movements in South Africa in 2015.

In a newspaper piece entitled 'I was not liberated by Mandela', Malaika wa Azania, a prominent figure among young black intellectuals in South Africa, questioned 'the Mandelafication of the Struggle against apartheid' in post-1994 public narratives. This phenomenon, she argued, has occluded the agency and anti-apartheid resistance of ordinary black South Africans.[31] Many critics have also drawn attention to Mandela's failures while in office, such as his neglect of the snowballing HIV/AIDS crisis and the adoption of the neoliberal Growth, Employment and Redistribution economic policy, which has exacerbated the country's profound economic inequality. Some, like South African politician Julius Malema, have gone further still, arguing that Mandela and the ANC negotiators effectively 'sold out' black South Africans during the negotiated transition to democracy by acceding to the demands of global (white) capital at the expense of those whose welfare they purported to promote.[32] Here, Slavoj Žižek's argument that Mandela's 'universal glory is also a sign that he really didn't disturb the global order of power' seems particularly trenchant.[33]

Viewed from this perspective, Mandela's symbolic nation-building efforts, such as his famous donning of the Springbok captain's jersey at the 1995 Rugby World Cup (mythologized by *Invictus*) and even the Truth and Reconciliation Commission's commitment to an ethic of forgiveness, have

---

31   Malaika wa Azania, 'I Was Not Liberated by Mandela', *The Sunday Independent* (19 July 2015) <http://www.iol.co.za/sundayindependent/i-was-not-liberated-by-mandela-1887330> accessed 22 January 2016.

32   Ranjeni Munusamy, 'Julius Malema and the Move towards #MandelaMustFall', *The Daily Maverick* (4 December 2015) <http://www.dailymaverick.co.za/article/2015-12-04-julius-malema-and-the-move-towards-mandelamustfall/> accessed 28 January 2016.

33   Slavoj Žižek, 'If Nelson Mandela Really Had Won, He Wouldn't Be Seen as a Universal Hero', *The Guardian* (9 December 2013) <https://www.theguardian.com/commentisfree/2013/dec/09/if-nelson-mandela-really-had-won> accessed 15 April 2016.

had harmful material consequences. Rhodes Must Fall activists emphasize that Mandela's inclusive humanism served the material interests of white South Africans in effect, if not in intention. Welcomed unreservedly into the new South Africa, they were absolved of having to acknowledge their benefit from, and complicity in, the apartheid system. The ongoing legacy of apartheid, not to mention practical questions of responsibility, restitution and justice, could likewise be ignored. To adapt Mandela's own analogy, the oppressors were liberated without comprehending their own imprisonment – no matter how many had a copy of *Long Walk to Freedom* on their bookshelves. As a result, gross economic inequality and white cultural supremacy have continued nearly unabated, to the marginalization, detriment and frustration of many black South Africans. Mandela's powerful and lauded work in the realm of the symbolic thus remains an insufficient substitute for the material changes necessary for the pursuit of equality and dignity for all.

Yet we may also regard the debate and critique spearheaded by these new post-Mandela political movements as reflecting the kind of robust conversation in public discourse that Mandela himself promoted. In an address to the Nelson Mandela Foundation when he retired from public life in the early 2000s, Mandela welcomed the questioning of his legacy, emphasizing that the Foundation did not 'need to protect him' from critique.[34] We might, in the end, view these developments as a necessary part of the 'longer and even more difficult road' towards a society that 'respects and enhances the freedom of others', which Mandela describes in the final passage of his autobiography, and to which he dedicated his life.[35] In the meantime, *Long Walk to Freedom*, along with Mandela's legacy, will remain a symbolic touchstone to be embraced, critiqued and contested as the project of decolonization continues.

---

34 Quoted in Nuttall and Mbembe, 'Mandela's Mortality', 283.
35 Mandela, *Long Walk*, 751.

Bibliography

Barnard, Rita, 'Afterword', in Rita Barnard, ed., *The Cambridge Companion to Nelson Mandela*, 291–4.
——, ed., *The Cambridge Companion to Nelson Mandela* (Cambridge: Cambridge University Press, 2013).
Benson, Mary, *Nelson Mandela* (Harmondsworth: Penguin, 1986).
Boehmer, Elleke, *Nelson Mandela: A Very Short Introduction* (Oxford: Oxford University Press, 2008).
Derrida, Jacques, 'Admiration of Nelson Mandela, or The Laws of Reflection', trans. Charles Gelman, *Law & Literature* 26/1 (2014), 9–30.
Grundlingh, Albert, Stéphane Robolin, Abigail Hinsman, Lily Saint, Sharrona Pearl and Samantha Pinto, 'Roundtable on *Invictus*', *Safundi* 13/1–2 (2012), 115–50.
Lodge, Tom, *Mandela: A Critical Life* (Oxford: Oxford University Press, 2006).
'Long Walk Sales Spike', *City Press* (8 December 2013) <http://www.news24.com/Archives/City-Press/Long-Walk-sales-spike-20150429> accessed 24 January 2016.
Mandela, Nelson, *Long Walk to Freedom: The Autobiography of Nelson Mandela* (London: Abacus, 1995 [1994]).
Meer, Fatima, *Higher than Hope: The Authorized Biography of Nelson Mandela* (London: Hamish Hamilton, 1990).
Modisane, Litheko, 'Mandela in Film and Television', in Rita Barnard, ed., *The Cambridge Companion to Nelson Mandela*, 224–43.
Munusamy, Ranjeni, 'Julius Malema and the Move towards #MandelaMustFall', *The Daily Maverick* (4 December 2015) <http://www.dailymaverick.co.za/article/2015-12-04-julius-malema-and-the-move-towards-mandelamustfall/> accessed 28 January 2016.
Nixon, Rob, 'Mandela, Messianism, and the Media', *Transition* 52 (1994), 42–55.
Nuttall, Sarah, and Achille Mbembe, 'Mandela's Mortality', in Rita Barnard, ed., *The Cambridge Companion to Nelson Mandela*, 267–90.
Pithouse, Richard, 'Nelson Mandela's Crossing', *The South African Civil Society Information Service* (6 December 2013) <http://www.sacsis.org.za/site/article/1865> accessed 15 April 2016.
Posel, Deborah, '"Madiba Magic": Politics as Enchantment', in Rita Barnard, ed., *The Cambridge Companion to Nelson Mandela*, 70–91.
Rentoul, John, 'The Top Ten: Books People Buy But Don't Read', *The Independent* (2 June 2013) <http://www.independent.co.uk/arts-entertainment/books/

features/the-top-ten-books-people-buy-but-dont-read-8636866.html> accessed 20 April 2016.

Roux, Daniel, 'Mandela Writing/Writing Mandela', in Rita Barnard, ed., *The Cambridge Companion to Nelson Mandela*, 205–23.

Sampson, Anthony, *Mandela: The Authorised Biography* (London: HarperCollins, 1999).

Sontag, Susan, 'For Nelson Mandela', *The Threepenny Review* 28 (1987), 27.

Soyinka, Wole, 'Views from a Palette of the Cultural Rainbow', in Xolela Mangcu, ed., *The Meaning of Mandela: A Literary and Intellectual Celebration* (Cape Town: HSRC Press, 2006), 24–40.

Steger, Manfred B., *The Rise of the Global Imaginary: Political Ideologies from the French Revolution to the Global War on Terror* (Oxford: Oxford University Press, 2008).

Van Robbroeck, Lize, 'The Visual Mandela: A Pedagogy of Citizenship', in Rita Barnard, ed., *The Cambridge Companion to Nelson Mandela*, 244–66.

Wa Azania, Malaika, 'I Was Not Liberated by Mandela', *The Sunday Independent* (19 July 2015) <http://www.iol.co.za/sundayindependent/i-was-not-liberated-by-mandela-1887330> accessed 22 January 2016.

Žižek, Slavoj, 'If Nelson Mandela Really Had Won, He Wouldn't Be Seen as a Universal Hero', *The Guardian* (9 December 2013) <https://www.theguardian.com/commentisfree/2013/dec/09/if-nelson-mandela-really-had-won> accessed 15 April 2016.

ANTOINETTE BURTON AND ISABEL HOFMEYR

Afterword: Plotting a Postcolonial Course in Fifteen Chapters

How should we teach postcolonial history and literature now? One cumulative effect of this volume is the prospect of new syllabi for the contemporary classroom: reading lists that both direct our attention to the work of canonical titles and suggest new textual, temporal and geopolitical parameters for our students' consideration. Just as a syllabus is not simply a reading list, so too *Fighting Words* is more than a mere set of titles. It is, rather, an orientation device: a guide to the relationship between time and space, genre and form, author and text. It's a way of making sense of bodies of knowledge and, in this particular case, of worlds shaped by modern imperialism and its aftermath. Any syllabus drawing on this collection for its facts and fictions would be registering a commitment to centring books in all their materiality and mobility in the study of anglophone empire. Taken together, these essays make the case that the politics of print culture mattered for the conditions through which imperialism took shape and that books themselves are indices of the global politics of postcolonial change.

The syllabi that emerge from this collection will take aim at some established conventions and reconfirm others. Students of British imperialism (and imperialism more broadly) might expect to see Jawaharlal Nehru; they may be surprised to see Anna Julia Cooper or to learn of the transnational, even global, reach of the Ugandan literary magazine, *Transition*. But their diverse authors and origins aside, the texts chosen for examination here tilt toward resistance – via noisy, disruptive narratives that antagonized colonial power and unsettled the social and political order it left in its wake. By leading from the presumption that such order could be, and was, routinely thrown on the defensive by books and other written forms that challenged the security of empire, contributors upend the Victorian notion that the British Empire was a force for peace and stability – 'Pax Britannica' by any other name. The story that emerges from these pages is one of restless motion, anticolonial movement and ungovernability at all scales. In that sense, 'fighting words' suggests a postcolonial history from the bottom up.

To be sure, many of the authors included here were colonial subjects who can hardly be considered common people, let alone subalterns. Nehru, Cheikh Anta Diop, Nelson Mandela and W. E. B. Du Bois were, effectively, the talented tenth. Yet what the collection maps are the radical subjects they took up and the ideas they networked through the combination of licit and illicit reading publics. Significantly, the deeply place-based contexts that generated the authors and allowed their writing to take off are closely attended to, as is the virality – literal and figurative – that made them dangerous and, in the case of Diop, seditious according to the letter of the law. If you had fifteen weeks to read through each chapter, you could easily make *Fighting Words* the foundational text in a course called 'Postcolonial History from Below: The Local and the Global'.

Historians looking for new narrative configurations of postcolonial time and place will also find valuable material here. Sol Plaatje represents an important chronological pivot in the volume. Roughly halfway between Marx and Mandela, his 1916 *Native Life in South Africa* shows the afterlife of imperial war and its impact on the shape of racial law and struggle across the rest of the twentieth century. The inclusion of Sally Morgan's 1987 *My Place* allows us to read back through Annie Besant and Cooper and to see how key intersectionality is to histories of imperial power. To paraphrase Paul Gilroy, gender was the modality in which indigeneity was lived – a social and economic fact that colonial officials simultaneously acknowledged and erased, setting up a complex and often contradictory form of identity politics at the heart of postcoloniality and its cognate historical condition, decolonization. In fact, *Fighting Words* raises more questions than it answers about the relationship between the time of decolonization (arguably well afoot by the mid-nineteenth century) and the time of the postcolonial (widely assumed to be a post-1945 phenomenon). Readers seeking to sync up these histories or, alternatively, to recalibrate them around insurgent ideas and their circulation between covers, would do well to think of the collection as the basis for a course on 'Decolonizing Postcolonial History'.

Recent work in the field anticipates just this kind of move, insofar as what Tracey Banivanua Mar calls 'procedural' histories of decolonization are coming under scrutiny for failing to capture the textured histories of postcolonial life, work and art.[1] This is in part because such top-down accounts have ignored the dense worlds of petitioning, letter writing and print culture that sustained a global imperial imaginary in which decolonizing activities – resistance by any other name – were the very stuff of the imperial experience itself. Rather than plotting a course serially – first colonialism, then postcolonialism – *Fighting Words* challenges received wisdom about the origins of postcolonial thought, showing time and again what a truly late Victorian phenomenon (via work by Marx, Besant, Nehru and even arguably Mandela) it was. Always future oriented, postcolonial thinking could also be prophetic, as with J. B. Danquah, whose publication laid the groundwork for an Afrocentric idiom that was to serve as the basis for 1960s Black Power in the US. Nehru too grappled with the futurity of the postcolonial Indian citizen, that indubitably national self whose emergence he choreographed out of his own autobiography. The template he laid down was to have an enduring effect on how late twentieth-century postcolonial leaders, from Mandela to Aung San Suu Kyi, narrated their journeys toward freedom. Surely these narratives could be the basis for a syllabus entitled 'Writing the History of Postcolonial Futures'.

Exploring the literary structure of Nehru's autobiography, as Elleke Boehmer does, underlines the rich formal and generic experiments that intellectuals in empire had of necessity to undertake as they sought to create new worlds and realities. Such experiments have of course constituted a core concern of postcolonial literary studies and many of the essays continue this tradition. We hear how Du Bois grappled with turning embodied experience into memorable literary form; how the Guatemalan writer Miguel Ángel Asturias's 1949 novel *Hombres de maíz* [*Men of Maize*] was one of the earliest experiments in fusing Mayan literary genres with avant-garde tropes, a mixture that long confounded academic critics who found

---

[1] Tracey Banivanua Mar, *Decolonisation and the Pacific: Indigenous Globalisation and the Ends of Empire* (Cambridge: Cambridge University Press, 2016).

the book incoherent and perplexing; and how the 'literary beatnik', Rajat Neogy, used the literary magazine *Transition* to invent the category of East African literature, carving out a space between colony, nation and empire.

This attention to literary form not only extends our appreciation of postcolonial literary canons but also helps us understand what exactly made these texts portable. *The Communist Manifesto* travelled as much via the currents of broader international socialist and anticolonial movements as through its memorable mottos and its supple self-reflexive structure. Indeed, the *Manifesto* came to embody these movements as its calling card. The collection illuminates other such intimate associations between book and social movements, with texts recruiting followers by recasting their experiences through new narrative modes. Social movements also created space for older texts to re-emerge, whether Anna Julia Cooper through black feminist thinkers; Emily Hobhouse via antinuclear pacifist campaigns of the 1980s; or Cheikh Anta Diop courtesy of contemporary hip-hop modes.

Importantly, the collection highlights moments when texts do not travel, when the traction of their address fails. One such case is Frank Hardy's *The Unlucky Australians*, which could not find a US publisher despite the resonances between Aboriginal politics, the Civil Rights movement and the position of Native Americans, as well as the concerted intercession of two influential academics with leading US publishers. Australia did not register in the world of US publishers who had forgotten their settler colonial past, whilst this nevertheless ensured that the book found traction in the Commonwealth.

The core business of book history is to grasp the relationship between the text, the object that conveys the text and the act that grasps it. Several of the essays take on the middle term of this equation, probing how the material form of the book itself enabled its traction in the world. Priyasha Mukhopadhyay examines an important but unacknowledged postcolonial form, namely the lecture, in both its spoken and printed modes. Paying careful attention to the accounts of the 'live' version and the subsequent printed version, the chapter teases out the different intellectual modes that Besant's lectures enabled. In addition to the charisma of the performance itself, Besant set out the desired aftereffect of her talks: 'A lecturer ought not to do the study for the hearer, much less to give out cut-and-dried opinions which the hearer is expected to adopt. The lecturer's work is to stimulate thought, rather than to do the thinking'. What a great caveat with which to begin any kind of syllabus writing, let alone course preparation in the age of TED talks, flipped classrooms and the largely disembodied experience of digital humanities.

In Besant's formulation, the reader has work and responsibilities, an important theme in studies of the postcolonial reader who often faced a 'loose-weave' text, cut and pasted from other publications. Such juxtapositional texts are reader-driven, requiring her to stitch together the 'syndicated universe of information' that Janet Remmington identifies in the 'Here, There and Everywhere' column in Plaatje's newspaper *Tsala ea Batho*.

The collection also provides a rich sense of the different publishing histories and biographies of texts, extending our appreciation of the world of postcolonial publishing and textual production. We follow the circuits of Asturias's novel through the routes of Spanish-language publishing and indeed beyond. We hear the touching life story of Danquah's book, its original manuscript form burned in a fire in 1941 caused by an electrical fault, a poignant anticipation of the anticolonial neglect (itself a type of intellectual malfunction) of the reworked and published version.

In his powerful account of *The Wretched of the Earth*, John Narayan sets out Fanon's prescient grasp of this malfunction, even in the euphoric moments of decolonization. Like Plaatje, Fanon was something of a prophet, delivering warnings on the pitfalls of anticolonial nationalism and the neo-imperialism to come. And, like the Black Panthers who wrestled with its 'bedeviling' meanings, students of the contemporary present may be surprised by its uncanny vision of the world in which they now live. This particular chapter might make a fitting final seminar to the proposed syllabus, looking both back and forward to the long postcolonial trajectory of fighting words and their changing targets. Because of how syllabi work, *The Wretched of the Earth* could also be used as the basis of the very first meeting of a world history or literature course, precisely because of how it looks forward to an uncertain global history via the tumultuous colonial and nascent postcolonial past it archives. Indeed, in the company of the other books whose lives are archived here, Fanon is just one of many texts with the capacity to remind us of the powerful spectres which animate books that change the world.

Notes on Contributors

ELLEKE BOEHMER is Professor of World Literature in English in the English Faculty at the University of Oxford, and Director of the Oxford Centre for Life Writing (OCLW), based in Wolfson College. Her most recent monograph is *Postcolonial Poetics: 21st-century critical readings*, and her 2015 study, *Indian Arrivals 1870–1915*, won the biennial ESSE 2016 prize for Literature in English. Her novels include *Nile Baby* (2008) and *The Shouting in the Dark* (2015).

ANTOINETTE BURTON teaches at the University of Illinois, Urbana-Champaign, where she is the director of the Illinois Program for Research in the Humanities. With Isabel Hofmeyr, she is the editor of *Ten Books That Shaped the British Empire* (2014). She is the author of *An ABC of Queen Victoria's Empire* (2017) and the general series editor of the six-volume *A Cultural History of Western Empires* (2018).

RUTH BUSH is Senior Lecturer in French and Comparative Literature at the University of Bristol. Her research interests include African literature, material print cultures, and decolonial epistemology. Her first book was *Publishing Africa in French: Literary Institutions and Decolonization 1945–67* (Liverpool University Press, 2016). She has also published a short history of New Beacon Books, the UK's first radical black bookshop and publishing house, and co-produced an exhibition and digital resource about *Awa: la revue de la femme noire*, an early African women's magazine.

DOMINIC DAVIES is a Lecturer in English at City, University of London. In 2018 he finished a British Academy Postdoctoral Fellowship at the University of Oxford, where he also completed his DPhil in 2015. He is the author of *Imperial Infrastructure and Spatial Resistance in Colonial Literature, 1880–1930* (Peter Lang, 2017) and *Urban Comics: Infrastructure & the Global City in Contemporary Graphic Narratives* (Routledge, 2019), and has written a number of articles and chapters on similar topics. He is also the co-editor of *Planned Violence: Post/Colonial Urban Infrastructure, Literature & Culture* (Palgrave Macmillan, 2018) and *Documenting Trauma in Comics: Traumatic Pasts, Embodied Histories & Graphic Reportage* (Palgrave Macmillan, 2019).

MICHAEL R. GRIFFITHS researches at the intersection of literature and history. His monograph *The Distribution of Settlement: Appropriation and Refusal in Australian Literature and Culture* was published by the University of Western Australia Publishing in 2018. He teaches at the University of Wollongong (Australia).

ISABEL HOFMEYR is Professor of African Literature at the University of the Witwatersrand in Johannesburg and Distinguished Global Professor in the English Department of New York University. Her most recent book is *Gandhi's Printing Press: Experiments in Slow Reading* (2013). Along with Antoinette Burton she has edited *Ten Books That Shaped the British Empire: Creating an Imperial Commons* (2014). She currently heads up a project entitled Oceanic Humanities for the Global South (www.oceanichumanities.com).

ROUVEN KUNSTMANN is a Postdoctoral Research Fellow on the ERC-funded project 'The Political Economy of African Development: Ethnicity, Nation and History' at the University of London, London Business School. He received his doctoral degree in history from the University of Oxford and focuses on print cultures, ethnicity, nationalism, decolonization and photography in West Africa, contributing to the understanding of global and local knowledge and information circulation. He is an editor of *The Global Histories of Books: Methods and Practices* (Palgrave, 2017) and his work has been recently published in *Social Dynamics: A Journal of African Studies*.

ERICA LOMBARD is a Postdoctoral Research Fellow at the University of Cape Town, where she works on South African literary publishing after apartheid. Her research interests include book history, memory and nostalgia in postcolonial contexts, and South Africa in the global imaginary.

Her work has appeared in the *Journal of Commonwealth and Postcolonial Studies*, *English in Africa* and the *Journal of Literary Studies*. She is also the designer and co-editor of the Oxford-based *Postcolonial Writers Make Worlds* (www.writersmakeworlds.com) website.

BENJAMIN MOUNTFORD is Senior Lecturer in History at the Australian Catholic University in Melbourne. He was formerly a David Myers Research Fellow at La Trobe University (2017–18) and a Michael Brock Junior Research Fellow in Modern British History at Corpus Christi College, University of Oxford. He is the author of *Britain, China, & Colonial Australia* (Oxford University Press, 2016) and co-editor of *A Global History of Gold Rushes* (University of California Press, 2018).

PRIYASHA MUKHOPADHYAY is Assistant Professor of English at Yale University. Her research focuses on South Asian literary and book cultures of the late nineteenth and early twentieth centuries. Her work has appeared in *Journal of Commonwealth Literature*, *Journal of Victorian Culture* and *Political Theology*. She is a co-editor of *The Global Histories of Books: Methods and Practices* (2017).

JOHN NARAYAN is Lecturer in Sociology at Birmingham City University. His current research focuses on the global politics of Black Power. His first book *John Dewey: The Global Public and its Problems* was published with Manchester University Press. And he is co-editor of *European Cosmopolitanism: Colonial Histories and Post-Colonial Societies*.

REILAND RABAKA is Professor of African, African American and Caribbean Studies in the Department of Ethnic Studies at the University of Colorado, Boulder. He is also a Research Fellow in the College of Human Sciences at the University of South Africa (UNISA). He is the author of more than fifty scholarly articles, book chapters, and essays, as well as more than a dozen books, including *Du Bois's Dialectics*; *Africana Critical Theory*; *Against Epistemic Apartheid: W.E.B. Du Bois and the Disciplinary Decadence of Sociology*; *Forms of Fanonism: Frantz Fanon's Critical Theory and the Dialectics of Decolonization*; *Concepts of Cabralism: Amilcar Cabral and*

Africana Critical Theory; *The Negritude Movement*; *Hip Hop's Inheritance*; *Hip Hop's Amnesia*; and *The Hip Hop Movement*.

JANET REMMINGTON combines her work as an editorial director at Routledge with her own research and writing. She was co-editor of *Sol Plaatje's Native Life in South Africa: Past and Present* (Wits University Press, 2016), which won the 2018 Non-Fiction Prize awarded by South Africa's Institute for Humanities and the Social Sciences. Her publications include articles in *Journal of Southern African Studies* and *Studies in Travel Writing* and a chapter on Plaatje's 1914 sea voyage in *Sea Narratives: Cultural Responses to the Sea, 1600-Present* (Palgrave, 2016). She has studied at the Universities of Cape Town, Oxford Brookes, Oxford and Royal Holloway, University of London. She is working on a cultural history of black South African travel texts as her doctoral research project at the University of York. Her African Studies Masters dissertation at the University of Oxford won the Terence Ranger Award.

JOHANNA RICHTER is Deputy Director of the IFK International Research Center for Cultural Studies, University of Art and Design Linz in Vienna, Austria. She grew up in Germany but has family in Argentina and Guatemala. After studying comparative literature, cultural studies and Latin American studies in Berlin, Buenos Aires and Mexico City, she received a PhD from the University of Potsdam with a thesis on the novel and the press in nineteenth-century Paris and London. Her research interests include the history of media and publishing since 1800, the serial form, the role of journalism in literary history, fiction as an anthropological device, and Hispanic-American cultural history.

ASHA ROGERS is Lecturer in Contemporary Postcolonial Literature at the School of English, Drama, American & Canadian Studies at the University of Birmingham. Her first book, *State Sponsored Literature: Britain and Cultural Diversity after 1945*, which explores how the modern British state became an integral, albeit conflicted, guardian of literary autonomy in the postcolonial world, is forthcoming.

CHRISTINA TWOMEY is Professor of History and Head of the School of Philosophical, Historical and International Studies at Monash University in Melbourne, Australia. She is the author of four books, including *The Battle Within: POWs in postwar Australia* (2018) and, with co-author Mark Peel, *A History of Australia* (2nd edn, 2017). A cultural historian of war, she has also published on the history of humanitarianism, photography and internment camps. Her work on Emily Hobhouse forms part of a broader project on the development of the concentration camp at the turn of the twentieth century.

IMAOBONG UMOREN is Assistant Professor in International History of Gender at the London School of Economics and Political Science. Her research interests focus on African American and Afro-Caribbean women's history in the nineteenth and twentieth centuries. She is the author of *Race Women Internationalists: Activist-Intellectuals and Global Freedom Struggles* (University of California Press, 2018).

Index

Aborigine(s) *see* Indigenous Australians
Achebe, Chinua 20, 183–4, 193, 247
activism 44, 46–7, 53–4, 69, 113–14, 116,
    201, 213, 224–5, 234, 252
African American(s) 21, 44–54, 73–7, 81–6,
    112–14, 143, 169, 202, 212, 224–5
African continent 2, 10, 18–23, 43–4, 54,
    61, 67–8, 81–3, 104, 112–18, 135–9,
    143–4, 147, 167, 169–71, 174–5,
    178, 183–9, 192–4, 213, 255
African culture 54, 135–6, 183, 186–9, 191,
    197, 252–3
African history fn. 83, 169, 173–4, 178
African National Congress (ANC) 35,
    104–5, 108, 110–13, 115, 212,
    250–1, 255–9
Afrikaner/Afrikaans 16, 57, 64, 66, 69, 117
Afrocentrism 167–8, 176–80
Amnesty International 183–4, 194–6
apartheid 16, 21, 57, 66, 68, 75, 84, 86,
    105, 114, 116, 185, 212, 227, 248,
    250, 252–3, 255, 258–60
Arab Spring 39, 212
Asante, Molefi 167–8, 176
Asia 13, 30, 35, 43–4, 204, 223
Asturias, Miguel Ángel 151–64, 265–7
    Men of Maize 15, 22, 151–64
Australia 3, 13, 23, 215–38, 242
autobiography 121–3, 125–30, 234–40,
    243, 247–9, 251, 256, 265

Baldwin, James 172, 189
Besant, Annie 21, 89–100, 264–7
    Wake Up, India 7, 16, 19, 21, 89–100
    Why I Became a Theosophist 89–90

Black Consciousness fn. 83, 116, 252
Black Lives Matter 18, 212
Black Panthers 201–2, 257, 267
Black Power movement 143, 202, 212,
    223, 265
Boehmer, Elleke 13–14, 252, 258
book, the 1, 4–5, 7–8, 10–11, 16, 18, 21,
    99–100, 106–8, 117, 129, 169, 175,
    184–5, 249
    global history of 4–10, 15–16, 19, 31,
        35, 53, 109, 225, 228, 231–2, 247,
        258, 266
bourgeoisie 32–4, 36–8, 206, 208–9
Bourne, Henry Fox 60–1, 68
Britain 2, 9, 21, 63–9, 90–1, 97, 104, 106,
    108, 112–16, 222–9, 232
British Empire 2–5, 13–15, 21, 57–8,
    60–4, 67–8, 91–6, 103, 106,
    110–13, 116–17, 183, 232, 263
British imperialism *see* British Empire

Canada 113, 161, 225, 227–9
Cape Town 65, 213, 254
    University of 18, 62
capitalism 20, 27, 30, 33–5, 37, 39–40,
    82, fn. 83, 128, 151, 154, 158, 195,
    206–12, 259
Castro, Fidel 35, fn. 158, 257
Césaire, Aimé 172, 210
China 2–4, 19, 28, 32, 35–7
Christianity 52, 57–8, 93, 136
Cold War 67–9, 184, 193, 195–7, 204–5
colonialism 2, 6–7, 12–19, 77, 82–4,
    92–3, 104, 109, 117, 125, 135, 148,
    159, 163, 169, 185, 196, 203–6,

209–10, 216, 219, 221–3, 227, 242–3, 266
    settler 18, 21, 103, 238–9, 266
color-line 73, 75–8, 80–2, 204, 207, 209, 211
Commonwealth 115, 194, 229, 232, 266
communism 27, 30–1, 34, 36–40, 197, 219, 225
Congress for Cultural Freedom (CCF) 190, 192–7
Cooper, Anna Julia 19, 21, 43–53, 263–4, 266
    Voice from the South, A 11, 19–20, 43–4, 46–53
Cuba 35, fn. 158, 205

Danquah, Joseph B. 135, 137–48, 265, 267
    Akan Doctrine of God, The 11, 19, 22, 135, 137–48
decolonization 7, 10, 15–16, 18–19, 22, 116, 136, 175, 183–5, 194, 201, fn. 202, 203, 205–6, 208, 211–12, 224, 227, 243, 247, 255, 260, 264–5, 267
    decolonial theory and studies 73, 86, 168, 174
    see also Rhodes Must Fall
democracy 39–40, 68, 82, 177, 204, 207, 250–2, 259
Diop, Cheikh Anta 19, 22, 167–81, 264, 266
    Nations nègres et culture 7, 167–81
Du Bois, W. E. B. 19, 21, 47, 51, 73–86, 114, 204, 264–5
    Souls of Black Folk, The 16, 19, 21, 73–86

Egypt 22, 81, 143, 167–8, 172, 174–6, 178, 180
Engels, Friedrich 6, 20, 28–34, 36–7, 39–40, 206
    Condition of the Working Class in England, The 32

Europe 12–13, 22, 27, 30, 32, 35, 43–4, 112, 144, 157–8, 160, 168, 172, 176, 196–7, 203–4, 206–10, 213, 223

famine 62–3, 154
Fanon, Frantz 19, 35, 116, 201–13, 267
    Wretched of the Earth, The 15, 19, 22–3, 201–3, 205–13, 267
feminism 64, 66–7, 69, 94
    black 20, 43–4, 46, 49–50, 52–4
First World War 103, 110, 113
France 2, 32, 45, 170–2, 175, 177, 222, 225, 228

Gandhi, M. K. 5–6, 65–6, 91, 96, 100, fn. 106, 122–3, 125–8
Garvey, Marcus 21, 114
Germany 2, 31, 33, 157, 222
    Berlin Wall 36
Ghana 11, 22, 35, 123, 135, 137–9, 141, 143–4, 146–8
Gilroy, Paul 17, 264
Global South 18, 122, 210–11
globalization 34, 103, 201, 203, 209–12, 248
Guatemala 151–2, 154, fn. 158, 160–3

Hardy, Frank 215–29, 266
    Unlucky Australians, The 10, 23, 215–29, 266
Hindus/Hinduism 91–5, 112
hip-hop 167–70, 176, 179–80, 266
Hobhouse, Emily 57–69, 266
    Brunt of the War and Where it Fell, The 16, 20–1, 57, 59, 61–9
Hobsbawm, Eric 2, 28, fn. 31
Hofmeyr, Isabel 4–5, fn. 6, 11, 15
human rights 20–1, 43–4, 52–4, 67–8, 253
humanism 203, 205, 205–12, 247, 252, 256–7, 260
humanitarianism 57, 68–9

'imperial commons' 5, 24
imperialism 1–7, 12–17, 22, 35–6, 43–4,
    54, 57, 68, 104, 125, 132, 151, 176,
    190, 204, 209, 211, 229, 263–6
India 3, 7, 14, 19, 22, 33, 35, 62, 66, 81,
    89–100, 121–3, 125–32, 208,
    212–13, 232
Indian National Congress 35, 100
Indigenous Australians 215–28, 231–43
interdisciplinarity 86
intersectionality 50, 52–4, 264

Kaunda, Kenneth 123, 125
Kenyatta, Jomo 123, 125

Latin America 15, 30, 151–6, 158–60, 213
Lenin, V. I. 35–6
London 3, 13, 31, 39, 47, 58, 92, 103,
    138–9, 145, 186–7, 194, 196,
    225, 227

Madras 21, 89, 99–100
Malcolm X 20
Mandela, Nelson 23, 122, 125, 247–60,
    264–5
    Long Walk to Freedom 6, 10–11, 23,
    122–3, 247–53, 256–60
Mao Zedong 36–7, 40
    Mao's Little Red Book 19
Marx, Karl 20, 28–40, 158, 193, 206, 264–5
    Communist Manifesto, The 6–7, 9, 11,
    19–20, 27–40, 206, 266
memory 57, 64–6, 69, 114
    appropriation of 66, 68–9
modernity/modernization 18, 22, 128,
    137, 157–8, 176, 189, 197, 204–8,
    212, 251, 253
Morgan, Sally 231–43, 264
    My Place 16, 23, 231–43

nation(s)/nationalism 7, 14, 16, 21–2, 27,
    30, 57, 64–9, 82–4, 90–1, 95–6,
    98, 106, 122–32, 137, 144, 170, 179,
    183–4, 195, 204–13, 216, 250–5,
    258–60, 266–7
Natives Land Act of 1913 21, 103–5, 108,
    116
Nehru, Jawaharlal 21, 121–32, 204, 250,
    263–5
    Autobiography, An 21–2, 121–4, 126,
    128–32
    Discovery of India, The 6–7, 21–2,
    121–3, 126, 128–32
neocolonialism/neo-imperialism 14,
    17–19, 23, 161, 163, 177, 192,
    201–4, 208–13, 267
Neogy, Rajat 183–97, 266
    Transition 7, 10, 16, 22, 183–97, 263,
    266
neoliberalism 23, 30, 37, 201, 210–12
network(s) 30, 58, 68, 89–90, 93, 99, 192,
    264
    imperial 15, 21, 103, 110–12
    print 103, 113–14, 135, 184
New Zealand 13, 227–9
Ngũgĩ wa Thiong'o 20, 184, 186
nineteenth century 6, 24, 31–2, 39, 43,
    53–4, 62, 75, 92, 168, 176, 264
Nkrumah, Kwame 35, 123, 138, 144,
    204–5, 250
Nobel Prize 66, 161, 195, 248, 255

Obote, Milton 183, 193–4, 196

pacifism 61, 63, 65–9, 266
Pan-Africanism 47, fn. 83, 113, 178–9,
    205, 252
Plaatje, Sol 21, 103–18, 264, 267
    Mhudi 113
    Native Life in South Africa 15, 21,
    103–6, 108–18, 264
    Tsala ea Batho 107, 109, 267
postcolonialism 7, 110, 115, 167, 169,
    223–4, 247, 263–7

postcolonial literature 7, 90, 183–4, 186–8, 222, 225, 229, 250–1, 256, 263, 265
postcolonial states and societies 21–3, 121–3, 125–6, 129, 135, 151, 163, 190
postcolonial studies 17, 20, 73, 86, 116, 173, 180
postcolonial world 1, 4–7, 12, 16–17, 23, 36, 68, 121, 132, 147–8, 164, 195–7, 203, 209, 211, 218, 229, 249, 251, 267
Prashad, Vijay fn. 202, 204, fn. 210–11
print culture 13, 15, 99, 103, 106, 108–9, 117, 183–5, 189, 196, 263
see also network(s)

race/racism 21, 23, 39, 43–7, 49–52, 54, 57, 60–4, 67–9, 73–8, 80–4, 86, 92, 96, 103, 109, 112, 115–16, fn. 160, 175, 188, 206, 209, 212, 215–16, 218–19, 221–6, 229, fn. 233–5, 237, 240–1, 248, 255–6, 258
anti-racism 19, 73–5, 80–1, 252–3
see also resistance
resistance 10, 12, 13–18, 21–3, 75, 91, 94, 97, 104, 114–15, 151–4, 157–8, 163, 183–6, 189, 196–7, 202, 215, 218, 223, 229, 232, 236, 238, 243, 247, 251, 253, 255, 259, 263, 265
anticolonial 1, 7–9, 14–16, 22, 35, 96–7, 115, 125, 135–6, 140, 147–8, 167, 169, 196, 204, 248, 250, 257, 264, 266–7
anti-imperial 1, 4–7, 16, 19, 21, 24, 27, 30, 35, 40, 89, 93, 100, 196, 204
revolution 32–7, 39, 45, 158, 205, 212–13
Rhodes Must Fall 18, 169, 212, 259–60
see also decolonization

Rive, Richard 186, 193
Royal Navy 3–4
Russia 2, 28–30, 36–7, 157, 161, 193, 222–4
Russian Revolution 32, 35

Said, Edward 14–15, 17, 93, 202, 210
Sartre, Jean-Paul 201, fn. 202
Second World War 28, 135, fn. 233
segregation 65, 75, 82–3, 104, 111–12, 114
Jim Crow laws 47, 75
Senegal 167–71, 176–81
Senghor, Léopold Sédar 171, 173, 177
slavery 39, 43–5, 77, 83, 112
Smuts, Jan 65, 113
socialism 37–8, 193, 206, 266
South Africa 16, 21, 35, 57–66, 68–9, 103–5, 108–13, 115–18, 122, 185–6, 212, 224, 227–8, 247–8, 250–60
Union of South Africa 103, 117
South African Natives National Congress *see* African National Congress (ANC)
South African War 16, 57–67, 69
Soviet Union *see* Russia
Soyinka, Wole 183, 186–7, 248
Stalin 36–7, 40, 222

Theosophy 89–91, 92–3, 96–7
Theosophical Society 89–90, 99
Third World 23, 35, 122, 128, 184, 190, 196, 201–10, 212–13
Non-Aligned Movement (NAM) 204
translation 9, 15, 32–5, 156–7, 174, 225, 232, 238
transnationalism 1, 7, 9–10, 18, 90, 93, 99, 179, 215, 218, 263
twentieth century 1, 6, 8–9, 11, 20, 23, 27, 35, 40, 44, 73, 75–6, 80, 82, 86, 89, 92, 114, 118, 157–8, 167,

169, 176, 183–4, 196, 203–4, 229, fn. 233, 256–7, 264

Uganda 178, 183–8, 190, 193–4, 263
United States of America 2, 39, 43–4, 53, 73–6, 81–4, 97, 103, 113–14, 144, 168–9, 179, 184–6, 190, 196, 202, 212–13, 222–6, 232, 266
   American Civil War 44, 223
   Civil Rights Movement 53, 75, 225–6, 266
University of Oxford 5, 12–13

violence 18–19, 43, 51, 76, 95, 205
   ecological 153, 161

Washington, Booker T. 21, 47, 51–2, 86, 114
white supremacy 52, 75–7, 80–4, 216, 235, 253, 260
world literature 31, 33–4, 40, 84, 187
World War I *see* First World War
World War II *see* Second World War

Žižek, Slavoj 35, 209, 259

RACE AND RESISTANCE ACROSS BORDERS IN THE LONG TWENTIETH CENTURY

Series Editors:
Tessa Roynon, University of Oxford (Executive Editor)
Elleke Boehmer, University of Oxford
Victoria Collis-Buthelezi, University of the Witwatersrand
Patricia Daley, University of Oxford
Aaron Kamugisha, University of the West Indies, Cave Hill
Minkah Makalani, University of Texas, Austin
Hélène Neveu Kringelbach, University College London
Stephen Tuck, University of Oxford

This series focuses on the history and culture of activists, artists and intellectuals who have worked within and against racially oppressive hierarchies in the first half of the twentieth century and beyond, and who have then sought to define and to achieve full equality once those formal hierarchies have been overturned. It explores the ways in which such individuals – writers, scholars, campaigners and organizers, ministers, and artists and performers of all kinds – located their resistance within a global context and forged connections with each other across national, linguistic, regional and imperial borders.

Disseminating the latest interdisciplinary scholarship on the history, literature and culture of anti-racist movements in Africa, the Caribbean, the United States, Europe, Asia and Latin America, the series foregrounds, through a cross-disciplinary approach, the transnational and intercultural nature of these resistance movements. The series embraces a range of themes, including but not limited to antislavery, intellectual and literary networks, emigration and immigration, anti-imperialism, church-based and religious movements, civil rights, citizenship and identity, Black Power, resistance strategies, women's movements, cultural transfer, white supremacy and anti-immigration, hip hop and global justice movements.

The series is affiliated with the Race and Resistance Research Programme at The Oxford Research Centre in the Humanities (TORCH), University of Oxford. Proposals are invited for sole- and joint-authored monographs as well as edited collections.

Editorial Advisory Board:
Funmi Adewole (DeMontfort University), Joan Anim-Addo (Goldsmiths, University of London), Celeste-Marie Bernier (University of Edinburgh), Alan Cobley (University of the West Indies, Cave Hill), Carolyn Cooper (University of the West Indies, Mona), Zaire Dinzey-Flores (Rutgers, State University of New Jersey), Tanisha Ford (University of Delaware), Maryemma Graham (University of Kansas), Christopher J. Lee (Lafayette College), Justine McConnell (King's College London), Pap Ndiaye (Sciences Po), David Scott (Columbia University), Hortense Spillers (Vanderbilt University), Imaobong Umoren (London School of Economics), Harvey Young (Boston University)

Published Volumes:

Dominic Davies, Erica Lombard and Benjamin Mountford (eds): Fighting Words: Fifteen Books that Shaped the Postcolonial World
2017. ISBN 978-1-906165-55-0. hb
2019. ISBN 978-1-78997-422-5. pb

Dominic Davies: Imperial Infrastructure and Spatial Resistance in Colonial Literature, 1880–1930
2017. ISBN 978-1-906165-88-8.

Claudia Gualtieri (ed.): Migration and the Contemporary Mediterranean: Shifting Cultures in Twenty-First-Century Italy and Beyond
2018. ISBN 978-1-78707-351-7.

Charlotte Baker and Hannah Grayson (eds): Fictions of African Dictatorship: Cultural Representations of Postcolonial Power
2018. ISBN 978-1-78707-681-5.

Rachel Knighton: Writing the Prison in African Literature
2019. ISBN 978-1-78874-647-2.